Mark Twain
in the
St. Louis *Post-Dispatch,*
1874-1891

Mark Twain
in the
St. Louis *Post-Dispatch*,
1874-1891

by

Jim McWilliams

The Whitston Publishing Company
Troy, New York
1997

Library of Congress Catalog Card Number 95-61176

ISBN 0-87875-469-5

Printed in the United States of America

Dedicated to Wolf

Acknowledgements

I could not have completed this book without the encouragement of my wife, Cynthia, and my daughter, Sophia, whose love always inspired me, even when it seemed as though my days in the microfilm room would never end. Special thanks for their continuous support are also due to my parents, Jim and Maryellen McWilliams; to my grandmother, Roberta Earnhardt; and to my aunt and uncle, Bob and Sandy White.

I would also like to recognize the contributions of five good friends: Thanks to Ed Malone for the many discussions about literary scholarship that have preoccupied us since we began as lowly master's students in 1986; and thanks to Nick Franke for all the advice—legal and personal—offered over the past decade. Also, thanks to Greg Jewell, president of the Humanities Defense League, who always knew how to turn pro when the going got tough. Finally, thanks to Cicero Bruce and Mike Given for the hundreds of visions and revisions that we shared at Booby's during the long, hot summer of '94.

Last, I would like to thank three eminent Twainians who have answered my questions with patience: Drs. Thomas Tenney, College of Charleston; Lawrence Berkove, University of Michigan-Dearborn; and Robert Hirst, University of California-Berkeley.

Jim McWilliams
Southern Illinois University-Carbondale
August 1994

Contents

Introduction

Although it eventually became the major newspaper in Missouri, the St. Louis *Post-Dispatch* had an inauspicious founding in 1862 as the St. Louis *Union*. Two years later, the newspaper was sold and renamed the *Dispatch*; it was subsequently resold so many times that it became the journalistic laughingstock of the city. By 1878 the newspaper had lost more than $250,000 for its investors. Since its future seemed dismal, the Circuit Court of St. Louis ordered the *Dispatch* and its few remaining assets sold at auction to reimburse the newspaper's many creditors. It seemed like the end of the *Dispatch*, but the bankruptcy sale was attended by a man who believed he could make something of the rundown newspaper.

Joseph Pulitzer (1847-1911) emigrated to the United States from Hungary during the Civil War as a recruit for the Union Army. When the war ended, he traveled to St. Louis and found work as a reporter on the German-language *Westliche Post*. Within a few years, Pulitzer had established himself as the best journalist in the city, which in turn helped him to make political and business connections throughout the state. After serving in the Missouri Legislature and making a fortune from investments, Pulitzer decided to buy a newspaper. He initially wanted the St. Louis *Post*, the most successful newspaper in the city, but its price was too high. Pulitzer then attended the 9 December 1878 bankruptcy auction of the *Dispatch* and was the high bidder at $2,500. He then owned a newspaper whose most valuable asset was its wire service. Since his primary competitor—John A. Dillon, owner of the St. Louis *Post*—desperately wanted to belong to a wire service, correctly judging that such an affiliation would be crucial to the future of journalism, Pulitzer agreed to merge the two newspapers and for both men to own jointly the newly created paper. By mid-December of 1878 the merger was in effect and the St. Louis *Post-Dispatch* was born.

After a year had passed, however, the venture failed to show much profit and Dillon sold his interest to Pulitzer. Under Pulitzer's critical eye and unstinted attention, the newspaper began to flourish and by 1883 it had become one of the leading newspapers in the Midwest. Although it generally supported the Democratic party and its platforms, the *Post-Dispatch* stood firmly against political corruption in all parties and earned a reputation for independent investigative reporting. With the *Post-Dispatch* a success, Pulitzer left his newspaper in the hands of capable editors and departed for New York and his next venture, the New York *World*.[1] The *Post-Dispatch* meanwhile enjoyed its new role as the leading newspaper in Missouri, and as such, it can serve as a unique biography of Missouri's favorite son—Mark Twain.

Indeed, Twain himself envisioned such a portrayal of his life—a biography composed of newspaper clippings. As Charles Neider points out in his introduction to *The Autobiography of Mark Twain*, Twain struggled throughout his later years to find a way to organize his autobiography, a way to impose logical structure on such a full and unstructured life. Twain had begun composing autobiographical chapters in the early 1870s, and continued to either write or dictate his autobiography for the next 40 years, but the project was still fragmentary at his death on 21 April 1910. At one point in this frustrating process, Twain considered placing into the autobiography objective opinions of himself as written by others:

> 'I shall scatter through this Autobiography newspaper clippings without end. When I do not copy them into the text it means that I do not make them a part of the Autobiography—at least not of the earlier editions. I put them in on the theory that if they are not interesting in the earlier editions, a time will come when it may be well enough to insert them for the reason that age is quite likely to make them interesting although in their youth they lack that quality.' (xi)

Ultimately, however, Twain rejected this odd way of completing his autobiography and died before he solved the problem of its structure. The fragments were left to his first literary executor and biographer, Albert Bigelow Paine, to edit into a formal autobiography published in 1912. Subsequently, Bernard DeVoto in 1940 and Charles Neider in 1959 tried their hands at editing the mass of fragments into an autobiography. Although none of the three "autobiographies" is wholly satisfactory, Neider's volume is certainly the best.

I do not mean to suggest that this annotated index of references to Mark Twain from the St. Louis *Post-Dispatch* can replace Twain's own autobiographies, or that this volume supersedes the many excellent biographies. Instead, my work complements those sources and offers a unique view of Twain—the view from his contemporaries. In fact, there was little that Twain did or said that the *Post-Dispatch* did not tell its readers. Through their scrupulous reporting of Twain and his activities, for instance, a twentieth-century reader can trace the growth of Twain's popularity. One illustration of this growth can be seen by a theater review from 25 September 1877:

> The laughable sketch of the "Pink Domino," as given
> by the Allen Combination, is enough to provoke the ris-
> ibles of a graven image, or to make Mark Twain's deaf
> and dumb man laugh.

This particular entry—referring to Twain's sketch entitled "A Deception"—makes it clear that an anonymous *Dispatch* drama critic could mention in passing one of Twain's sketches printed more than three years earlier in the *Dispatch* (on 29 June 1874) and assume that his audience would fully understand the allusion.[2] Although the editors of the *Post-Dispatch* occasionally reserved some of their sharpest sarcasm for Twain, they could not ignore the man. In fact, between 1874 and 1891 the *Dispatch*, the *Post*, and the *Post-Dispatch* printed nearly 300 interviews, articles, stories, memoirs, and anecdotes about or by Mark Twain. My index collects and annotates this wealth of material, much of which has never before been reprinted.

The methodology for my study is simple. Beginning with January 1874, I read every issue of the *Dispatch*, the *Post*, and the *Post-Dispatch* and made a record of each time Mark Twain was mentioned. (All three newspapers have been microfilmed back to 1874 and are available under the general title of the *St. Louis Post-Dispatch*.) I ended my search in 1891, when Twain closed his house in Hartford, Conn., and moved to Europe. Over the next decade, he suffered from a number of tragedies, including his bankruptcy in 1894 and the death of his favorite daughter in 1896. Unfortunately, these events—as well as his chronic depression—led to Twain's decline as a writer. Although he returned to the United States in 1904, he had already published the works for which he is best known today. He did not literally die until 1910, but it is not an exaggeration to say that creatively he had died in 1891.

Throughout this index the names "Mark Twain" and "Samuel L. Clemens" will be used without discrimination by the many writers whose work appears here. Indeed, Twain/ Clemens himself did not seem to distinguish between the two names as clearly as his twentieth-century critics would like. He often signed humorous letters "S. L. Clemens," for example, and just as often signed serious letters "Mark Twain." It can be convenient in our century to assume "Twain" refers to a fictitious person who loved rough humor, while "Clemens" refers to a very real, very proper Victorian gentleman. But this distinction was not made in the lifetime of Twain/Clemens. The two names were interchangeable, although it was not until the mid-1880s that readers of the *Post-Dispatch* came to understand that fact. As late as 10 July 1884, as this index shows, at least one confused subscriber wrote to ask what Mark Twain's real name was. And just three months later (27 October 1884), a *Post-Dispatch* writer would spell Twain's name "Clements." At any rate, in my introduction and annotations I always use the name "Mark Twain" for consistency.

The material I uncovered about and by Twain can be divided into three types: Items either written or said by Twain (the latter quoted through newspaper reporters); longer items about Twain and his life written by friends or reporters; and short items that frequently are nothing more than gossip or speculation. Obviously, material under the first two headings hold the most interest, but the gossip, even when false, should not be neglected as it so clearly demonstrates the fascination of the *Post-Dispatch* with anything connected with Mark Twain. It is worth noting, for example, that the tone of many of the short items written between 1878 and 1882 (in gossip columns about celebrities under titles like "Personal," "Our Spice Box," and "Pencilings") are sarcastic toward Twain. On 3 September 1870, upon Twain's return from a tour of Europe, an anonymous *Post-Dispatch* writer noted:

> When he gets here [back in the United States] and finds that every respectable newspaper has its own 'funny man,' he will linger long enough to read their scintillations, and then double on his track by the next steamer. And in all human probability that will be the last we will ever see of Mark Twain.

In all "human probability" this jealous editorialist considered himself to be the *Post-Dispatch's* own "funny man" and resented

Twain's success as a humorist. While some of the shorter references are indeed slight, in the interests of comprehensive scholarship, I decided to note every reference to Mark Twain and to his works, no matter how trivial it seemed. In short, this index is an exhaustive record of Mark Twain in the St. Louis *Post-Dispatch* between 1874 and 1891.

For all entries, I give the day and date the reference to Twain appeared and its title (when one was given), as well as the page upon which it appeared. Following this information is the entry itself. Any words or punctuation within brackets is material I have added to help a reader understand the text; question marks within brackets, however, denote places where the newspaper is torn or otherwise unreadable. To aid the reader, I silently correct all typographical or stylistic errors from the *Post Dispatch*; factual errors I let stand, although I correct the error in an annotation. For nearly all entries, I also provide annotations to place them within the context of Twain's life and work. To give an example of this latter type of annotation, for the very first entry of this index—that of 9 January 1874—I reprint the material that appeared in the *Dispatch*, then supply information about Charles Warren Stoddard and his relationship with Twain. To give another example, for the entry of 12 May 1882, I reprint the *Post-Dispatch* interview with Twain, and then in an annotation give additional information about Twain's 1882 visit to St. Louis. I also explain an obscure reference ("Commodore Rollingpin") and note that the St. Louis *Globe-Democrat* published an interview with Twain the next day.[3] Because there are hundreds of people mentioned in the entries, I faced a particularly difficult problem in deciding who deserved annotation. Finally, I decided to annotate all of Twain's relatives, as well as all of his friends and business associates. I also annotate any names that would especially help a reader to understand the point of an entry, such as on 29 May 1884 when Henry Bergh is mentioned. But when a name is not particularly important to the understanding of an entry, I do not annotate it. Nor do I annotate famous names that can be readily found in an encyclopedia or other reference work, e.g. Ralph Waldo Emerson or George Eliot. Even though Twain specialists will probably decide I annotated the obvious, for the sake of non-specialists I chose to err on the side of verbosity. In my annotations, however, I have undoubtedly missed references that deserve fuller explication. I trust that fellow Twainians will correct these deficiencies, as well as find the material in my index of use in their own studies of Twain.

Notes

[1] Two excellent sources that detail the early history of the St. Louis *Post-Dispatch* are Don Carlos Seitz's *Joseph Pulitzer: His Life and Letters* (New York: Simon & Schuster, 1924); and Julian S. Rammelkamp's *Pulitzer's Post-Dispatch, 1878-1883* (Princeton: Princeton University Press, 1967).

[2] Many other newspapers also printed this sketch, which was written in 1872 and subsequently reprinted in Twain's *Sketches, New and Old* (1875).

[3] This interview, as well as two articles about Twain from the *Globe-Democrat*, I reprint in an appendix. I have not read all the issues of the *Globe-Democrat*; in fact, I only examined a few issues that I felt certain contained articles about Twain.

Abbreviations

The following titles have been abbreviated for the citations used in this volume:

Autobiography   Mark Twain, *The Autobiography of Mark Twain*, ed. Charles Neider (New York: Harper & Row, 1959);

Autobiography I   Mark Twain, *Mark Twain's Autobiography*, 2 volumes, ed. Albert Bigelow Paine (New York: Harper & Brothers, 1924);

Collected Tales   Mark Twain, *Collected Tales, Sketches, Speeches, & Essays*, 2 volumes, ed. Louis J. Budd (New York: Library of America, 1992);

Complete Essays   Mark Twain, *The Complete Essays of Mark Twain*, ed. Charles Neider (Garden City, New Jersey: Doubleday, 1963);

Jane Clemens   Rachel M. Varble, *Jane Clemens: The Story of Mark Twain's Mother* (Garden City, New York: Doubleday, 1964);

Landslide Case   Mark Twain, *The Great Landslide Case: Three Versions*, ed. Frederick Anderson and Edgar M. Branch (Berkeley: University of California, 1972).

Lecture Tours   Fred W. Lorch, *The Trouble Begins at Eight: Mark Twain's Lecture Tours* (Ames, Iowa: Iowa State University Press, 1968);

MT Abroad   Dewey Ganzel, *Mark Twain Abroad: The Cruise of the "Quaker City"* (Chicago: University of Chicago Press, 1968);

MT: Bachelor   Margaret Sanborn, *Mark Twain: The*

	Bachelor Years (New York: Doubleday, 1990);
MT Boyhood Home	Henry Sweets, *Mark Twain Boyhood Home Rededication* (Hannibal: n.p., 1991);
MT & Elisha Bliss	Hamlin Hill, *Mark Twain and Elisha Bliss* (Columbia, Missouri: University of Missouri Press, 1964);
MT Himself	Milton Meltzer, *Mark Twain Himself* (New York: Wings Books, 1960);
MT & His World	Justin Kaplan, *Mark Twain and His World* (New York: Harmony Books, 1974);
MT & Howells	Mark Twain and W. D. Howells, *Selected Mark Twain-Howells Letters 1872-1910*, eds. Frederick Anderson, William M. Gibson, and Henry Nash Smith (New York: Atheneum, 1968);
MT Speaking	Paul Fatout, *Mark Twain Speaking* (Iowa City: University of Iowa Press, 1976);
MT Speaks	Paul Fatout, *Mark Twain Speaks for Himself* (West Lafayette: Purdue University Press, 1978);
MT & the Theatre	Von Thomas Schirer, *Mark Twain and the Theatre* (Nürnberg, Germany: Verlag Hans Carl, 1984);
MT: Virginia City	George Williams III, *Mark Twain: His Life in Virginia City, Nevada* (Riverside, California: Tree by the River Publishing, 1986);
Mark & Livy	Resa Willis, *Mark and Livy: The Love Story of Mark Twain and the Woman Who Almost Tamed Him* (New York: Atheneum, 1992);
Mr. Clemens & MT	Justin Kaplan, *Mr. Clemens and Mark Twain: A Biography* (New York: Simon & Schuster, 1966);
Nook Farm	Kenneth R. Andrews, *Nook Farm: Mark Twain's Hartford Circle* (Seattle: University of Washington Press, 1969);
Sam Clemens	Dixon Wecter, *Sam Clemens of Hannibal* (Boston: Houghton Mifflin, 1961);
Sketches & Tales	Mark Twain, *The Complete Humorous*

	Sketches and Tales of Mark Twain, ed. Charles Neider (Garden City, New Jersey: Doubleday, 1961).
Susy & MT	Edith Colgate Salsbury, ed., *Susy and Mark Twain: Family Dialogues* (New York: Harper & Row, 1965);
Twins of Genius	Guy A. Cardwell, *Twins of Genius* (East Lansing: Michigan State College Press, 1953).

1874

9 January (Friday)
"Among the Celebrities"; p. 2

George Warren Stoddard writes home from London in a private letter: "I have been very busy—have dined at the 'White Friars,' 'Savage,' and 'Westminster'—have seen George Eliot in her own house, and am invited to her receptions—have come upon lots of interesting people, and am forever full of delightful engagements in viewing the wonders of this grand old city. Yet California is the place for me, and I shall bless God the hour I am able to set my face toward it. I am with Mark Twain; we have our suite of rooms and have gorgeous times. He begins his lectures Monday night, and I expect to be with him till he sails from home; and then, ho! for the continent. Mark and I lunched with Charles Kingsley today at the Cloisters, Westminster Abbey; Ouida was in the house. You cannot open your door here without stumbling upon a celebrity."

The *Dispatch* misattributes this letter which is actually from Charles Warren Stoddard (1843-1909), a California poet and a friend of Twain's. The two men met in San Francisco in 1865, and eight years later Twain hired Stoddard to be his private secretary during his 1873-74 lecture tour of England (*Mr. Clemens & MT* 172). When Charles Kingsley (1819-75), a prominent English clergyman and novelist, lectured in Salem, Mass., on 14 February 1875, Twain introduced him to the audience; *Mark Twain Speaking* reprints the text of his speech (83-84). Ouida, pseudonym of Maria Louise Ramée (1839-1908), gained fame in England and the United States for her flamboyant romance stories.

16 January (Friday)
"News and Notes"; p. 2

Some critics, more honest than flattering, say that a collection of the last specimens of Mark Twain's wit would make a
good lead mine.

This comment is about *The Gilded Age*, coauthored by Twain and his
friend and neighbor Charles Dudley Warner (1829-1900). Warner, already well-established in the community as co-owner of the Hartford
Courant, befriended Twain when the humorist moved his family to
Hartford, Conn., in 1871. *The Gilded Age*, published simultaneously
in the United States and England on 23 December 1873, sold relatively
well for a few months, but by 1880 it had sold only 56,484 copies, which
disappointed Twain since he had considered it a certain bestseller (*MT
& Elisha Bliss* 84-85). See 25 May 1874 for another short item about this
novel.

11 February (Wednesday)
"Personalities"; p. 2

Mark Twain is coming home to lecture.

Twain actually arrived in Boston on 26 January, although he did not
lecture until later in the year.

18 February (Wednesday)
"Personalities"; p. 2

Mark Twain's *Innocents Abroad* enabled him to regard,
with about $22,000 worth of complacency, the multiplication
of innocents at home.

By early 1874, Twain's first book had sold more than 100,000 copies,
earning him between $1,000 and $1,500 a month in royalties since its
initial publication on 15 August 1869 (*MT & Elisha Bliss* 39-40).
It would remain one of his most popular books throughout the century.

24 February (Tuesday)
"Personalities"; p. 2

The latest developments show that Chang and Eng resembled our popular humorist. Being two and not one, their
distinctive mark is Mark Twain.

As they neared death, the original Siamese Twins were discussed in
the *Dispatch* nearly every day. Lurid accounts of their passing and subsequent autopsies were also printed. Twain, just as fascinated by the
Twins as were his contemporaries, wrote in 1869 a burlesque account

of how difficult their lives together must be. Entitled "Personal Habits of the Siamese Twins," it is reprinted in *Collected Tales I* (296-99). In the 1890s, as he labored with the writing of *Pudd'nhead Wilson*, Twain returned to the idea of Siamese twins. His sketch of "Those Extraordinary Twins," however, was left unfinished.

25 February (Wednesday)
no headline; p. 2
>   Henry W. Longfellow, John G. Whittier, Oliver Wendell Holmes, Henry Wilson, Josiah Quincy, Samuel L. Clemens, T. W. Higginson, E. P. Whipple, and J. T. Trowbridge attended the Wilkie Collins banquet in Boston on Monday night. Mr. Holmes presented a little poem on the double significance of the name of Wilkie Collins, which closed as follows:
>   And so his double name comes true.
>   They christened better than they knew.
>   And art proclaims him twice her son,
>   Painter and poet, both in one!

The banquet took place on 16 February 1874. Although Twain delivered a speech in which he discussed his recent trip to England, no copy of his remarks is extant (*MT Speaking* 651). This invitation into Boston's high literary society, however, illustrates very well his growing reputation as an author.

31 March (Tuesday)
"News and Notes"; p. 2
>   Rumors are heard of another humorous weekly, to which Mark Twain, Charles Dudley Warner, and Bret Harte are named contributors.

1 April (Wednesday)
"Personalities"; p. 2
>   Mark Twain says he will never again heave his leaden jokes from the lecture platform.

As much as he had come to loathe public lecturing, financial difficulties were to force him onstage again throughout his career. In 1895-96, for example, Twain delivered lectures around the world—from North America to Asia, from South Africa to Europe—to raise enough money to repay his creditors after his 1894 bankruptcy. His book *Following the Equator*, published November 1898, resulted from the long tour and also helped to repay creditors. Even after he had officially retired from the lecture circuit, however, Twain continued to give many private and public speeches. Without a doubt, he was the most popular speaker of his day.

3 April (Friday)
"Personalities"; p. 2

It is said that Mark Twain will experiment with a weekly paper somewhat after the style of the Danbury *News*.

Whoever "said" this is wrong. Frequently asked to edit a newspaper or magazine, Twain declined all such proposals after he became a full-time writer with the success of *The Innocents Abroad*, published 15 August 1869.

14 April (Tuesday)
"News and Notes"; p. 2

Mark Twain has a window put just above each fireplace in his new house, which will allow the female members of the family to keep themselves warm without neglecting to observe what is going on in the street and across the way.

Mr. Clemens & MT describes in detail Twain's odd-shaped residence with its "forest of chimneys" and many windows (181-82), while *MT & His World* prints a full-color photograph of the house (102-03) and *MT Himself* gives its floorplans (132). Located at 351 Farmington Avenue in Hartford, Conn., Twain's house was finally completed in 1875 although renovations continued for many years afterward. As much as he loved his house, however, financial reverses in 1891 necessitated the family's move to Europe where they could live more cheaply. After his daughter Susy's death five years later, it became evident that the family would never again live in Hartford and the house was sold in 1903 by a real estate agency that billed it as "Mark Twain's Home for Sale" (*MT Himself* 243). Today, the house stands as a museum to Twain.

20 April (Monday)
"News and Notes"; p. 2

London papers appreciate the jokes of *The Gilded Age*, and praise the book highly. It is published across the water in three volumes.

In general, the novel received better reviews in England than in the United States, where it was often attacked as poorly written and inferior to previous work by either Twain or Warner (*MT & Elisha Bliss* 79-81).

21 April (Tuesday)
"Mark Twain's Pretended Brother Perpetrates a Joke"; p. 1

Duburque, Iowa, April 21—

A man representing himself as the brother of Mark Twain has been about here several days preparing to lecture. He announced that he would appear last night, sold $200 worth of tickets, and then skipped.

28 April (Tuesday)
"News and Notes"; p. 2

Duburque people have a new appreciation for Mark Twain's story of a jumping frog since that bogus brother of his swindled them out of $200 worth of lecture tickets.

People impersonating him (or his relatives) would continue to plague Twain throughout his career. See 19 May 1889 for an interview in which Twain addresses the problem. His story "The Celebrated Jumping Frog of Calaveras County," first published on 18 November 1865 as "Jim Smiley and His Jumping Frog" in the *Saturday Press*, brought Twain national recognition. Subsequently reprinted many times, by 1874 it is doubtful that anybody in the United States would not have known the tale of the jumping frog or who wrote it. See 1 June 1881 for an account of the genesis of this story.

2 May (Saturday)
"Mark Twain a Confederate"; p. 2

It transpires that Mark Twain was a soldier, having served two weeks with Jeff Thompson in the rebel army in Missouri. That he never made much of a military record is ex-plained in a letter which he has just written to Thompson. "We never won any victories to speak of. We never could get the enemy to stand still when we wanted to fight, and we were generally on the move when the enemy wanted to fight."

Twain's two-week service in the Confederate army would continue to be a news item for more than a decade; see, for example, 19 May 1883, 21 November 1885, 23 February 1886, and 30 April 1887 for more stories the *Post-Dispatch* printed about Twain's activities during the war. To explain his war record, Twain wrote an account of his service and published it in the *Century*, which ran first-person memoirs of the war in 1885. Most of the pieces for the *Century* attempted to show the Civil War as noble and glamorous, but Twain's essay—entitled "The Private History of a Campaign that Failed"—depicted insubordination and cowardice and served as an ironic contrast to the other essays. See 11 December 1885 for an excerpt.

15 May (Friday)
"News and Notes"; p. 2
Charles Dudley Warner and Mark Twain are said to have realized $40,000 from their book, *The Gilded Age*. That is where the gilt edge came in.

While he may have made this much money from the novel, Twain considered it a failure since its sales did not exceed those of *The Innocents Abroad* or *Roughing It*.

18 May (Monday)
"News and Notes"; p. 2
Charles Dudley Warner and Mark Twain are said to have realized $40,000 from their book, *The Gilded Age*. Almost any man would experience a sense of guilt in defrauding the public with such a book.

5 June (Friday)
"Cormorants: Mark Twain Gives the Fishers Another Showing Up"; p. 2
So the Fisher heirs have come again. I wrote a full account of the performance of these insatiable blood-suckers, and published it in the *Galaxy* magazine in 1870—August of that year, I think. My facts were drawn from official sources, that is to say from printed documents of the House and Senate—documents which the favorably reporting military committee can see at any moment if they are really ignorant of the fact that the Fisher claim is a vile swindle upon the government. The committee need only send to the document department of the Capitol for H. R. Ex. No. Doc. 21, 36th Congress, 2nd session, and for S. Ex. Doc. No. 166, 41st Congress, 2nd session, if they really do not know the history of the Fisher pirates.
These Fishers are the only people who ever did me the high honor to try to bribe me. I call it a high honor because it seems to suggest that I am worth bribing. After the *Galaxy* article appeared they sent a former Californian congressman all the way to Buffalo to intimate to me that I could make it very profitable to myself if I would promise to be silent about the Fisher claim in the future. That was all. I was only to keep still and let the Fishers alone. I was really so much flattered by this attention that I did not destroy the messenger. I said I would keep perfectly still without charge, until the Fishers

moved upon Congress again, and then I would say all I could against them, even if it did no sort of good. So I want to keep my promise now. There are people whose words can be effective, whether mine are or not, and I beg Gen. Hawley or Sunset Cox or Mr. Beck to do a plain duty to the country and extinguish these importunate vampires.

If your readers are not acquainted with the Fisher conspiracy, let me state the facts in brief. Sixty years ago, the Creek war being then in progress in Florida, the crops, hands, and houses of a Mr. George Fisher were destroyed by the said Creek Indians. George Fisher seems to have known that he could not collect damages from the government [the next two or three words are illegible]. Fisher died, and his widow married again. The new husband, nearly 20 years after the Indian raid, petitioned for damages, and tried to prove that some of the destruction was done by the troops that pursued the Indians. The Congress of that day smiled a bland smile at that ingenious idea, and decidedly declined to see it.

The Fishers waited another 16 years, and then petitioned again. They got $8,873, being half of the whole damage originally sustained. The auditor said the testimony showed that at least half the destruction was done by the Indians "before the troops started in pursuit."

The Fishers came once more the same year. This time they got interest on the original award dated back to 1813, the date of the raid, said interest amounting to $19,004.89.

The Fishers lay quiet for five years, and came back in 1854, but James Guthrie, an honest man, was chief of the Treasury then, and he sent them about their business with the pointed remark that they had "been paid too much already."

The Fishers rested till 1858—four years—and came back famishing. They got their claim removed from the Treasury to the War Office, where a man of their own sort was in authority—John B. Floyd, of particular renown. Floyd figured at it and decided that nearly three-fourths of the damage was done by the United States troops—on what evidence, God knows. So he paid the Fishers a fraction under $40,000 and so appeased them for a little while. The (originally) worthless Fisher farm had now yielded the heirs nearly $67,000 in cash.

The Fishers kept away just two years and then swarmed in upon Floyd once more. They brought their same old musty documents, but largely improved with erasures and interlineations (which forgeries were known to Floyd) whereby the values of many of the articles in the list of the destroyed property were doubled; and by the help of the said forgeries and by the force of his own foul genius, and by attributing all the destruction to the soldiers this time and none to the Indians, Mr. Floyd discovered that the nation still owed the Fishers $66,519.85, "which," Mr. Floyd sweetly remarked, "will be paid accordingly, to the administrator of the estate of George Fisher, deceased, or to his attorney in fact."

But it wasn't. A new president came in just at this time, and the first thing Congress did in 1861 was to rescind the resolution of June 1, 1860, under which Floyd had been ciphering.

The Florida Fishers survived the war and came back in July 1870 to beg for that $66,000-odd. Mr. Garret Davis was their noble champion, and I would greatly like to know the name of their present cat's-paw in Congress—not that I take any more interest in him than in any other individual of his kidney who has wandered into Congress when he ought to be serving his country in the chain-gang—but just for curiosity's sake.

The above are the facts; and as they are all taken from congressional documents, how is it that the Committee on Military Affairs have been induced to look favorably upon this most infamous swindle once more?

Originally printed in the New York *World*, this essay continues Twain's attack on the Fishers begun four years earlier in the "Case of George Fisher, Deceased," to which he alludes in the first paragraph. Twain is incorrect, however, in his dating of the earlier piece; it actually appeared in the January 1871 issue of the *Galaxy* and was later published in *Sketches, New and Old* and is reprinted in *Collected Tales I* (500-06). Of the three politicians to whom he appeals for help in defeating the Fisher claim, the most important is his neighbor and friend Gen. Joseph R. Hawley (1826-1905), former governor of Connecticut and representative from that state to the U. S. Congress. In 1881 Twain worked to elect him to the U. S. Senate. S. S. "Sunset" Cox (1824-89) was a prominent representative and later served as Minister to Turkey, while James C. Beck was a Kentucky representative with a reputation for honesty.

20 June (Saturday)
"Venerated Relics"; p. 1
    A Boston correspondent tells the following: "Mark Twain,

in one of his articles, speaks of the lady who treasures a precious slice of bread from which Dickens had taken a bite. This sounds like the broadest burlesque, but the following anecdote, which is literally true, and illustrates many people's foolish desire for relics, shows that Twain was hardly burlesquing in his essay. The last time that Mr. Dickens was in this country he happened one morning to breakfast at the common table of the hotel where he was stopping. When he had eaten his egg, he dropped the empty shell into his egg-cup, and, after finishing his breakfast, he left the table. As soon as he had gone, a lady who had sat next to him arose and, taking up the cup, went to the hotel proprietor and offered to purchase it from him at any price; and the unwashed egg-cup, containing the broken shell, is now kept by her as a souvenir of the great novelist."

The complete text of Twain's anecdote about Dickens memorabilia is reprinted in *Collected Tales I* as "The Approaching Epidemic" (447-48). Twain had witnessed firsthand the frenzy surrounding a Dickens reading tour when he heard him perform in New York City in December 1867. In his later years, Twain said that he had found the performance compelling; in *Autobiography*, for example, Twain states that Dickens's appearance was "striking and picturesque" (174-75). But in a February 1868 review written for the *Alta California*, Twain describes Dickens as barely audible and boring: "Mr. Dickens' reading is rather monotonous . . . his voice is husky; his pathos is only the beautiful pathos of his language—there is no heart, no feeling in it. . . ." (qtd. in *MT Himself* 111). This discrepancy can perhaps be explained by the fact that in 1868 Twain had just embarked upon his own lecture career; consequently, he may have felt a need to criticize more popular lecturers in order to gain publicity for his own appearances.

22 June (Monday)
"News and Notes"; p. 2

Among the subscribers to the stock of a new insurance company is Samuel L. Clemens, Mark Twain, who takes $50,000.

In *Autobiography*, Twain reports the amount he initially invested into the Hartford Accident Insurance Company as $5,000 (230-31). In either case, the amount was enough for him to be named a director of the company although he apparently took no part in its daily affairs. On 12 October 1874 Twain delivered a humorous speech in which he points out how accident insurance has helped the lives of many "freshly mutilated" people; it is reprinted in *Sketches & Tales* (286-87).

By the end of 1876, however, the company was in danger of bankruptcy and Twain stood to lose a total of $23,000. But since the company's primary investor—Sen. John P. Jones (1829-1912)—had indemnified him against loss, Twain was allowed to withdraw his money without penalty (*Mr. Clemens & MT* 303, *Autobiography* 231-32).

24 June (Wednesday)
"News and Notes"; p. 2
> Mark Twain has taken $50,000, Senator Jones of Nevada $75,000, and David Clark $10,000 in the stock of a new Hartford Accident Insurance Company.

29 June (Monday)
"Mark Twain Deceived"; p. 4
> You may remember that I lectured lately for the young gentlemen of the Clayonian Society. During the afternoon of that day I was talking with one of the young gentlemen referred to, and he said he had an uncle who, from some cause or other, seemed to have grown permanently bereft of all emotion, and, with tears in his eyes, this young man said: "Oh, if I could only see him laugh once more! Oh, if I could only see him weep!" I was touched. I could never withstand distress. I said: "Bring him to my lecture. I'll start him for you." "Oh, if you could but do it. If you could but do it, our family would bless you forevermore; for he is very dear to us. Oh, my benefactor, could you make him laugh? Can you bring soothing tears to those parched orbs?"
> I was profoundly moved. I said: "My son, bring the old party around. I have got some good jokes in my lecture that will make him laugh, if there's any laugh in him; and, if they miss fire, I have got some others that will make him cry or kill him, one or the other."
> Then the young man wept on my neck, and presently spread both hands on my head and looked up toward heaven, mumbling something reverently, and then went after his uncle. He placed him in full view, in the second row of benches that night, and I began on him. I tried him on mild jokes, then with severe ones; I dosed him with bad jokes, and ridiculed him with good ones; I fired old stale jokes into him, and peppered him fore and aft with red-hot new ones. I warmed up to my work, and I assaulted him on the right and left; in front and behind; I fumed, and charged, and ranted, till I was hoarse and sick, frantic and furious; but I

never moved him once—I never started a smile or a tear!
Never a ghost of a smile, and never a suspicion of moisture!
I was astounded. I closed the lecture at last with one despair-
ing shriek—with one wild burst of humor—and hurled a
joke of supernatural atrocity full at him. It never phased
him! Then I sat down bewildered and exhausted.

The president of the society came up and bathed my head
with cold water and said:

"What made you carry on so towards the last?"

I said: "I was trying to make that confounded old idiot
laugh in the second row."

And he said: "Well, you were wasting your time; because
he is deaf and dumb, and as blind as a badger."

Now, was that any way for that old man's nephew to impose on a stranger, and an orphan, like me?"

Originally written in 1872, Twain later included this anecdote under
the title "How the Author was Sold In Newark" in his *Sketches, New
and Old*, published 25 September 1875. The book's modest sales—only
23,556 copies sold by 1880—disappointed Twain, who resolved to publicize his next book more thoroughly to increase his profit (*MT &
Elisha Bliss* 98).

2 July (Thursday)
"News and Notes"; p. 2

Mark Twain thus concludes a business letter to his agent:
"Daughter born, a few days ago. Weight, seven and three-
quarters pounds. All well, yours, Mark."

This excerpt from a letter refers to Twain's daughter Clara, born 8 June
1874, his second daughter of three and the only one to survive him.

6 July (Monday)
"News and Notes"; p. 2

Mark Twain is putting $100,000 worth of humor into his
new Hartford home. Most of it is in fancy brick work and ve-
randahs.

20 July (Monday)
"Mark Twain Gets a Customer"; p. 2

A correspondent sends us the following, which, though
not endorsed by Gov. Bramlette or by the trustees of the library, is good enough to be published in an amusing
bagotelle:

"Messrs. Mark Twain & Barnum:

"Gentlemen—

"We read with great interest and with sincere gratification of your lease of the comet *Coggia*, and of the trip of which we propose to avail ourselves. In our five gift concerts we have pretty much exhausted the advertising facilities of this mundane sphere, and like new Alexanders, only awaited new worlds to conquer. Thanks to your enterprise and management, this facility is now afforded us. We desire to know your price for 100 double staterooms, as near amidships as possible, and not more than 30- or 40,000 miles apart. We wish you to deposit one of our agents on every star of respectable magnitude and particularly on each of the planets. These agents will await your return. For the return trip we will, of course, expect from you security for the vast sums of money with which each of these agents will be loaded, and shall expect you to preserve their incognito from all the other passengers.

"Our enterprise is one of no ordinary magnitude, and, therefore, our agents will be men of high degree who must be supposed to be guests of yours, invited for a pleasure trip. We shall also need about 100 square miles in the hold of the *Coggia* for circulars, library papers, and tickets to the last gift concert. Please make this freight a separate item in your bid. Of course, as each agent leaves the comet to stop at a star, the freight will be diminished by the amount he takes ashore with him. Mr. Geo. Francis Train will get off at Mercury, Mr. Henry Ward Beecher at Venus. Gen. John Pope at Mars. The agent for Jupiter will be appointed by President Grant and will probably consist of Matt Carpenter.

"Efforts are on foot to get Boss Tweed pardoned in time to send him to Saturn, where his acquaintance with rings will be of value to us. Should this effort fail, Boss Shepherd will take his place. Old Probabilities will go as far as U-rain-ia. People of less note will go to stars of less magnitude. If you prefer to take a part of the risk, we will give you a commission on all the tickets sold on the trip.

"All of our agents you will positively prohibit from going near the railing, as their enthusiastic nature might peril their valuable lives. An early reply, and oblige,

"Yours truly,

"Public Library of Kentucky."

Reprinted in the *Dispatch* from the *Public Library Paper*, this article by an anonymous writer is in response to Twain's own piece about a plan supposedly hatched by himself and P. T. Barnum (1810-91) to use a newly discovered comet as a ship to explore space. Entitled "A Curious Pleasure Excursion," Twain's essay originally appeared in the New York *Herald* in 1874 and is reprinted in *Collected Tales I* (573-77). Of the celebrities mentioned in this response, Train (1829-1904) was a wealthy but eccentric lecturer and political agitator; Beecher (1813-87), a prominent minister accused of adultery (see 24 January 1890); Pope (1822-92), a noted Union general; Matthew H. Carpenter (1824-81), a senator from Wisconsin; William Marcy Tweed (1823-78), a New York City politician convicted in 1871 of corruption; and Alexander Robey Shepherd (1835-1902), a former public official in Washington D.C. widely suspected—though never convicted—of corruption. "Old Probabilities" was a common pseudonym for a newspaper weather prognosticator. Incidentally, Twain had an affinity for comets since he was born two months premature on 30 November 1835 when Halley's comet shone in the winter skies. He predicted late in his life that he would not die until the comet reappeared 75 years later: "I came in with Halley's comet in 1835. It is coming again next year, and I expect to go out with it. . . . The Almighty has said, no doubt, 'Now there go those two unaccountable frauds; they came in together, they must go out together'" (qtd. in *MT Himself* 288). Twain held to his prediction and died 21 April 1910 with the comet again streaking across the sky.

7 August (Friday)
"News and Notes"; p. 2

A five-act drama entitled *Colonel Sellers* by Mark Twain is soon to be brought on the stage. Mark, says the New York *Graphic*, having become a bear in the humor market, is disposing of his wit at "sellers" option.

Basing his play upon the most popular character from *The Gilded Age*, Twain wrote *Colonel Sellers* in 1874 as he worked on *Tom Sawyer*. His first play proved to be his greatest financial success of the decade, primarily because of the comic acting of John T. Raymond in the title role; a photograph of Raymond in *MT Himself* shows the actor—dressed as Sellers—shaking Twain's hand (176). Twain boasted in July 1876 that he had already made $23,000 from the play, a figure which would more than compensate for the slow sales of *The Gilded Age* (*MT & the Theatre* 56). See 6 March 1875 for a review of the play.

19 August (Wednesday)
"Twain's Interview with a Book Pedlar"; p. 2

A book pedlar visited Mark Twain at home to get his subscription for a new work, of which he carried a copy. He found the genial Mark hoeing in his garden. He was kindly received, and asked to take a seat. He took a seat. The seat was on top of a fence, the uppermost rail of which was sharp. He was not happy as he sat down, and got no happier as he remained. He remained there, too, a very long time, and Mr. Twain was very kind. He talked to him about the book and its author, whom he knew; about the pictures, and the press, and then he branched off into other and very deep literary subjects, of which the agent knew nothing. After an hour or so, Twain hospitably asked the agent into his house, and then talked to him some more. The agent was getting very tired and very hungry. Twain excused himself for a moment, and stayed away an hour, during which time the agent suspects he took dinner. He came back, and was still very kind, and talked again. It was now nearly six p.m., and the agent had come about 11 a.m. He had had nothing to eat, and not a word had been said about a subscription. He grew desperate and asked Twain if he would subscribe. "I think I will," drawled Twain, "but not today; come tomorrow, and we will talk about it." The agent decamped, and now he swears—though he had a nice time and Twain is a good talker—that he will never go back again—no, never.

17 November (Tuesday)
"News and Notes"; p. 2

Mark Twain is emulous of Weston. He wrote as follows from Hartford Monday to Boston:

"Dear Redpath: Rev. J. H. Twichell and I expect to start at 8 o'clock Thursday morning to walk to Boston in 24 hours—or more. We shall telegraph Young's Hotel for rooms for Saturday night, in order to allow for a low average of pedestrianism,

"Yours, S. L. Clemens."

News of this trek, which began 10 November 1874 but was aborted after only 10 hours of walking, made newspapers across the country (*Autobiography* 214-15), surely Twain's intention since his agent, James Redpath, promoted the event by sending the above letter as a telegram to various newspapers (*Mr. Clemens & MT* 185-86). Redpath (1833-91), founder of the Boston Lyceum Bureau, booked lecture tours for Ralph Waldo Emerson and Horace Greeley, as well as Twain. Joseph Twichell (1838-1918), pastor of the Asylum Hill Congregational

Church, was Twain's neighbor in Hartford and his best friend. Twain points out in *Autobiography* that the two men typically took a 10-mile hike through the countryside surrounding Hartford every Saturday, using the opportunity to tell each other off-color stories (269). The "Weston" referred to by the *Dispatch* is Edward Payson Weston (1839-1929), who billed himself as a "professional walker." He became famous in 1867 for walking from Portland, Maine, to Chicago in just 26 days. When he was 70, Weston walked from New York City to San Francisco and then back to New York in less than two years.

1875

7 January (Thursday)
"Personalities"; p. 2

> Mark Twain is hashing up another play, said to be a dramatization of "Roughing It in the Sandwich Islands."

As early as 1870 Twain attempted to write a series of dramatic sketches about his experiences in Nevada and California; eventually, however, he rejected those sketches and decided to tell his story in prose (*MT & the Theatre* 33-34). The result of his decision was *Roughing It*, published in February 1872. Its success—it sold 96,083 copies by 1880 (*MT & Elisha Bliss* 63)—led Augustin Daly (1838-99) to dramatize the book in late 1872. His version of *Roughing It* had only a tenuous connection with Twain's book and was a failure. *MT Himself* reprints a copy of Daly's playbill for *Roughing It* (174). If, as the *Dispatch* states, Twain attempted to do his own theatrical version of the book in 1875, nothing came of it.

19 January (Tuesday)
"Mark Twain's Boyhood Home"; p. 4

> On Third Street, a short distance from a cross street—it is Bird Street, Rock Street, or Collier Street, no one seemed to be certain which was the correct name—stands the building in which little Sammy Clemens lived 20 years ago. It is a square, two-story frame house, of the plainest possible architecture. The half-decayed weather-boarding is deeply streaked with age, and the roof is green with moss. It has a stone foundation, large brick chimney outside the building, and fronts eastward, being faced by four sprawling locust trees. Otherwise, there is not a single distinguishing mark. It has no front yard, and the fences in the immediate vicinity are ancient and frail. The upper part of the house is given to old boxes and the spiders, while the lower floor is used as a cabi-

net-shop by some desecrator of regard for button-bursting and sides-splitting genius. Many of the people of the town remember the boy, but with different opinions. One old lady, Mrs. Martin, says he "used to come up and play with her girls, and that he weren't such an awful smart fellow till he got away, and then folks began to see lots of him." Another person, however, of the masculine persuasion, says he "knew the boy well, and that he was as smart as a steel trap." A third says that "old man Clemens married a second cousin of his (citizen's) sister, so that he came near being in the family." Still another avers that an emissary of *Harper's* came once to sketch the scene and write an account, and had been willingly informed that the house where the future Mark Twain was born, in Florida, Monroe County, had been torn down; but that he (citizen) knew it to be in good preservation, and that the *Harper's* man had gone away from the state without seeing it. Most of the Hannibal people, on being asked about Mark Twain, reflectively exclaim, "Twain! Twain! You don't mean the man that bosses Smith's stone quarry and used to work at the T. W. and W. shops, do you?"

At 206 Hill Street in Hannibal, a scant block from the Mississippi River but facing to the south, stands the boyhood home of Mark Twain; the Clemens family lived there from 1844-53. In that latter year, 18-year-old Twain left for New York City to be a typesetter and his older brother, Orion, bought an interest in an Iowa newspaper. Consequently, Twain's mother sold the house and moved to Iowa with Orion and his wife. After the departure of the family, a number of people owned the house, but it was allowed to fall into general disrepair. The above article, originally published in the Terre Haute *Journal*, may very well be an accurate description of the home's condition in 1875. But in 1911, after it was scheduled to be demolished for the construction of a new building, George A. Mahan, a prominent Hannibal attorney, purchased the house and donated it to the city with the provision that it become a museum to Twain (*MT Boyhood Home* 2). Over the next 70 years, some repairs were made to the home but in 1984 an engineer recommended that it be closed to visitors because of its poor condition. For seven years, however, Hannibal worked to not only make the house structurally sound for visitors but also to restore it to its 1844 appearance. Completed in April 1991, Twain's boyhood home is now a monument to the humorist. *MT Boyhood Home*, a pamphlet available at the home itself, provides many photographs of the house and details its step-by-step reconstruction. Twain's birthplace in Florida, Mo., also stands today, although it has been relocated from its original site to a state park a mile to the south. Like Twain's boyhood home, the Florida house—a rough two-room cabin—fell into such disrepair that it was scheduled for demolition. In 1924, however, M. A. Violette, a prominent citizen of Monroe County, purchased the house and donated it to the Mark Twain Memorial Park Association with the stipulation that it become part of a museum, which it did. In 1960, the state of Missouri constructed the Mark Twain Memorial Shrine around the house to protect it from the elements and to hold an extensive collection of Twain's belongings and memorabilia. *MT's World* prints a photograph of the house as it appeared before its enclosure (14).

30 January (Saturday)
"Personalities"; p. 2

They say Mark Twain has been offered the Constantinople mission because he is a harum-scarum kind of fellow. He would not remain an "innocent abroad" very long.

6 March (Saturday)
"Col. Mulberry Sellers"; p. 2

We do not mean to criticize the play, which like *Solon Shingle*, or *Rip Van Winkle*, has only a certain amount of background to the one prominent figure, nor do we mean to analyze the character of Col. Sellers himself save to remark in passing, that Raymond is well nigh perfect in the part; but we do desire to draw a few conclusions from the bearing of each audience who has visited it of a rather philosophical kind. There appears upon the scene from the first scene to the fifth a certain Senator Dilworthy—that is to say, his presence is felt, understood to be present, referred to so inimitably by the Colonel as to make him an everyday acquaintance, talked of as though he were just gone out for a moment, and so absolutely considered a part of every speculation as to cause wonderment why Napoleon was not called Dilworthy, and the Asiatic Eye Water some name more in consonance with the name of the Christian statesman.

But with all the general laughter that greeted the broad national fun of the Colonel, all the real delight manifested in more ways than one at his quaint good humor, and the strong Western heart that beat at the bottom of every ebb and flow in the tide of fortune, it gave almost real pain to hear the derisive shouts that rose loud and high at every mention made of an American Congress, and to witness the unmistakeable evidences of contempt held by all classes of people for our national law-givers. Their honor was caricatured, and all the audience applauded: their honesty was burlesqued in a public place, and everybody shouted, their patriotism the playwright made farcical, and all play-goers yelled with delight—indeed, it was real public opinion, both on and off the stage, telling the true story of national and official dishonor. But while the lesson is severe, it may be wholesome. Blessings are liable to come in disguise at any time from men like Col. Mulberry Sellers. How keenly and accurately his admirers felt the degradation of the Dilworthy ascendancy and that of his whole corrupt and venal following, their derisive shouts and jeers best gave idea: but how well and truly they are the representatives of a correct but latent public sentiment which has lost faith and heart in all things manipulated by Christian statesmen or Christian law-givers—will endeavor to clear out and break up the whole brood in God's own good time, it is best to be judged by the present hatred of every class to the men of subsidy and scheme—to the tail of the Mobiler serpent that is not alone on Dilworthy, but a host of other men in authority and unknown to the world as yet, but who, for all that, are in high and exalted places.

Colonel Sellers, with noted comic actor John T. Raymond (1836-87) in the title role, opened 16 September 1874 at the Park Theatre in New York City. The great success of his play gave Twain the illusion that he could be a playwright; his other attempts at drama, however, were failures. See 24 September 1887 for a particularly scathing review of *The American Claimant.* The character of Dilworthy in the play was based primarily upon Sen. Samuel C. Pomeroy (1816-91), nationally known for accepting bribes and buying votes (*Mr. Clemens & MT* 162), but he was just one of many corrupt politicians that plagued America during its "Gilded Age." Later in life, Twain would quip, "It could probably be shown by facts and figures that there is no distinctly native American criminal class except Congress." *Solon Shingle* and *Rip Van Winkle* were both popular dramatic monologues at the time.

27 March (Saturday)
"Personalities"; p. 2

Mark Twain says he is so tired of traveling around the country that he would rather stay at home than lecture, and as he is only worth half a million, he will probably fail in starving.

Although the figure of $500,000 is much too high, Twain certainly enjoyed a luxurious standard of living in Hartford without having to resort to the lecture circuit.

31 March (Wednesday)
"Mark Twain"; p. 1

Coming out of the Erie railway building, I yesterday saw Mark Twain, whom we used to know in the old Frisco days as Sam Clemens. He wears the same old brigand hat and cloak, and one is always sure when looking at him that he would rather look shabby than wear a pink overcoat with yellow buttons. It is now just 10 years since I sat one day on the steps of the American House in Honolulu, Sandwich Islands, with Clemens and happened to mention that I was writing letters to the New York *Herald*. He was then unknown except as an odd character in San Francisco, and the writer of letters to the Sacramento *Union*, and he very timidly mentioned that he had received an offer from a [?] monthly to write a page for it for $5. He wanted to know whether it would pay him to go to New York. I had never read anything of his, and I told him that if he went to New York he couldn't earn his salt. Yet there he stood yesterday, with his saucy moustache and gimlet eyes, as unconcerned as if he hadn't married a girl with more salt lying around loose than would pickle all Honolulu.

This anecdote is attributed to the New York correspondent of the Danbury *News*, who otherwise remains anonymous. Twain's penchant for wearing well-worn, frontier-style coats and hats was just one aspect of his public personality at this time in his life. A photograph reproduced in *Mr. Clemens & MT* shows the humorist in his sealskin overcoat and hat and depicts very well his image of being a rough-hewn humorist. Later in his life, Twain developed a new public personality—that of an elder statesman of letters who courageously speaks the truth—and so took to wearing impeccable white suits to reflect his new image. He argued in *Autobiography* that the white suits helped him to feel pure: "I am considered eccentric because I wear white clothes both winter and summer. I am eccentric, then, because I prefer to be clean in the matter of raiment—clean in a dirty world; absolutely the only cleanly-clothed human being in all Christendom north of the tropics" (370). Twain did indeed marry a woman with a great deal of "salt lying around." In late 1867 he met Olivia Louise Langdon (1845-1904), daughter of a rich coal and iron baron of Elmira, N.Y. Although he almost immediately fell in love with Livy and began to court her, her father, a staid businessman, disapproved of her potential match with a humorist. Eventually, though, the couple's love for each other swayed his heart and Jervis Langdon (1809-70) gave his consent for the wedding, which then took place 2 February 1870 (*Mr. Clemens & MT* 79-100). Twain and Livy went on to thirty-seven years of complete happiness. As *Mark & Livy* makes clear, Twain came to regard his wife as indispensable: "She read and proposed changes on nearly everything he wrote. She attended many of his lectures and made constant suggestions regarding material. . . . He relied upon her judgment as to what readers would and wouldn't accept" (xi). See 23 March 1876 and 1 December 1888 for two accounts the *Post-Dispatch* printed about their courtship.

31 March (Wednesday)
"News and Notes"; p. 2

Mark Twain says: "To the poor whites along the Mississippi River chills are a merciful provision of Providence, enabling them to take exercise without exertion."

This joke is taken from the fourth of Twain's articles for the *Atlantic* about the river; the articles were later collected and, after Twain supplemented them with new material, published in May 1883 as *Life on the Mississippi*. The book sold poorly (only 50,000 copies sold in the first few years after its publication), and Twain blamed his publisher James R. Osgood for its failure (*Mr. Clemens & MT* 249-50). The book's lack of success proved to be an impetus for Twain to set up his own publishing company with his nephew Charles L. Webster as its head (*Mr. Clemens & MT* 256). This move to self-publication, initially a success with *Huckleberry Finn* in February 1885, eventually hastened Twain's financial ruin because Webster was clearly not capable of running such a complex business and because the firm overextended itself by publishing works by other authors. In *Autobiography*, which he wanted published only after his death, Twain's memories of Webster are bitter (245-49, 253-58). But Twain himself— with his prodigal spending of the firm's assets and endless bickering with Webster—was just as guilty for the publishing company's failure.

26 April (Monday)
"News and Notes"; p. 2

"Mark Twain used to run a boat down here, didn't he?" inquired a traveler of a Mississippi pilot, lately. "Mark Twain; do you mean him as was Sam Clemens? Wal, yes, he did try pilotin' yer awhile, but he couldn't do it, couldn't do 'tall, hadn't the gen'us. But, I tell you," continued the grizzly veteran, giving his wheel a twist, "if ye'd agin him boats 'nough while he was a-practicin', he'd a-clared the river of snags, for shuah."

Like all steamboat pilots, Twain had his share of incidental groundings, but there is no record of him being a poor pilot as this anecdote suggests.

3 May (Monday)
"Some Successful Literary People"; p. 2

Clemens, the humorist, better known as Mark Twain, has done better than any man in his turn of labor. He has been seven years before the public, and during that time has become rich enough to live on his income. His property in Hartford is worth more than $80,000.

This story from the Troy *Times* also mentions other authors, including Harriet Beecher Stowe (1811-96) and Josh Billings, pseudonym of Henry Wheeler Shaw (1818-85).

4 May (Tuesday)
"News and Notes"; p. 2

We hope Mark Twain's appeal for subscriptions to erect a Shakespeare Memorial building will meet with the generous response it deserves. The walls and rafters of the house where William was born are so covered with signatures that the American visitor is now obliged to write his name on a piece of paper and hang it over the fireplace. We see no way of relieving this crowded condition of things except by putting up a new building.

This piece is reprinted from the Brooklyn *Argus*. *MT Speaks for Himself* gives the text of Twain's appeal, in which he asks the New York *Times* to publicize the drive for money to build an elaborate monument to Shakespeare in Stratford-upon-Avon (93-97). Ironically, later in his life Twain, convinced that Shakespeare could not have written the plays attributed to him, argued that Francis Bacon was the probable author. The humorist attempts to prove his theory in a long essay entitled "Is Shakespeare Dead?" (*Complete Essays* 407-54).

19 May (Wednesday)
"Mark Twain on Spelling: The Beauty of Unfettered Originality in Orthography"; p. 2

There was a spelling match at the Asylum Hill Congregational Church, Hartford, Conn., on Wednesday evening, and

Mr. Samuel L. Clemens (Mark Twain) being called upon for a few preliminary remarks spoke as follows:

"Ladies and gentlemen: I have been honored with the office of introducing these approaching orthographical solemnities with a few remarks. The temperance crusade swept the land some time ago, that is, that vast portion of the land where it was needed, but it skipped Hartford. Now comes this new spelling epidemic, and this time we are stricken. So, I suppose we needed the affliction. I don't say we needed it, for I don't see any use in spelling a word right, and never did. I mean, I don't see any use in having a uniform and an arbitrary way of spelling words. We might as well make all clothes alike and cook all dishes alike. Sameness is tiresome; variety is pleasing. I have a correspondent whose letters are always a refreshment to me, there is such a breezy, unlettered originality about his orthography. He always spells 'Kow' with a large K. Now, that is just as good as to spell it with a small one. It is better. It gives the imagination a broader field, a wider scope. It suggests to the mind a grand, vague, impressive kind of a cow. Superb effects can be produced by variegated spelling. Now there is Blind Tom, the musical prodigy. He always spells a word according to the sound that is carried to his ear. And he is an enthusiast in orthography. When you give him a word, he shouts it out—puts his soul into it. I once heard him called upon to spell orang-outang before an audience. He said, 'O, r-a-n-g, orang, ger, ger, oranger, t-a-n-g, orangger tang!' Now a body can respect an orang-outang that spells his name in such a vigorous way like that. But the feeble dictionary makes a mere kitten of him. In the old times people spelled just as they pleased. That was the right idea. You had two chances at a stranger then. You know a strong man from a weak one by his ironclad spelling and his handwriting helped you to verify your verdict. Some people have an idea that correct spelling can be taught—and taught to anybody. This is a mistake. The spelling faculty is born in a man, like poetry, music, and art. It is a gift; it is a talent. People who have this gift in a high degree only need to see a word once in print, and it is forever photographed upon their memory. They cannot forget it. People who haven't it must be content to spell more or less like—like thunder—and expect to splinter the dictionary wherever their orthographical lightning happens to strike.

There are 114,000 words in the unabridged dictionary. I know a lady who can spell only 130 of them right. She steers clear of all the rest. She can't learn any more. So her letters always consist of these constantly recurring 130 words. Now and then, when she finds herself obliged to write upon a subject which necessitates the use of some other words, she—well, she don't write on that subject. I have a relative in New York who is almost sublimely gifted. She can't spell any word right. There is a game called Verbarium. A dozen people are each provided with a sheet of paper across the top of which is written a word like 'kaleidoscopal,' or something like that, and the game is to see who can make up the most words out of that in three minutes, always beginning with the initial letter of that word. Upon one occasion the word chosen was 'cofferdam.' When time was called, everybody had built from five to 20 words except this young lady. She had only one word—'calf.' We all studied for a moment, and then said, 'Why, there is no 'l' in cofferdam.' Then we examined her paper. To the eternal honor of that uninspired, unconscious, sublimely independent soul be it said, she had spelt that word 'caff'! If anybody here can spell 'calf' any more sensibly than that, let him step to the front and take his milk. The insurrection will now begin."

An excellent speller himself (*Autobiography* 109, 202-03), Twain was nevertheless fascinated by schemes to change spelling; in "A Simplified Alphabet" (*Complete Essays* 544-50), for example, he advocates the use of a purely phonetic alphabet. This particular spelling match, the highlight of a fund-raising carnival by the youth of the church, took place on 12 May 1875 and proved to be a popular entertainment. The Twain family donated the prizes for the contest—an assortment of books and objets d'art—and participated in the "insurrection." Twain, among the last to lose, spelled "chaldron" without its "h" (*MT Speaking* 94-96).

21 May (Friday)
"News and Notes"; p. 2

The Rochester (Minn.) *Post* gives the following as a sign painted on a fence in the neighborhood: "Kash pade fur littel kalves nut mourn to daze old." How a letter from that man would warm the heart of Mark Twain.

25 May (Tuesday)
"News and Notes"; p. 2

Mark Twain denies that his *Gilded Age* was a failure. He says it gave a poor, worthy bookbinder a job.

7 June (Monday)
"Mark Twain's Brother: The Principle Land Owner of Fentress County"; p. 2

Late in the evening we came to Jamestown, Tenn. This is the county seat of Fentress County. Here, a few years ago, Calvin Logston paid the debt of nature, and of the law. The gibbet where he suffered stands yet upon the green, a terrible warning to evil-doers. At this place I had the good fortune to form the acquaintance of Mr. Orien [sic] Clemens, a brother of the celebrated Mark Twain. Their father, John M. Clemens, was clerk of the circuit court at Jamestown for several years, along about 1823 and 1830. He was afterward postmaster at Pall Mall in the same county for a number of years. In looking over the musty records at Jamestown I find that he located some 40,000 acres of mountain land in this county. This wild land, I am told, plays a prominent part in Twain's novel *Gilded Age*. From here, they moved to Missouri, where Mark was born. About the year 1856, Twain and the other heirs transferred their interest in most or all of this land to their brother Orien [sic], "for $1 and other considerations." Suppose Twain, instead of generously handing his interest over to his quiet, inoffensive brother (who never did him any harm), had held on to it, and had spent his time in trying to work up and straighten out these mountain titles. *The Gilded Age, Roughing It,* and *Innocents Abroad* would never have been written, the thousands of believers and practicers of the doctrine of "laugh and grow fat" would today be lean, gaunt spectres, monuments of a thwarted providence; and the immortal Mark himself would, in all human probability, have been ere this a raving, roaring, ranting inmate of an insane asylum. But he shoved the thing off on his brother, went to work and turned the whole thing into a huge joke, and is making more money out of it than any man ever made out of mountain land before. I shall ever after this believe in special providences. I found the brother a quiet, social gentleman, and not puffed up over the fact that he is brother to the most distinguished humorist of the age.

This article is attributed to a correspondent of the Knoxville *Chronicle*, who otherwise remains anonymous. Twain's father, John Marshall Clemens (1798-1847), actually purchased more than 75,000 acres of the Tennessee land as an investment, but it was never to return a profit for his heirs. Twain himself came to regard it as a "curse" since it made the family feel rich but only bled them dry through taxes (*Autobiography* 18-19, 22-25). In 1866, Twain found a man who wanted to purchase the land for $200,000 and use it for vineyards, but Orion—an advocate of abstemiousness at the time—refused to sign the contract. His refusal remained a source of conflict between the brothers for some months afterward (*MT: Bachelor* 274-75). Presumably, this correspondent misspells Orion's name because he only heard it pronounced (the Clemens family pronounced it "Or-ean") and had not seen it spelled. Orion (1825-97) tried all his life to be a success like his younger brother, but he was doomed to failure by a mediocre intelligence and decided lack of perseverence. See 12 June 1879 and 8 June 1885 for two additional items about him.

9 June (Wednesday)
"News and Notes"; p. 2

Mark Twain says: "I have seen slower people than I am—and more deliberate than I am—even quieter, and more listless than I am. But they were dead."

24 July (Friday)
"Mark Twain's Scientific Calculation"; p. 2

Mark Twain in the August *Atlantic* mourns over the diminished length of the Mississippi in this strain:

"Therefore, the Mississippi between Cairo and New Orleans was 1,200 miles 176 years ago. It was 1,180 after the cut-off of 1822. It was 1,040 after the American Bend cut-off (some 16 years ago). It has lost 67 miles since. Consequently its length is only 9,733 miles at present.

"Now, if I wanted to be one of these ponderous scientific people, and 'let on' to prove what had occurred in the remote past by what had occurred in a given time in the recent past, or what will occur in the far future by what has occurred in late years, what an opportunity is here! Geology never had such a chance nor such exact data to argue from. Nor 'development of species' either! Glacial epochs are strange things, but they are not vague. Please observe:

"In the space of 176 years the lower Mississippi has shortened itself 242 miles. That is an average of a trifle over one mile and a third per year. Therefore, any calm person, who is not blind or idiotic, can see that in the old Oolitic Silurian period, just a million years ago next November, the lower Mississippi River was upwards of 1,300,000 miles long, and stuck out over the Gulf of Mexico like a fishing rod. And by the same token any person can see that 742 years from now the lower Mississippi will be only a mile and three quarters long, and Cairo and New Orleans will have joined their streets together, and be plodding comfortably along under a single mayor and a mutual board of aldermen. There is something fascinating about science. One gets such wholesale returns out of conjectures out of such a trifling investing of fact."

This long joke, taken from the seventh article of Twain's "Old Times on the Mississippi," illustrates perfectly how Twain loved to twist statistics until they became meaningless. Other more serious "scientists" used statistics in similar ways; see 30 November 1878 for an example.

7 August (Saturday)
"Animated Journalism: An Eventful Three Hours' Experience on a Tennessee Newspaper"; p. 2

I was told by the physician that a southern climate would improve my health, so I went down to Tennessee and got a berth on the *Morning Glory and Jefferson County Warwhoop* as associate editor.

When I went on duty, I found the chief editor tilted back in a three-legged chair, with his feet on a pine table. There was another pine table in the room and another afflicted chair, and both were half-buried under newspapers and scraps and sheets of manuscript. There was a wooden box of sand sprinkled with cigar stubs and "old soldiers," and a stove with a door hanging upon its upper hinge. The chief editor had a long-tailed, black-cloth, frock coat on and white linen pants. His boots were small and neatly blacked. He wore a ruffled shirt, a large seal ring, a standing collar of obsolete pattern and checked neckerchief with the ends hanging down. Date of costume about 1848. He was sucking a cigar and trying to think of a word and in pawing his hair for it he had rumpled it a great deal. He was scowling fearfully and I judged he was concocting a particularly knotty editorial. He told me to take the exchanges and skim through them, and write up "The Spirit of the Tennessee Press," condensing into the article all of their contents that seemed to be of interest.

"SPIRIT OF THE TENNESSEE PRESS.

"The editors of the *Semi-Weekly Earthquake* evidentaly labor under misapprehension with regard to the Ballyhack railroad. It is not the object of the company to leave Buzzardsville off to one side. On the contrary, they consider it one of the most important points on the line, and, consequently, can have no desire to slight it. The gentlemen of the *Earthquake* will, of course, take pleasure in making the correction.

"It is pleasant to note that the city of Blathersville is endeavoring to contract with some New York gentlemen to have its well-impassable streets paved with the Nicolson pavement. But it is difficult to accomplish a desire like this since Memphis got some New Yorkers to do a like service for her and then declined to pay for it. However, the *Daily Hurrah* still urges the measures with ability, and seems confident of success.

"We are pained to learn that Col. Bascom of the *Dying Shriek for Liberty* fell in the street a few evenings since and broke his leg. He has lately been suffering from debility, caused by overwork and anxiety on account of sickness in his family, and it is supposed that he fainted from the exertion of walking too much in the sun."

I passed my manuscript over to the editor for acceptance, alteration, or destruction. He glanced at it and his face clouded. He ran his eye down the paper and his countenance grew portentous. It was easy to see that something was wrong. Presently he sprang up and said:

"Thunder and lightning! Do you suppose I'm going to speak of those cattle that way? Do you suppose my subscribers are going to stand such gruel as that? Give me the pen."

I never saw a pen scrape and scratch its way so viciously, or plow through another man's verbs and adjectives as relentlessly. While he was in the midst of his work, somebody shot at him through the open window and marred the symmetry of his ear.

"Ah!" said he, "that is that scoundrel Smith of the *Moral Volcano*. He was due yesterday." And he snatched up a navy revolver from his belt and fired. The shot crippled Smith's aim, who was taking a second chance, and he crippled a stranger. It was me. Merely a finger shot off.

Then the chief editor went on with his erasures and inter-lineations. Just as he finished them, a hand grenade came down the stove pipe, and the explosion shivered the stove into fragments. However, it did no further damage, except that a vagrant piece knocked a couple of my teeth out.

"That stove is perfectly ruined," said the chief editor.

I said I believed it was.

"Well, no matter, don't want it this kind of weather. I know the man that did it. I'll get him. Now, here is the way this stuff ought to be written."

I took the manuscript. It was scarred with erasures and interlineations till its mother wouldn't have known it, if it had had one. It now read as follows:

"SPIRIT OF THE TENNESSEE PRESS.

"The inveterate liars of the *Semi-Weekly Earthquake* are often endeavoring to palm off upon a noble and chivalrous people another of their vile and brutal falsehoods with regard to that most glorious conception of the 19th century, the Bally-hack railroad. The idea that Buzzardsville was to be left off at one side originated in their own fulsome brains, or rather, in the settlings they regard as brains. They had better swallow this lie, and not stop to chew it either, if they want to save their abandoned reptile carcasses the cowhiding they so richly deserve.

"That ass Blossom of the Higginsville *Thunderbolt and Battlecry of Freedom* is down here again, bumming his board at the Van Buren.

"We observe that the besotted blackguard of the Mud Springs *Howl* is giving out with his usual propensity for lying that Van Werter is not elected. The heaven-born mission of journalism is to disseminate truth—to eradicate error—to educate, refine, and elevate the tone of public manners and morals, and make all men more gentle, more virtuous, more charitable, and, in all ways, better and holier, and happier—and yet this black-hearted villain, this hell-spawned miscreant, prostitutes his great office persistently to the dissemination of falsehood, calumny, vituperation, and degrading vulgarity. His paper is notoriously unfit to take into people's homes and ought to be banished to the gambling halls and brothels where the mass of reeking pollution which does its duty as its editor lives and moves and has his being.

"Blathersville wants a Nicolson pavement—it wants a jail and a poorhouse more. The idea of pavement in a one-horse town with two gin-mills and a blacksmith's shop in it, and that mustard-plaster of a newspaper, the *Daily Hurrah*! Better borrow of Memphis, where the article is cheap. The crawling insect Buckner, who edits the *Hurrah*, is braying about the pavement business with his customary loud-mouthed imbecility, and imagining that he is talking sense. Such foul, mephitic scum as this verminous Buckner is a disgrace to journalism.

"That degraded ruffian Bascom of the *Dying Shriek for Liberty* fell down and broke his leg yesterday—pity it wasn't his neck. He says it was debility caused by overwork and anxiety! It was debility caused by trying to lug six gallons of 40-rod whisky around town when his hide is only gauged for four, and anxiety where he was going to bum another six. 'He fainted from the exertion of walking too much in the sun'! And well he might say that—but if he would walk straight he would get just as far and not have to walk as much. For years the pure air of this town has been made perilous by the deadly breath of this perambulating pestilence, this pulky bleat, this steaming animated tank of mendacity, gin, and profanity, this Bascom! Perish all such from the sacred and majestic mission of journalism."

"Now, that is the way to write—peppery and to the point. Mush-and-milk journalism gives me the Pan-Tod."

About this time a brick came in at the window with a splintering crash, and gave me a considerable jolt in the middle of the back. I moved out of range. I began to feel in the way. The chief said:

"That was the colonel, likely. I've been expecting him for two days. He will be up now, right away."

He was correct. The "colonel" appeared in the door a moment afterward with a dragoon revolver in his hand. He said: "Sir, have I the honor of addressing the blatant, black-hearted scoundrel Capt. Blatherskite Tecumseh?"

"The same."

"I have a little account to settle with you. If you are at leisure, we will begin."

"I have an article on the 'encouraging progress of moral and intellectual development in America' to finish, but there is no hurry. Begin."

Both pistols rang out their fierce clamor at the same instant. The chief lost a lock of hair, and the colonel's bullet ended its career in the fleshy part of my thigh. The colonel's left shoulder was clipped a little. They fired again. They both missed their men this time, but I got my share, a shot in the arm. At the third fire both gentlemen were wounded slightly, and I had a knuckle clipped. I then said I would go out and take a walk, as this was a private matter and I had a delicacy about participating in it further. Both gentlemen begged me to keep my seat, and assured that I was not in the way. I had thought differently up to this time.

They then talked about the elections and the crop awhile, and I fell to tying up my wounds. But presently they opened fire again with animation, and every shot took effect—but it is proper to remark that five out of six fell to my share. The sixth one mortally wounded the colonel, who remarked with fine humor that he would have to say good morning now as he had business up town. He then inquired the way to the undertaker's and left. The chief turned to me and said:

"I am expecting company to dinner and shall have to get ready. It will be a favor to me if you would read proof and attend to customers."

I winced a little at the idea of attending to customers, but I was too bewildered by the fusilade that was still ringing in my ears to think of anything to say.

"Jones will be here at three. Cowhide him. Gillespie will call earlier, perhaps—throw him out of the window. Ferguson will be here about four. Kill him. That is all for today, I believe. If you have any odd time, you may write a blistering article on the police—give the chief inspector rats. The cowhides are under the table, weapons in the drawer, ammunition up there in the corner, lint and bandages up there in the pigeon holes. In case of accident, go to Lancet, the surgeon downstairs. He advertises—we take it out in trade."

He was gone. I shuddered. At the end of the next three hours I had been through perils so awful that all peace of mind and all cheerfulness had gone from me. Gillespie had called, and thrown me out of the window. Jones arrived promptly, and when I got ready to do the cowhiding, he took the job off my hands. In an encounter with a stranger not in the bill of fare, I had lost my scalp. Another stranger by the name of Thompson left me a mere wreck and ruin of chaotic rags.

Originally written for the Buffalo *Express* in 1869, this story was later published in *Sketches, New and Old* under the title "Journalism in Tennessee." The *Dispatch's* version is incomplete because it lacks the concluding paragraph in which the protagonist resigns from the paper and departs for a hospital. Although fictional, this story captures very well the spirit of journalism on the frontier. In 1864, for example, Twain, assistant editor on a newspaper, tried to provoke a duel through his insults about the editor of a rival newspaper; see 10 April 1876 for Twain's account of that incident.

20 November (Saturday)
"Our Spice Box"; p. 2

One of Mark Twain's funniest stories is that of a Scripture panorama, the proprietor of which engaged a pianist to play appropriate music. The musician, when the picture for the Prodigal Son was passing, struck up "When Johnny Comes Marching Home" which excited the indignation of the moral lecturer. Recently, in a neighboring town the drama of *Joseph and his Brethren* was played, and the tune to which Jacob and his family journeyed into Egypt was "Marching Through Georgia."

This joke is a summary of one of Twain's earliest pieces written under the pseudonym of "Mark Twain." Entitled "'Mark Twain' on the Launch of the Steamer *Capitol*," it was originally written in early November of 1865 for the *Californian*, a literary journal edited by Bret Harte, and was later included in *Sketches, New and Old* under the title of "The Scriptural Panoramist." Its full text is reprinted in *Collected Tales I* (178-83).

11 December (Saturday)
"My Late Senatorial Secretaryship"; p. 3

I am not private secretary to a senator any more, now. I held the berth two months in security and in great cheerfulness of spirit, but my bread began to return from over the waters then—that is to say, my works came back and revealed themselves. I judged it best to resign. The way of it was this. My employer sent for me one morning tolerably early, and, as soon as I had finished inserting some conundrums clandestinely into his last great speech upon finance, I entered his presence. There was something portentous in his appearance. His cravet was untied, his hair was in a state of disorder, and his countenance bore about it the signs of a suppressed storm. He held a package of letters in his tense grasp, and I knew that the dreaded Pacific mail was in. He said:

"I thought you were worthy of my confidence?"

I said: "Yes, sir."

He said: "I gave you a letter from certain of my constituents in the state of Nevada asking the establishment of a post office at Baldwin's Ranch, and told you to answer it as ingeniously as you could, with arguments which should persuade them that there was no real necessity for an office at that place."

I felt easier. "Oh, if that is all, sir, I *did* do that."

Yes, you *did*. I will read your answer for your own humiliation."

"'Washington, Nov. 24.

"'Messrs. Smith, Jones, and others—

"'Gentlemen:

"'What the mischief do you suppose you want of a post office at Baldwin's Ranch? It would not do you any good. If letters came there, you couldn't read them, you know; and, besides, such letters as ought to pass through with money in them for other localities would not be likely to *get* through, you must perceive at once; and that would make trouble for us all. No, don't bother about a post office in your camp. I have your best interests at heart, and feel that it would only be an ornamental folly. What you need is a nice jail, you know—a nice substantial jail and a free school. These will be a lasting benefit to you. These will make you really contented and happy. I will move in the matter at once. Very truly, etc.,

"'Mark Twain.

"'For James W. N----, U. S. Senator.'

"That is the way you answered the letter. Those people say they will hang me, if I ever enter that district again; and I am perfectly satisfied they *will*, too."

"Well, sir, I did not know I was doing any harm. I only wanted to convince them."

"Oh. Well, you *did* convince them, I make no manner of doubt. Now, here is another specimen. I gave you a petition from certain gentlemen of Nevada, praying that I would get a bill through Congress incorporating the Methodist Episcopal Church of the State of Nevada. I told you to say in reply that the erection of such a law came more properly within the province of a state legislature, and to endeavor to show them that, in the present feebleness of the religious element in that new commonwealth, the expediency of incorporating the church was questionable. What did you write?"

"'Washington, Nov. 24.

"'Rev. John Halifax, and others—

"'Gentlemen:

"'You will have to go to the state legislature about that speculation of yours—Congress don't know anything about religion. But don't you hurry to go there, either; because the thing you propose to do out in that new country isn't expedient—in fact, it is ridiculous. Your religious people there are too feeble in intellect, morality, in piety—in everything, pretty much. You had better drop this—you can't make it work. You can't issue stock on an incorporation like that, or if you could it would only keep you in trouble all the time. The other denominations would abuse it, and 'bear' it, and 'sell it short,' and break it down. They would do with it just as they would with one of your silver mines out there—they would try to make all the world believe it was 'wildcat.' You ought not to do anything that is calculated to bring a sacred thing into disrepute. You ought to be ashamed of yourselves, that is what I think about it. You close your petition with the words: 'And we will ever pray.' I think you had better—you need to do it. Very truly, etc.,

"'Mark Twain.

"'For James W. N----, U. S. Senator.'

"*That* luminous epistle finishes me with the religious element among my constituents. But that my political murder might be made sure, some evil instinct prompted me to hand you this memorial from the grave company of elders composing the board of aldermen of the city of San Francisco to try your hand upon—a memorial praying that the city's right to the water-lots upon the city front might be established by law of Congress. I told you this was a dangerous matter to move in. I told you to write a non-committal letter to the aldermen—an ambiguous letter—a letter that should avoid as far as possible all real consideration and discussion of the water-lot question. If there is any feeling left in you—any shame—surely this letter you wrote in obedience to that order ought to evoke it when its words fall upon your ears.

"'Washington, Nov. 27.

"'The Honorable Board of Aldermen, etc.

"'Gentlemen:

"'George Washington, the reverend father of his country, is dead. His long and brilliant career is closed, alas! forever. He was greatly respected in this section of the country, and his untimely decease cast a gloom over the whole community. He died on the 14th day of Dec. 1799. He passed peacefully away from the scene of his honors and his great achievements, the most lamented hero and best beloved that ever earth hath yielded unto Death. At such a time you speak of water-lots!—what a lot was his!

"'What is fame? Fame is an accident. Sir Issac Newton discovered an apple falling to the ground—a trivial discovery truly, and one which a million men had made before him—but his parents were influential and so they tortured that small circumstance into something wonderful, and lo! the simple world took up the shout and, in almost the twinkling of an eye, that man was famous. Treasure these thoughts:

"'Poesy, sweet poesy, who shall estimate what the world
          owes to thee!

"'Mary had a little lamb, its fleece was white as snow—

"'And everywhere that Mary went, the lamb was sure to
          go.

"'Jack and Jill went up a hill

"'To get a pail of water;

"'Jack fell down and broke his crown,

"'And Jill came tumbling after.

"'For simplicity, elegance of diction, and freedom from immoral tendencies, I regard these poems in the light of gems. They are suited to all grades of intelligence, to every sphere of life—to the field, to the nursery, to the guild. Especially should no board of aldermen be without them.

"'Venerable fossils! write again. Nothing improves one so much as friendly correspondence. Write again—and if there is anything in this memorial of yours that refers to anything in particular, don't be backward about explaining it. We shall always be happy to hear you chirp. Very truly, etc.

"'Mark Twain.

"'For James W. N.----, United States Senator.'

"This is an atrocious, a ruinsome epistle! Distraction!"

"Well, sir, I am really sorry if there is anything wrong

about it—but—but—it appears to me to dodge the water-lot question."

"Dodge the mischief! Oh!—but never mind. As long as the destruction must come now, let it come complete. Let it be complete—let this last of your performances, which I am about to read, make a finality of it. I am a ruined man. I had my misgivings when I gave you the letter from Humboldt, asking that the best route from Indian Gulch to Shakespeare Gap and intermediate points be changed partly to the old Morman trail. But I told you it was a delicate question and warned you to deal with it deftly—to answer it dubiously and leave them a little in the dark. And your fatal imbecility impelled you to make this disastrous reply. I should think you would stop your ears, if you were not dead to all shame.

"'Washington D.C, Nov. 30.

"'Messrs. Perkins, Wagner, et. al.

"'Gentlemen:

"'It is a delicate question about this Indian trail, but, handled with proper deftness and dubiousness, I doubt not that we shall succeed in some measure or otherwise, because the place where the route leaves the Lassen Meadows, over beyond where those two Shawnee chiefs, Dilapidated-Vengeance and Biter-of-the-Clouds, were scalped last winter, this being the favorite direction to some, but others preferring something else in consequence of things, the Morman trail leaving Mosby's at three in the morning, and passing through Jawbone Flat at Blucher, and then down by Jug-Handle, the road passing to the right of it and naturally leaving it on the right, too, and Dawson's on the left of the trail, where it passes to the left of said Dawson's, onward thence to Tomahawk, thus making the route cheaper, easier of access, and compassing all the desirable objects so considered by others, and therefore, conferring the most good upon the greatest number, and consequently I am encouraged to hope we shall be ready, and happy, to afford you still further information upon the subject, from time to time, as you may desire it and the post office department be enabled to furnish it to me. Very truly, etc.

"'Mark Twain.

"'For James W. N.----, U. S. Senator.'

"There—now, *what* do you think of that?"

"Well, I don't know, sir. It—well, it appears to me—to be

dubious enough."

"Du—leave the house! I am a ruined man. Those Humboldt savages never will forgive me for tangling up their brains up with this inhuman letter. I have lost the respect of the Methodist Church, the board of aldermen—"

"Well, I haven't anything to say about that, because I may have missed it a little in their cases, but I *was* too much for the Baldwin's Ranch people, General."

"Leave the house! Leave it forever, and forever, too!"

I regarded that as a sort of covert information that my services would be dispensed with, and so I resigned. I never will be a private secretary to a senator again. You can't please that kind of people. They don't know anything. They can't appreciate a party's efforts.

This story, which surely exaggerates Twain's mischief during his few weeks as private secretary to U. S. Senator William M. Stewart (1827-1909) in late 1867, was originally printed in the New York *Galaxy* in May 1868 and was later included in *Sketches, New and Old*.

1876

4 January (Tuesday)
"Our Spice Box"; p. 2

Mark Twain, the author of *The Gilded Age*, now regrets that he didn't kill "Carenel Selby" in the first act.

15 January (Saturday)
"Personal, Professional, and Political"; p. 2

Col. Mulberry Sellers is pointed this way and will arrive next month.

See 29 February 1876 for another announcement about the play.

16 February (Wednesday)
"Mark Twain on Biblical Geography"; p. 3

When I was a boy I somehow got the impression that the River Jordan was 4,000 miles long and 35 miles wide. It is only 90 miles long, and so crooked that a man does not know which side of it he is on half the time. In going 90 miles it does not get over more than 50 miles of ground. It is not any wider than Broadway in New York. There is the Sea of Galilee and the Dead Sea—neither of them 20 miles long or 13 wide. And yet when I was in Sunday school I thought they were 60,000 miles in diameter.

Travel and experience mar the grandest pictures and rob us of the most cherished traditions of our boyhood. Well, let them go. I have already seen the Empire of Solomon diminish to the size of the state of Pennsylvania. I suppose I can bear the reduction of seas and the river.

Throughout *The Innocents Abroad*, his first travel book, Twain explains how he felt disillusioned by the sights of Europe, Asia Minor, and the Holy Land. In the latter region, for instance, he was constantly amazed at how small all the geographical features seemed to be in comparison with the grandiose descriptions provided by the Bible.

29 February (Tuesday)
"Amusements"; p. 1

The bulk of this long column, which ran nearly every day in the *Dispatch* and covered the St. Louis theater scene, describes a number of different productions. However, there is one line in reference to Twain: "John T. Raymond will appear at the Olympic next week in *Mulberry Sellers*." Over the course of the next two weeks, nearly all the "Amusement" columns carried a similar line previewing the comedy and encouraging people to attend.

22 March (Wednesday)
"Mark Twain on St. Patrick"; p. 1

The following letter was read at the supper of the Knights of St. Patrick at Hartford, Conn., on Friday night:

"Hartford, March 16,

"Richard McCloud, etc.

"Dear Sir—I am very sorry that I cannot be with the Knights of St. Patrick tomorrow evening. In this Centennial year we ought all to find a peculiar pleasure in doing honor to the memory of a man whose good name has endured through 14 centuries. We ought to find pleasure in it for the reason that at this time we naturally have a fellow-feeling for such a man. He wrought a great work in his day. He found Ireland a prosperous republic, and looked about him to see if he might find some useful thing to turn his hand to. He observed that the president of that republic was in the habit of sheltering his great officials from deserved punishment, so he lifted up his staff and smote him, and he died. He found that the Secretary of War had become so unbecomingly economical as to have laid up $12,000 a year out of a salary of $8,000, and he killed him. He found that the Secretary of the Interior always prayed over every separate and distinct barrel of salt beef that was intended for the unconverted savage, and then kept that beef himself, so he killed him also. He found that the Secretary of the Navy knew more about handling suspicious claims than he did about handling a ship, and he at once made an end of him. He found that the very foul Private Secretary had been engineered through a sham trial, so he destroyed him. He discovered that the Congress which pretended to prodigious virtue was very anxious to investigate an ambassador who had dishonored his country abroad, but was equally anxious to prevent the appointment of any spotless man to a similar post; that this Congress had no God but party, no system of morals but party policy; no vision but a bat's vision, and no reason or excuse for existing anyhow. Therefore he massacred that Congress to the last man.

"When he had finished his great work he said in a figurative way, 'Lo, I have destroyed all the reptiles in Ireland.'

"St. Patrick had no politics; his sympathies lay with the right—that was politics enough. When he came across a reptile he forgot to inquire whether he was a Democrat or a Republican, but simply exalted his staff and 'let him have it.' Honored be his name—I wish we had him here to trim us up for the Centennial. But that cannot be. His staff, which was the symbol of real, not sham reform, is idle. However, we still have with us the symbol of truth—George Washington's little hatchet—for I know [where] they've buried it. Yours truly,

"S. L. Clemens."

This piece contrasts the traditional honesty of St. Patrick with the venality of many American politicians during the "Gilded Age" by rather pointedly attacking President Grant for allowing corrupt officials to continue in his cabinet. Grant's second term (1872-76) was plagued by one scandal after another, the worst of which was Crédit Mobilier, a scheme to rob the treasury through fraudulent contracts for railroad construction. Twain's disgust with politics is quite clear from this letter, and it is no surprise that he eagerly joined the burgeoning movement to reform the American political system. Unfortunately, not much changed even after reformist candidates were elected in 1876 and 1880. For some reason, the *Dispatch* leaves out the crucial word "where" from the last sentence of the letter. *Sketches & Tales*, however, reprints the letter and fills in the missing word (302-03).

23 March (Thursday)
"Mark Twain's References"; p. 1

When Mark Twain was courting the girl who became his wife, her father, thinking matters had gone pretty far for a stranger, called the young man aside and said: "Mr. Clemens, you seem to be paying continued attention to my daughter. Now, we all like you pretty well, you know, and we are of course all acquainted with your reputation as a literary man. Still, in other respects you are a stranger to us, and some references as to your character and standing are desirable."

"That's very reasonable," said Mark. "That's very natural and paternal. It's just what I should do were I in your position. I guess I can give you some names that will satisfy you. Now, there's Mr. Goodman of the *Territorial Enterprise*. And there's Mr. Frederick McCrellish [sic], of the *Alta California*. You write to them. I guess they'll give me a good character. I guess they will lie for me. I've done the same for them whenever a requisition has been made upon me."

But Mark married the girl notwithstanding.

Twain himself relates a similar story of his references in *Autobiography*, noting that two letters stated he would "fill a drunkard's grave" (188-90). In that version of the story, however, Twain does not use Goodman as a reference, although it is plain that he should have. Joseph T. Goodman (1838-1917), owner and editor of the *Territorial Enterprise* of Virginia City, Nev., befriended the penniless humorist and offered him a position on his newspaper; the two grew to become close friends. Conversely, Twain's relations with Frederick MacCrellish were not nearly as cordial. MacCrellish, owner of the *Alta* of San Francisco, employed Twain in 1866 as a traveling correspondent for his newspaper and subsequently paid him $20 for each letter that Twain sent to the *Alta* during the *Quaker City* cruise of 1867 (*Mr. Clemens & MT* 69-70). In 1868, after he had signed a book contract with the American Publishing Company of Hartford, Twain wanted to use the 50 letters he had mailed to the *Alta* for his first book, *The Innocents Abroad*. MacCrellish initially refused Twain permission to reprint his own letters but later relented with the proviso that Twain acknowledge the *Alta* in the preface to his book, which he did. *The Innocents Abroad*, published in 1869, went on to become a best seller and established Twain's reputation as a humorist. Given the copyright feud between the two men, MacCrellish very well might have given Twain a bad reference had he asked for one. On 1 December 1888 the *Post-Dispatch* printed another version of Twain's courtship of Livy.

4 April (Tuesday)

"Mark Twain: How He Edited an Agricultural Newspaper"; p. 3

I did not take the temporary editorship of an agricultural newspaper without misgivings. Neither would a landsman take command of a ship without misgivings. But I was in circumstances that made the salary an object. The regular editor of the paper was going off for a holiday, and I accepted the terms he offered and took his place.

The sensation of being at work again was luxurious, and I

wrought all the week with unflagging pleasure. We went to press, and I waited a day, with some solicitude, to see whether my effort was going to attract any notice. As I left the office toward sundown, a group of men and boys at the foot of the stairs dispersed with one impulse and gave me passage-way, and I heard one of them say: "That's him!" I was naturally pleased by this incident. The next morning I found a similar group at the foot of the stairs, scattered couples and individuals standing here and there in the street and over the way, watching me with interest.

The group separated and fell back as I approached, and I heard a man say: "Look at his eye!" I pretended not to observe the notice I was attracting, but secretly I was pleased with it, and was purposing to write an account of it to my aunt. I went up the short flight of stairs and heard cheery voices and a ringing laugh as I drew near the door, which I opened and caught a glimpse of two young rural-looking men, whose faces blanched and lengthened when they saw me, and then they both plunged through the window with a great crash.

In about half an hour an old gentleman, with a flowing beard and a fine but rather austere face, entered and sat down at my invitation. He seemed to have something on his mind. He took off his hat and set it on the floor, and got out of it a red silk handkerchief and a copy of our paper.

He put the paper in his lap, and, while he polished his spectacles with his handkerchief, he said: "Are you the new editor?"

I said I was.

"Have you ever edited an agricultural newspaper before?"

"No," said I, "this is my first attempt."

"Very likely. Have you ever had any experience in agriculture practically?"

"No; I believe I have not."

"Some instinct told me so," said the gentleman, putting on his spectacles and looking over them with asperity while he folded his paper into a convenient shape. "I wish to read you what must have made me have that instinct. It was this editorial. Listen and see if it was you who wrote it:

"'Turnips should never be pulled; it injures them. It is much better to send a boy up and let him shake the tree.'

"Now, what do you think of that?—for I really suppose

you wrote it."

"Think of it? Why, I think it is good. I think it is sense. I have no doubt that every year millions and millions of bushels of turnips are spoiled in this township alone by being pulled in half-ripe condition, when if they had sent a boy to shake the tree—"

"Shake your grandmother! Turnips don't grow on trees!"

"Oh, they don't, don't they? Well, who said they did? The language was intended to be figurative—wholly figurative. Anybody that knows anything will know that I meant that the boy should shake the vine."

Then this old person got up and tore his paper all into small shreds, and stamped on them, and broke several things with his cane, and said I did not know as much as a cow; and then went out and banged the door after him, and, in short, acted in such a way that I fancied he was displeased about something. But, not knowing what the trouble was, I could not be any help to him.

Pretty soon after this, a long, cadaverous creature, with lanky locks hanging down to his shoulders and a week's stubble bristling from the hills and valleys of his face, darted within the door and halted motionless, with finger on lip, and head and body bent in listening attitude. No sound was heard. Still he listened. No sound. Then he turned the key in the door, and came elaborately tip-toeing toward me till he was within long reaching distance of me, when he stopped, and, after scanning my face with intent interest awhile, drew a folded copy of our paper from his bosom and said:

"There, you wrote that. Read it to me quick. Relieve me, I suffer."

I read as follows, and as the sentences fell from my lips I could see the relief come. I could see the drawn muscles relax and the anxiety go out of the face and rest and peace steal over the features like the merciful moonlight over a desolate landscape:

"'The guano is a fine bird: but great care is necessary in rearing it. It should not be imported earlier than June or later than September. In the winter it should be kept in a warm place, where it can hatch out its young.

"'It is evident that we are going to have a backward season for grain. Therefore it will be well for the farmer to begin setting out his cornstalks, and planting his buckwheat cakes in

July instead of August.

"'Concerning the pumpkin. This berry is a favorite with the natives of the interior of New England, who prefer it to the gooseberry for the making of fruit cake, and who likewise give it the preference over the raspberry for feeding cows, as being more filling and fully as satisfying. The pumpkin is the only esculent of the orange family that will thrive in the North, except the gourd and one or two varieties of the squash. But the custom of planting it in the front yard with the shrubbery is fast going out of vogue, for it is now generally conceded that the pumpkin as a shade tree is a failure.

"'Now, as the warm weather approaches, and the ganders begin to spawn—'"

The excited listener sprang toward me to shake hands and said:

"There, there—that will do. I know I am all right now, because you have read it just as I did word for word. But, stranger, when I first read it this morning, I said to myself, I never, never believed it before, notwithstanding my friends kept me under watch so strict, but now I believe I *am* crazy; and with that I fetched a howl that you might have heard two miles and started out to kill somebody, because, you know, I knew it would come to that sooner or later, and so I might as well begin. I read read one of them paragraphs over again so as to be certain, and then I burned my house down and started. I have crippled several people, and have got one fellow up a tree, where I can get him if I want him. But I thought I would call in here as I passed along and make the thing perfectly certain; and now it *is* certain, and I tell you it is lucky for that chap that is in the tree. I should have killed him sure as I went back. Good-bye, sir, good-bye; you have taken a great load off my mind. My reason has stood the strain of one of your agricultural articles, and I know that nothing can ever unseat it now. Good-bye, sir!"

I felt a little uncomfortable about the cripplings and arson this person had been entertaining himself with, for I could not help feeling remotely accessory to them. But the thoughts were quickly banished, for the regular editor walked in. (I thought to myself, now, if you had gone to Egypt, as I had recommended you to, I might have had a chance to get my hand in, but you wouldn't do it, and here you are. I sort of expected you.)

The editor was looking sad, and perplexed, and dejected.

He surveyed the wreck which that old rioter and those two young farmers had made, and then said: "This is a sad business—a very sad business. There is the mucilage bottle broken, and six window panes of glass, and a spittoon, and two candlesticks. But that is not the worst. The reputation of the paper is injured—permanently, I fear. True, there never was such call for the paper before, and it never sold such a large edition or soared to such celebrity; but does one want to be famous for lunacy, and prosper on the infirmities of his mind? My friend, as I am an honest man, the street out here is full of people, and others are roosting on the fence, waiting to get a glimpse of you, because they think you are crazy. And well they might after reading your editorials. They are a disgrace to journalism. Why, what put it into your head that you could edit a paper of this nature? You do not seem to know the first rudiments of agriculture. You speak of a furrow and a harrow as being the same thing; you talk of the moulting season for cows, and you recommend the domestication of the pole-cat on account of its playfulness and its excellence as a ratter. Your remark that clams will lie quiet if music is played to them was superfluous—entirely superfluous. Nothing disturbs clams. Clams always lie quiet. Clams care nothing whatever about music. And heavens and earth, friend! If you had made the acquiring of ignorance the study of your life, you could not have graduated with higher honor than you could today. I never saw anything like it. Your observation of the horse-chestnut as an article of commerce steadily gaining in favor is simply calculated to destroy this journal. I want you to throw up your situation and go. I want no more holiday—I could not enjoy it if I had it. Certainly not with you in my chair. I would always stand in dread of what you might be going to recommend next. It makes me lose all patience every time I think of you discussing oyster beds under the head of 'Landscape Gardening.' I want you to go. Nothing on earth could persuade me to take another holiday. O! why didn't you tell me you didn't know anything about agriculture?"

"Tell you, you cornstalk, you cabbage, you son of a cauliflower! It's the first time I've ever heard such an unfeeling remark. I tell you I have been in the editorial business going on 14 years, and it is the first time I ever heard of a man's having to know of anything in order to edit a newspaper. You turnip! Who write the dramatic critiques for the second-rate players? Why, a parcel of promoted shoemakers and apprentice apothecaries, who know just as much about good acting as I do about good farming, and no more. Who review the books? People who never wrote one. Who do up the heavy leaders on finance? Parties who have the largest opportunities for knowing nothing about it. Who criticize the Indian campaigns? Gentlemen who do not know a warwhoop from a wigwam, and who never have had to run a foot race with tomahawk, or pluck arrows out of several members of their families to build the evening campfire with. Who write the temperance appeals and clamor about the flowing bowls? Folks who will never draw another sober breath till they do it in the grave. Who edit the agricultural papers, you yam? Men, as a general thing, who fail in the poetry line, yellow-covered-novel line, sensation-drama line, city-editor line, and finally fall back on the agriculture as a temporary reprive from the poorhouse. You try to tell me anything about the newspaper business! Sir, I have been through it from Alpha to Omaha, and I tell you the less a man knows the bigger noise he makes and the higher salary he commands. Heaven knows, if I had been ignorant, instead of cultivated, and impudent instead of diffident, I could have made a name for myself in this cold, selfish world. I take my leave, sir. Since I have been treated as you have treated me, I am perfectly willing to go. But I have done my duty. I have fulfilled my contract as far as I was permitted to do it. I said I could make your paper of interest to all classes—and I have. I said I could run your circulation up to 20,000 copies, and if I had had two more weeks, I'd have done it. And I'd have given you the best class of readers that ever an agricultural paper had—not a farmer in it, nor a solitary individual who could tell a watermelon tree from a peach vine to save his life. You are the loser by this rupture, not me, pie-plant. Adios."

I then left.

Originally printed in the July 1870 edition of the New York *Galaxy*, this story was also published in *Sketches, New and Old*.

10 April (Monday)
"Mark Twain's Duel: His Wonderful Escape"; p. 3

Mark Twain contributes the following to *Tom Hood's Annual*:

The only merit I claim for the following narrative is that it is a true story. It has a moral on the end of it, but I claim nothing on that, as it is merely thrown in to curry favor with the religious element.

After I had reported a couple of years on the Virginia City (Nev.) *Daily Enterprise*, they promoted me to be editor-in-chief, and I lasted just a week by the watch. But I made an uncommonly lively newspaper while I did last, and when I retired I had a duel on my hands and three horsewhippings promised me.

The latter I made no attempt to collect, however; this story concerns only the former. It was the old "flush times" of the silver excitement, when the population was so wonderfully wild and mixed; everybody went armed to the teeth, and all slights and insults had to be atoned for with the best article of blood your system could furnish. In the course of my editing I made trouble with a Mr. Lord, the editor of a rival paper. He flew up about some trifle or other that I said about him—I do not remember now what it was. I suppose I called him a thief, or a body-snatcher, or an idiot, or something like that; I was obliged to make the paper readable, and I couldn't fail in my duty to a whole community of subscribers merely to save the exaggerated sensitiveness of an individual. Mr. Lord was offended, and replied in his paper. Vigorously means a good deal when it refers to a personal editorial in a frontier newspaper. Dueling was all the fashion among the upper classes in that country, and very few gentlemen would throw away an opportunity of fighting one. To kill one man in a duel caused a man to be even more looked up to than to kill two in the ordinary way. Well, out there if you abused a man and that man did not like it, you had to call him out and kill him, otherwise you would be disgraced. So I challenged Mr. Lord, and I did hope he would not accept; but I knew very well that he did not want to fight, and so I challenged him in the most violent and implacable manner. And then I sat down and snuffed and snuffed till the answer came. All the boys—the editors—were in the office "helping" me in the dismal business and telling me about duels, and discussing the code with a lot of ruffians, who had experience in such matters, and al-together there was a loving interest taken in the matter that made me unspeakably uncomfortable. The answer came— Mr. Lord declined. Our boys were furious, and so was I on the surface.

I sent him another challenge, and another, and the more he did not want to fight the more bloodthirsty I became. But at last the man's tone began to change. He appeared to be waking up. It was becoming apparent that he was going to fight me after all. I ought to have known how it would be— he was a man who could never be depended upon. Our boys were jubilant. I was not, though I tried hard to be.

It was now time to go out and practice. It was the custom there to fight duels with navy six shooters at 15 paces—load and empty till the game for the funeral was secure. We went to a ravine just out of town and borrowed a barn door for a target—borrowed it from a gentleman who was absent—and we stood his barn door up, and stood a rail on the end against the middle of it to represent Lord, and put a squash on top of the rail to represent the head. He was a very tall lean crea-ture, the poorest sort of material for a duel; nothing but a line shot could fetch him, and even then he might split your bul-let. Exaggeration aside, the rail was, of course, a little too thin to represent the body, but the squash was all right. If there was any intellectual difference between the squash and the head it was in favor of the squash.

Well, I practiced and practiced at the barn door, and could not hit it; and I practiced at the rail, and could not hit that; and I tried for the squash, and could not hit that. I would have been entirely disheartened but that occasionally I crip-pled one of the boys, and that gave me hope.

At last we began to hear pistol shots near by in the next ravine. We know what that meant! The other party was out practicing, too. Then I was in the last degree distressed, for of course they would hear our shots and then send over the ridge, and the spies would find my barn door without a wound or mark, and that would simply be an end to me, for of course, the other man would immediately become as bloodthirsty as I was.

Just at that moment a little bird no larger than a sparrow flew by and lit on a bush about 30 paces away, and my little second, Steve Gillis, who was a dead shot with a pistol—

much better than I was—snatched out his revolver and shot the bird's head off! We all ran to pick up the game, and sure enough, just at this moment, some of the other duelists came reconnoitering over the little ridge. They ran up to our group to see what the matter was, and when they saw the bird Lord's second said:

"That was a splendid shot. How far off was it?"

Steve said with some indifference:

"Oh, no great distance. About 30 paces."

"Thirty paces! Heavens alive! Who did it?"

"My man—Twain."

"The mischief he did! Can he do it often?"

"Well, yes. He can do it about four times out of five."

I knew the little rascal was lying, but I never said anything. I never told him so. He was not of a disposition to invite confidence of that kind, so I let the matter rest. But it was a comfort to see those other people look sick, and see their jaws drop when Steve made that statement. They went off and got Lord and took him home; when we got home, half an hour later, there was a note stating that Mr. Lord peremptorily declined to fight.

We found out afterward that Lord hit his mark 13 times in 18 shots; if he had put those 13 bullets into me it would have narrowed my sphere of usefulness a good deal. True they could have put pegs in the holes and used me as a hat-rack; but what is a hat-rack to a man who feels he has intellectual powers?

I have written this true incident of my history for one purpose only—to warn the youth of today against the practice of dueling, and to plead with them to war against it. I was young and foolish when I challenged the gentleman, and I thought it very fine and grand to be a duelist and stand upon the "field of honor." But I am older and more experienced now, and am inflexibly opposed to the dreadful custom. I am glad, indeed, to be able to lift up my voice against it. I think it is a bad, immoral thing. It is every man's duty to do all he can to discourage dueling.

If a man were to challenge me I would go to that man and take him by the hand and lead him to a retired room—and kill him.

After its appearance in *Tom Hood's Comic Annual for 1873*, this story was published in *Sketches, New and Old*. A similar version of

Twain's escape from a duel is related in *Autobiography* (112-18). *MT: Bachelor*, however, gives a good summary of what really occurred, including the fact that Twain acted shamefully throughout the entire episode (230-41). Apparently, Twain repeatedly insulted rival newspaperman James Laird in an attempt to goad him into a duel. But Laird, who had no quarrel with Twain, never accepted the challenge. Because of Nevada Territory's strict laws forbidding dueling or the sending of challenges, Twain and Steve Gillis—his close friend who did act as his second in the affair—then decided to leave Virginia City for California. This move to California proved pivotal to Twain's career, for it was in San Francisco that he met Bret Harte and other writers, and where—during a visit to the gold fields—that he heard the story of the jumping frog which was to be his springboard into a literary career.

25 April (Tuesday)
"Mark Twain's Report of an Accident"; p. 2

Mark Twain recently tried his hand at writing up a distressing accident for a Boston local newspaper, and this is how he did it:

"Last evening about six o'clock, as William Schuyler, an old and respected citizen of Hyde Park, was leaving his residence to go down town, as has been his custom for many years, with the exception of only one short interval in the spring of 1850 during which he was confined to his bed by injuries received in attempting to stop a runaway horse by thoughtlessly throwing up his hands and shouting, which even if he had done so a single moment sooner, would inevitably have frightened the animal still more instead of checking its speed, although disastrous enough to himself as it was, was rendered more melancholy and distressing by reason of the presence of his wife's mother, who was there and saw the occurence, notwithstanding it is at least likely, though not necessarily so, that she should be reconnoitering in another direction when incidents occur, not being vivacious and on the lookout, as a general thing, but even in the reverse, as her mother is said to have stated, who is no more, but who died in the full hope of a blessed resurrection upward of three years ago, aged 86, being a Christian woman without guile, as it were in property, in consequence of a fire in 1849, which destroyed every solitary thing she had in the world. But such is life. Let us all take warning by this solemn occurence, and let us endeavor so to live that when we come to die we can do it. Let us place our hands upon our hearts and say with earnestness and sincerity that, from this day forth we will beware of the intoxicating bowl."

This burlesque is an excerpt from a sketch entitled "Mr. Bloke's Item"; the entire piece is reprinted in *Sketches and Tales* (57-59).

28 April (Friday)
"Our Spice Box"; p. 2
>   Mark Twain will appear as Peter Spuyk in the *Loan of a Lover* on Wednesday evening at Hartford.

While he lived in Hartford, Twain took an interest in amateur dramatic performances. Consequently, he and some like-minded members of the community performed *Loan of a Lover*—a popular melodrama of the time—for their friends. The performance was not without controversy, however, since the play allegedly contained profanity (*Nook Farm* 97-99).

5 June (Monday)
no headline; p. 2
>   Mark Twain has had a Canada canal boat named after him. That's the way fame plods along the tow-path of glory.

30 June (Friday)
"Our Spice Box"; p. 2
>   Mark Twain, speaking of a new mosquito netting, writes: "The day is coming when we shall sit under our nets in church and slumber peacefully while the discomfited flies club together and take it out of the minister."

10 July (Monday)
"Mark Twain: How Tom Sawyer Got His Fence Whitewashed"; p. 3
>   Tom Sawyer having offended his sole guardian, Aunt Polly, is by that sternly affectionate dame punished by being set to whitewash the fence in front of the garden. The world seemed a hollow mockery to Tom, who had planned fun for that day, and who knew that he would be the laughing-stock of all the boys as they came past and saw him work like a "nigger." But a great inspiration burst upon him and he went tranquilly to work. What that inspiration was will appear from what follows. One of the boys, Ben Rogers, came by and paused, eating a particularly fine apple. Tom does

nothing. Ben stared a moment and then said:

"Hi-yi! You're up a stump, ain't you?"

No answer. Tom surveyed his last touch with the eye of an artist, then he gave another gentle sweep and surveyed the results as before. Tom's mouth watered for the apple, but he stuck to his work. Ben said:

"Hello, old chap, you go to work, hey?"

"Why, it's you, Ben; I wasn't noticing."

"Say, I'm going in a swimming, I am. Don't you wish you could? But, of course you'd druther work, wouldn't you? Course you would."

Tom contemplated the boy a bit, and said:

"What do you call work?"

"Why, ain't that work?"

Tom resumed his whitewashing, saying:

"Well, maybe it is, and maybe it ain't. All I know is it suits Tom Sawyer."

"O, come now, you don't mean to let on that you like it?"

The brush continued to move.

"Like it? Well, I don't see why I oughtn't to like it. Does a boy get a chance to whitewash a fence every day?"

That put the thing in a new light. Ben stopped nibbling his apple. Tom swept his brush daintily back and forth— stepped back to note the effect—added a touch here and there—criticized the effect again, Ben watching every move, and getting more and more interested, more and more absorbed. Presently he said:

"Say, Tom, let me whitewash a little."

Tom considered; was about to consent; but he altered his mind: "No, no, I reckon it won't hardly do, Ben. You see, Aunt Polly's awful particular about this fence—right here, on the street, you know—but if it were the back I wouldn't mind and she wouldn't. Yes, she's awful particular about this fence; it's got to be done very careful; I reckon there ain't but one boy in a thousand, maybe two thousand, that can do it in the way it's got to be done."

"No—is that so? Oh, come now, lemme, just only try a little. I'd let you, if you was me, Tom."

"Ben, I'd like to, honest Injun; but Aunt Polly—well, Jim wanted to do it and she wouldn't let Sid. Now, don't you see how I am fixed. If you was to tackle this fence, and anything was to happen to it—"

"Oh, shucks; I'll be just as careful. Now lemme try. Say—I'll give you the core of my apple."

"Well, here. No, Ben; now don't; I'm feard."

"I'll give you all of it!"

Tom gave up the brush with reluctance in his face, but alacrity in his heart. And while Ben worked and sweated in the sun, the retired artist sat on a barrel in the shade close by, dangled his legs, munched his apple and planned the slaughter of more innocents. There was no lack of material; boys happened along every little while; they came to jeer, but remained to whitewash. By the time Ben was flagged out, Tom had traded the next chance to Billy Fisher for a kite in good repair; and when he played out, Johnny Miller bought in for a dead rat and a string to swing it with; and so on, and so on, hour after hour. And when the middle of the afternoon came, from being a poor, poverty-stricken boy in the morning, Tom was literally rolling in wealth. He had, besides the things I have mentioned, 12 marbles, part of a jewsharp, a piece of blue bottleglass to look through, a spool cannon, a key that wouldn't unlock anything, a fragment of chalk, a glass stopper of a decanter, a tin soldier, a couple of tadpoles, six firecrackers, a kitten with only one eye, a brass door knob, a dog collar—but no dog—the handle of a knife, four pieces of orange peel, and a dilapidated old window sash. He had had a nice, good, idle time all the while—plenty of company—and the fence had three coats of whitewash on it. If he hadn't run out of whitewash, he would have bankrupted every boy in the village.

Tom said to himself that it was not such a hollow world after all. He had discovered a great law of human action without knowing it, namely, that in order to make a man or boy covet a thing, it is only necessary to make the thing difficult to attain. If he had been a great and wise philosopher, like the writer of this book, he would now have comprehended that work consists of whatever a body is obliged to do, and that play consists of whatever a body is not obliged to do. And this would help him to understand why constructing artificial flowers, or performing on a treadmill is work, whilst rolling nine-pins or climbing Mount Blanc is only amusement. There are wealthy gentlemen in England who drive four-horse passenger coaches 20 or 30 miles on a daily line in the summer because the privilege costs them considerable money; but if they were just offered wages for the service, that would turn it into work, and then they would resign.

Published 8 December 1876 to mediocre reviews, *The Adventures of Tom Sawyer* generated only modest sales (just 35,000 copies were sold by 1885), much to Twain's disappointment. It was a commercial failure for a number of reasons, but the primary culprit was Twain's publisher, Elisha Bliss (1822-80), who mishandled the novel's publicity (*MT & Elisha Bliss* 117-21). One of the more famous incidents from the novel, this excerpt is from chapter two of *Tom Sawyer*.

22 July (Saturday)
no headline; p. 2

Had Mark Twain been selected by the various Indian tribes to christen the various chiefs, he could not have hit upon such streaks of the ridiculous as is seen in the present nomenclatures of the "big Injuns." Nobody but Mark or the untutored savage could have invented funnier names than Sitting Bull, Shack Nasty Jim, and the like.

28 August (Monday)
"The Boy, the Beetle, and the Dog: A Sketch from Mark Twain's *Tom Sawyer*"; p. 3

The minister gave out his text, and droned along monotonously through an argument which was so prosy that many a head, by-and-by, began to nod, and yet it was an argument that dwelt in limitless fire and brimstone, and thinned the predestined elect down to a company so small as to hardly be worth the saving. Tom counted the pages of the sermon; after church he always knew how many pages there had been, but he seldom knew anything else about the discourse. However, this time he was readily interested for a little while. The minister made a grand and moving picture of the assembling together of the world's hosts at the millennium, when the lion and the lamb shall lie down together and a little child shall lead them. But the pathos, the lesson and the moral of the greatest spectacle were lost upon the boy; he only thought of the conspicuousness of the principle character before the onlooking nations, his face lit up with the thought, and he said to himself that he wished he could be that child, if it were a tame lion. Now he lapsed into suffering again as the dry argument was resumed. Presently he bethought himself of a treasure he had and got it out. It was a large black beetle with formidable jaws—a "pinch bug" he called it. It was in a percussion-cap box. The first thing the beetle did was take him by the finger. A natural flip followed, and the beetle went floundering into the aisle and lit on its back, and the hurt finger went into the boy's mouth. The beetle lay there, working its helpless legs, unable to turn over. Tom eyed it and longed for it, but it was safe out of his reach. Other people, uninterested in the sermon, found relief in the beetle, and they eyed it, too. Presently a vagrant poodle-dog came idling along, sad at heart, lazy with the summer's softness and the quiet, weary with captivity, sighing for change. He spied the beetle; the drooping tail lifted and wagged. He surveyed the prize, walked around it, smelt it from a safe distance, walked around it again, grew bolder and took a closer smell, then lifted up his lip and made a gingerly snatch at it, just missing it; made another, subsided to his stomach with the beetle between his paws, and continued his experiments; grew weary at last and then indifferent and absent-minded. His head nodded and little by little his chin descended and touched the enemy, who seized it. There was sharp yell, a flirt of the poodle's head, and the beetle fell a couple of yards away and lit on its back once more. The neighboring spectator shook with a gentle inward joy, several faces went behind fans and handkerchiefs and Tom was happy. The dog looked foolish and probably felt so, but there was resentment in his heart, too, and a craving for revenge. So he went back to the beetle, and began a wary attack on it again, jumping at it from every point of a circle, lighting with his forepaws within an inch of the creature, making even closer snatches at it with his teeth, and jerking his head until his ears flapped again. But he grew tired once more, after a while; tried to amuse himself with a fly, but found no relief; followed an ant around, with his nose close to the floor, and quickly wearied of that; yawned, sighed, forgot the beetle entirely, and sat down on it. Then there was a wild yelp of anger, and the poodle went sailing up the aisle; the yelps continued, and so did the dog; he crossed the house in front of the altar: he flew down the other aisle; he crossed before the doors; he clambered up the home stretch; his anguish grew with his progress, till presently he was a wooly comet, moving in its orbit, with the gleam and speed of light. At last the frantic sufferer sheered from his course and sprang into his master's lap; he flung it out of the window, and the voice of distress quickly thinned away and died in the distance.

Tom Sawyer went home quite cheerful, thinking to himself that there was some satisfaction about divine service when there was a bit of variety in it. He had but one marring thought: he was willing that the dog should play with his pinch bug, but he didn't think it was upright to carry it off.

This excerpt is from the conclusion of chapter 5 of *Tom Sawyer*, although *The Dispatch* omits the penultimate paragraph which points out that the dog's performance was enjoyed by all the congregation even though their laughter could not be expressed aloud.

8 October (Friday)
no headline; p. 2

Mark Twain has been betrayed into making a few campaign stump speeches, and combines humor with politics quite successfully. He is a believer of civil service reform, and justly observes that the practice of giving office to the incompetent is "enough to make the very gods of solemnity laugh"—for, he says, we insist that tradesmen and mechanics shall know their business, while "we serenely fill our political places with ignoramuses," and confide our custom houses to the hands of men "who do not know a bill of lading from a transit of Venus, never having heard of either of them before."

The full text of his speech, which was delivered to a Hartford Republican rally on 30 September 1876, is reprinted in *Mark Twain Speaking* (97-99). Although he had misgivings about the Republican Party's ability to govern the country, Twain remained loyal to it until 1884 when he joined with the Mugwumps in support of Grover Cleveland's bid for the presidency. See 24 October 1884 for an account of Twain's support for Cleveland.

27 October (Friday)
"Mark Twain at Home: A Visit to His House in Hartford—His Singular Behavior"; p. 2

The New York *Sun* has the following extract from a private letter to a gentleman in New York City:

"I called yesterday upon our old friend Clemens, better known to the police as Mark Twain, for the purpose of ascertaining the truth of certain stories which have reached me of late regarding the present condition of his fine mind.

"Clemens lives in a surprising house on Farmington Avenue in the outskirts of the city. The resources of taste and wealth have been lavished upon his residence, and the result is a structure architectually midway between a medieval church and a modern game of baseball. Herein Mark lives the elegant life of a man of leisure, cutting coupons, smoking long and strong pipes from morning to night, and drinking lager beer, which he buys by the keg, and often.

"I was shown into the library, the appointments of which are characteristic of the owner's originality. The tints are all neutral and the furniture of the homeliest and plainest description. On the study table stood a plaster bust of John Calvin, on whose face somebody had inked a goatee and festooned moustaches. The charm of the room is in the open fireplace, where generous logs were burning upon old-fashioned brass andirons. The mantelpiece is of heavy black oak, purchased by Mr. Clemens in England. Over the fireplace is a brass plate, on which the following inscription is engraved in old English text:

"'A HAND: ONE MAN IS THE ORNAMENT OF HIS OWN HOUSE.'

"While I was reading this legend our friend came in. He is as tall and as sad-eyed as ever. The unequal disposition of flesh upon his face, which is pulpy in places and lean in others, tells of the struggle for supremacy that is going on within his tissues between the fat-producing beer and the fat-destroying tobacco. The tobacco appears to be getting the better of the beer.

"Clemens came in, wearing a long dressing gown of sombre hue, and after glancing furtively around the room, advanced and shook my hand. 'Hello,' he said. 'You must go instantly. We are observed. Do you not hear their derisive laughter? Fly, my friend; fly at once!'

"'They are not laughing at us,' I replied, humoring his strange fancy. 'They are laughing over your books—your jokes.'

"'Now look here, pard,' he said, laying his sinewy hand upon my shoulder and dragging me toward the door. 'That was a million, ten million years ago. I know the humorous laugh and I know the political laugh. Escape without delay. If they capture us here together they will make you president and me inspector of elections for this ward.'

"I tried to soothe him, but in vain.

"'There was a time, ages and ages now gone by,' he continued, gazing abstractly into the fire, 'when it was my ambition to be inspector of elections for this ward. I worked for it; I pulled wires for it; I prevaricated, aye, falsehooded to compass it. They promised to make me inspector of elections if I would preside at a political meeting in Hartford—a town on the Connecticut River—and make a funny speech. Ha! I hear their fiendish laughter still. It has rung in my ears these centuries. They gave the place to another man. I staked my soul and lost it. You come here to jeer at me, to scoff! But I am a desperate man. See here!'

"He seized the tongs and with one powerful blow scattered John Calvin into a thousand fragments. Then he turned on me. Seeing that it was useless to reason with him in his present frame of mind, I fled.

"Clemens has done many things lately which give his friends natural alarm. Last week he hoisted a little flag of black crepe on each of the numerous lightning rods which adorn his mansion. Last Sunday he walked slowly up the aisle of the Rev. Mr. Twichell's church, stood a moment before the desk, and then turned and fled, uttering piercing shrieks. Yesterday he attended a match game of the California polo players, who are exhibiting at the trotting park, insisted on mounting an almost unmanageable mustang, known as the 'bucking horse,' and rode wildly up and down Asylum Street shouting, 'Woe! woe unto Israel!' His actions are especially queer at or near the full of the moon."

Unfortunately, no author is given for this piece. Presumably, however, it was written by the same person who wrote the story published nearly three weeks later on 15 November.

15 November (Wednesday)
"The Bust and the Brain: Some Further Light of the Sad Case of a Great Humorist"; p. 2

Hartford, Nov. 10—

The true story of the destruction of Mark Twain's plaster bust of Calvin has been so twisted and distorted by certain newspapers that Clemens' conduct is placed in a rather unpleasant light. In justice to him I consider it my duty, as the original narrator of the facts, to give you the complete and correct version of this unfortunate affair.

The bust of Calvin was a wedding present to Mr. and Mrs. Clemens from a pious clergyman who had accompanied Mark Twain upon his expedition to the Holy Land. The appropriate gift was highly valued by both husband and wife. The former always treated it with grave reverence, and made a point every spring and fall of providing it with a new silk hat of the latest style. Calvin stood, not upon the mantel, but upon the center table in Mark's study.

What, therefore, was Mrs. Clemens' astonishment, upon returning a few weeks ago from a brief visit to her father's home, to find that in her absence the cherished features of John Calvin had been ornamented by the addition of a pair of spiral moustaches and a fanciful goatee done in ink! The austere theologian now looked like a French barber.

Mark protested his innocence in the most solemn manner and neither blanched nor blushed beneath the searching gaze of his indignant wife. "It may have been the cat," he suggested.

"Sam Twain Clemens!" replied the lady, with some animation, "you are deceiving me. The cat could never have done that shameful deed. More likely it was Charles Warner, or that Joe Hawley, or some of those that have been here carousing while I was away. Now, I wish to know what has been going on in this house."

Mark's explanation that the cat might have jumped upon the table, dipped the end of her tail in the inkstand, and thus accomplished the work of the desecration, was thrust aside as contemptibly inadequate.

"An improbability isn't an impossibility," muttered Mark.

"No, Samuel Clemens, nor is this home a place for wild carousings and sacrilegiousness," was the logical and conclusive rejoinder.

The next day Twain tried to throw the blame on Prof. Huxley, and the day after that he admitted in confidence that Bob Ingersoll was the real culprit. But as he was unable to show that either Prof. Huxley or Bob Ingersoll had been entertained at the Clemens Mansion during the absence of the mistress the explanations were sternly rejected as miserable subterfuges.

The subject was not recurred to again, but the besmeared face of John Calvin remained in Mark's study, a silent accuser, a dumb yet terrible witness.

In vain Clemens tried to scrap off the moustache. In vain he endeavored to erase the goatee with the blade of his penknife. Scrape deep as he might the ink went deeper still, and the only result of his effort was to make Calvin's face more ghastly than ever. More awful yet was the expression that would come over Mrs. Clemens' face as she pointed to the bust, and by looks more significant than words, reminded her wretched husband of the mysterious proceedings that must have occurred in the establishment during her absence.

It was about this time that John Calvin disappeared. A week later he was accidentally discovered buried beneath several tons of hay in the stable loft, and was rescued and restored to his place on the study table. Mark denied all knowledge of the abduction. The next day, however, Calvin was again gone, and not until the favorite pipe of the great humorist had been seized and held as a hostage did the theologian reappear.

All this was wearing on the mind of my friend Clemens. Perhaps it was the accusing voice of a guilty conscience—perhaps it was the weight of unjust suspicions—that made him moody, fretful and morose. It was now that he went into politics, with the sad results narrated in the previous letter. It was now that he began to see strange things and do still stranger. It was now that it began to be whispered about Hartford that a once powerful intellect was tottering—perhaps tottered.

When I visited Clemens on the 17th of last month, the morbid horror with which he had come to regard the countenance of John Calvin had worked itself into desperate recklessness, and it was in my presence that he seized the tongs and smashed the eminent theologian into a thousand little pieces. This is the whole story.

No author is given for this article, which was reprinted from the New York *Sun*. Like Charles Dudley Warner, General Joseph Hawley (1826-1905) was a friend and neighbor of Twain's; he would later serve four terms in the U. S. Senate. T. H. Huxley (1825-95) was a prominent English biologist then touring the United States, while Robert Ingersoll (1833-99) was a popular orator and Republican politician from Illinois.

1877

9 February (Friday)
"Mark Twain's Eulogy of a Watch"; p. 2

A jeweler in New Haven, Conn., has a remarkable watch made by a foreign watchmaker, which Mark Twain describes as follows:

"I have examined the wonderful watch made by M. Matile, and indeed it comes nearer to being a human being than any piece of mechanism I ever saw before. In fact, it knows considerable more than the average voter. It knows the movements of the moon and keeps exact record of them; it tells the day of the week, the day of the month and the month of the year, and will do this perpetually; it tells the hour of the day and the minute and the second, and even splits the seconds into fifths and marks the division with 'stop' hands; having two stop hands it can take accurate care of two race horses that start, not together but one after the other; it is a repeater wherein the voter is suggested again, and musically chimes the hour, the quarter, the half, the three-quarter hour, and also the minutes that have passed of an uncompleted quarter hour—so that a blind man can tell the time of day by it to the exact minute.

"Such is this extraordinary watch. It ciphers to admiration; I should think one could add another wheel and make it read and write; still another and make it talk; and I think one might take out several of the wheels that are already in it and it would still be a more intelligent citizen than some that help to govern the country. On the whole I think it is entitled to vote, that is if its sex is the right kind."

This anecdote, which sounds suspiciously like an endorsement, illustrates Twain's fondness for mechanical gadgets of all sorts. As *Mr. Clemens & MT* points out, Twain considered complex machines—

when they worked properly—to be more intelligent than many men (280-88). His fascination with these machines helped lead to his bankruptcy, however, since he was rarely able to resist any inventor with a contraption that needed funding. One such inventor was James W. Paige and his automatic typesetter; see 23 February 1891 for Twain's involvement. Unlike Twain, who repaid his creditors and became wealthy again, Paige's decline continued after the failure of his machine; he died in a poorhouse in Oak Forest, Ill., in 1917.

29 May (Tuesday)
"Mark Twain's Title: How He Ordered His Drinks to be Chalked Down"; p. 2

We knew Clemens in the early days, and know exactly how he came to be dubbed "Mark Twain." John Piper's saloon on B Street used to be the grand rendezvous for all of the Virginia City Bohemians. Piper conducted a cash business and refused to keep any books. As a special favor, he would occasionally chalk down drinks to the boys on the wall back of the bar. Sam Clemens, when localizing for the *Enterprise*, always had an account with the balance against him on Piper's wall. Clemens was by no means a Coal Oil Tommy; he drank with the pure and unadulterated love of the ardent. Most of his drinking was conducted in single-handed contests, but occasionally he would invite Dan de Quille, Charley Parker, Bob Lowery, or Alf Doten, never more than one of them, however, at a time, and whenever he did, his inevitable parting injunction to Piper was to "mark twain," meaning two chalk marks, of course. It was in this way that he acquired the title which has since become famous wherever the English language is read or spoken.

Reprinted from the Eureka, Nev., *Sentinal*, this anecdote by George W. Cassidy explaining Twain's nom de plume is false. Twain himself points out the significance of the phrase "mark twain" in *Autobiography*: After he had stirred up some trouble in the Nevada State Legislature in 1863, Twain—who desired to remain as anonymous as possible—"presently began to sign the letters [that he wrote for the *Territorial Enterprise*] using the Mississippi leadsman's call, 'Mark Twain'" (105). The call, which means literally "two fathoms," indicates a deep enough channel for safe steamboat passage. Later in his career, Twain would claim that he merely borrowed the sobriquet from another riverboat pilot, one Isaiah Sellers. *MT: Bachelor*, however, refutes this claim by pointing out that no records exist of Sellers ever using the name. Of the men mentioned in Cassidy's piece, Dan de Quille—

pseudonym of William Wright (1829-98), a long-time reporter on the *Enterprise's* staff—was probably Twain's best friend and drinking companion during the Virginia City years of 1862-64. The other men—Parker, Lowery, and Doten—were fellow journalists and heavy drinkers. *MT: Virginia City* prints a photograph of John Piper and gives many details about his saloon and its patrons (102-06).

11 June (Monday)
"Personal"; p. 2
     Mark Twain is 42 and has cleared $50,000 or more by his books and lectures.

7 August (Tuesday)
"Mark Twain's Last Joke: How He Organized a Wedding in the House and Persuaded the Young Man"; p. 3
     Hartford, July 21—
     A good story about Mark Twain is just beginning to leak out here. Some time ago he went on a visit to Elmira, N. Y., leaving his quaint house among the trees on Farmington Avenue in charge of his servants. Nearly two weeks ago an item was published in the Hartford daily papers chronicling an ineffectual attempt to rob the humorist's residence.
     The story was that a man presented himself at the door one day, saying that he had been sent by the gas company to inspect the meter and pipes. The servant, who had not the slightest suspicion, allowed the stranger to enter and do as he pleased. When he supposed no one was watching his movements he hid himself away in a dark corner, of which there are many in that old chalet, and waited for darkness. But the girl, who had watched his movements, went and procured assistance and had the intruder "bounced" without ceremony.
     When Mr. Clemens heard the story in Elmira, he thought he smelled a very large rat, and hastened to Hartford with the purpose of ferreting it out. His theory was that one of the servant girls must have a beau who was admitted to the house at unusual hours, and that, being caught in the act, this means of concealing the real truth of the case was adopted. With all the sagacity of an ex-journalist he followed his clue, but could not establish the theory he had formed.
     But while pursing his investigation he learned that one of the girls who had been a member of his family for a long time was really guilty of having a male admirer, who occa-

sionally shared the hospitality of the house, unknown to the proprietor. She was a buxom English girl, with a handsome form and a bright, cheerful face. Faithful in the performance of her duties, and always solicitous for the best interests of the family, she had made herself almost invaluable to the household. The high esteem in which Mr. Clemens had always held her no doubt influenced his course. He was sorry to part with the girl who had served him so well, but seeing no other alternative, quickly matured a plan that "should let her down easy." After a long hunt he succeeded in discovering the young fellow's name. When that was gained, Mr. Clemens went downtown and procured a marriage certificate. Returning, he stopped at the residence of the Rev. Mr. Twichell, pastor of the Asylum Street Church, and took him into his carriage. Arrived home, the first thing done was to send for the young man, who soon appeared, somewhat frightened at the summons. From his dress and general appearance of decay, it was evident that his circumstances were not those of violent prosperity. When he was brought in, Mark braced up and tried to look dignified. This was about the dialogue that ensued:

Mark—So, young man, you have been in the habit of making a hotel of my house—with all the modern improvements. (Silence unbroken by the young man.) Well, as you don't offer any objections we'll take that part of the matter for granted. If your offense had stopped at that point it would have been all right. I am always glad to entertain company—yes, if you had mentioned it I would have had the house refurnished for you. All that, and more, I would have done gladly for a guest. But when you (dignity and pathos)— you alienate the affections of Maria Jane, when you descend upon this peaceful fold with base designs—like a wolf in sheep's clothing, as it were, that I cannot forgive.

Y. M. (with humility)—If you please, sir, I ain't got no sheep's clothing.

Mark (examining the fabric of the young man's coat)— Ah, I perceive my error; it is cotton, not wool. However, I was speaking metaphorically. As I intimated before, I cannot endure the thought of having my home, which, until your fell presence, had been the abode of innocence, turned into a kennel of wrong-doing. When you sought that end, you not only wounded me mortally, but you aroused my wrath; and, young man, when I'm mad I'm a bad crowd. In the first throes of my passion I was doubtful whether to have you arrested for murder in the first degree, or—

At this point, the young man showed symptoms of terror. "But," continued Mark, "it suddenly occurred to me that a certain Pennsylvania judge—Joe Bradley, I believe—once ruled that in case of arson the fellow must marry the girl; and so, I conclude you must answer to the crime of arson; in other words, you must get hitched to Maria Jane."

Apparently, Mark's victim was relieved, but he still seemed doubtful. He said: "If you please, sir, I'd be glad to marry Maria, but I couldn't support her. I ain't got no money, and I can't get no work. I mean to marry her some time, sir; honest and true, I do."

Mark—That's altogether too thin, young man. You must marry Maria right here and now, or you go for arson.

Y. M.—Well, sir, if it comes to that, of course I'll marry her.

Mark—That's the kind of talk I like. Here Twichell! Maria Jane! Come here!

And the two people, named, followed by the other servant, entered the room; the marriage ceremony was performed, and Mark and the second girl signed the certificate as witnesses. After that, Mark paid the minister, gave the couple $290 in cash, and sent them adrift with an injunction—which, by the way, he ascribed to Hoyle—to "go and sin no more."

Attributed to the Boston *Herald*, this story is partially true. Apparently, the young servant Maria also claimed to be pregnant by her lover, who refused to marry her until Twain threatened to have him arrested. Her claim of pregnancy was later proven to be false (*Nook Farm* 107-08).

16 August (Thursday)
"Our Spice Box"; p. 2

In private Mark Twain is full of jests, keeping them up even at his domestic hearth. His wife asked him one day when he was fondling his first-born, "You do love the little thing, do you not, Samuel?" "I can't say I love it, but I respect it sincerely for its noble father's sake."

Twain's "first-born" was a son named Langdon, born 7 November 1870. Since he died of diphtheria on 2 June 1872, this joke refers to

Twain's first daughter, Olivia Susan (Susy), born 19 March 1872. See 1 December 1888 for another item about Susy.

3 September (Monday)
"Personal"; p. 3

The best thing Mark Twain ever said, if he ever said it, was when he replied to his wife who had just asked him if he loved their child that he was fondling, "I can't say I love it, but I respect it sincerely for its noble father's sake."

6 September (Thursday)
"Personal"; p. 3

Mark Twain's birthplace was Hannibal, Mo., and the house in which he was born, a miserable wreck of a building, is still standing on Third Street, between Bird and Hill. It is the residence of a wretchedly poor family, employed in varnishing furniture. Mark's bedroom is reached by a crazy ladder, the floor is full of holes, the plaster has peeled away from the ceiling, and the whole place is in desolation.

Born in Florida, Mo., some 30 miles to the south of Hannibal, Twain did not move to the city most associated with him until the summer of 1839 when he was three years old. This accurate description of his boyhood home is consistent with the one printed on 19 January 1875.

6 September (Thursday)
"Amusements"; p. 4

A brief blurb notes that *Colonel Sellers* was once again playing in St. Louis at the Olympic Theatre; it also mentions that the play *Ah Sin* had recently opened at De Bar's Opera House. The latter play, coauthored by Twain and Bret Harte (1836-1902), was a failure. Upon its completion in February 1877, the two authors bickered and never made any of the necessary revisions (*MT & the Theatre* 53-59). After a moderately successful Washington D.C. premier on 7 May 1877, the play moved to New York City in July to begin a run at one of the leading dramatic houses. Its reviews, however, were scathing. After five weeks of dwindling attendence, the play closed in New York and was taken on the road, where it fared no better (*MT & the Theatre* 63-64). In a speech on 31 July 1877, Twain himself acknowledged how wretched the play was but said it improved every time the manager cut it. He adds, "He cut out, and cut out, and cut out, and I do believe this would be one of the best plays in the world today if his strength had held out, and he could have gone on and cut out the rest of it" (*MT Speaking* 103-05). Because he blamed the play's failure on Harte, and because Harte had allegedly insulted Livy Clemens, Twain ended his friendship with the Californian; by the mid-1870s, he so thoroughly despised his former partner that in *Autobiography* he remembers Harte as "bad, distinctly bad; [with] no feeling and . . . no conscience" (294-302).

7 September (Friday)
no headline; p. 2

Mark Twain believes in three months of working, followed by three months of loafing, and so on as a steady business, with no loafing to interfere with the work, and no work to interfere with the loafing.

21 September (Friday)
"That Burial Lot: The Story Mark Twain Heard on a New Haven Steamer"; p. 3

All the journeyings I had ever done had been purely in the way of business. The pleasant May weather suggested a novelty, namely, a trip for pure recreation, the bread and butter element left out. The reverend said he would go, too—a good man, one of the best of men, although a clergyman. By 11 o'clock at night we were in New Haven and on board the New York boat. We bought our tickets, and then went wandering around, here and there, in the solid comfort of being free and idle, and of putting distance between ourselves and the mails and telegraphs.

After a while I went to my stateroom and undressed; but the night was too enticing for bed. We were moving down the bay now, and it was pleasant to stand at the window and take the cool night breeze and watch the gliding lights on shore. Presently, two elderly men sat down under the window and began a conversation. Their talk was properly no business of mine, yet I was feeling friendly towards the world and willing to be entertained. I soon gathered that they were brothers, that they were from a small Connecticut village, and that the matter at hand concerned the cemetery. Said one:

"Now, John, we talked it over among ourselves, and this is what we've done. You see, everybody was a'movin' from the old buryin' ground, and our folks was most about left to theirselves, as you may say. They were crowded, too, as you know; lot wa'n't big enough in the first place; and last year, when Seth's wife died we couldn't hardly tuck her in. She

sort o' overlaid Deacon Shorb's lot, and he soured on her, so
to speak, and on the rest of us, too. So we talked it over, and I
was for a layout in the new simitery on the hill. They wasn't
unwilling, if it was cheap. Well, the two best and biggest
plots was No. 8 and No. 9—both of a size; nice comfortable
room for 26 full-growns, that is; but you reckon in children
and other shorts, and strike an average, and I should say you
might lay in 30, or maybe 32 or 3, pretty genteel—no crowdin'
to signify."

"That's a'plenty, William. Which one did you buy?"

"Well, I'm a'coming to that, John. You see, No. 8 was $13,
No. 9 $14—"

"I see. So'st you took No. 8."

"You wait. I took No. 9. And I'll tell you for why. In the
first place, Deacon Shorb wanted it. Well, after the way he'd
gone on about Seth's wife overlappin' his premises, I'd a'best
him out of that No. 9 if I'd a had to stand $2 extra, let alone
one. That's the way I felt about it. Says I, what's a dollar
anyway? Life's on'y a pilgramage, says I; we ain't here for
good, and we can't take it with us, says I. So I just dumped it
down, knowin' the Lord don't suffer a good deed to go fur
nuthin', and calklatin' to take it out o' somebody in the
course o' trade. Then there was another reason, John. No.
9's a long way the handiest lot in the simitery, and the likeli-
est for situation. It lays right on top of a knoll in the dead
center of the buryin' ground; you can see Millport from there,
and Tracy's, and Hopper Mount, and a raft o' farms, and so
on. There ain't no better outlook from a buryin' plot in the
state. Well, and that ain't all. Course Shorb had to take No.
8; wa'n't no help for it. Now, No. 8 jines on to No. 9, but it's
on the slope of the hill, and ev'ry time it rains it'll soak right
down on the Shorbs. Si Higgins says 't when the deacon's
time comes, he'd better take out fire and marine insurance
both on his remains."

Here, there was a sound of a low, placid duplicate chuckle
of appreciation and satisfaction.

"Now, John, here's a little rough draft of the ground that
I've made on a piece of paper. Up here in the left-hand corner we've bunched the departed; took them from the old
graveyard and stowed them along one side o' t'other on a
first-come-first-served plan, no partialities, with gran'ther
Jones as a starter, only because it happened so, and windin'

up indiscriminate with Seth's twins. A little crowded towards the end of the layout, maybe, but we reckoned 't wa'n't best to scatter the twins. Well, next comes the livin'. Here, where it's marked A, we're goin' to put Mariar and her family when they're called; B, that's for brother Hosea and his'n; C, Calvin and tribe. What's left is these two lots here—just the gem of the patch for general style and outlook; they're for me and my folks and you and yours. Which of them would you rurther be buried in?"

"I swear you've took me mighty unexpected, William! It sort of started the shivers. Fact is, I was thinkin' so busy about makin' things comfortable for the others I hadn't thought about being buried myself."

"Life's only a fleetin' show, John, as the sayin' is. We've all got to go, sooner or later. To go with a clean record's the main thing. Fact is, it's the on'y thing worth strivin' for, John."

"Yes, that's so, William, that's so; there ain't no getting around it. Which of these lots would you recommend?"

"Well, it depends, John. Are you particular about outlook?"

"I don't say I am, William; I don't say I ain't. Reely, I don't know. But mainly, I reckon, I'd set store by a south exposure."

"That's easy fixed, John. They're both south exposure. They take the sun and the Shorbs get the shade."

"How about sile, William?"

"D's sandy sile, E's mostly loom."

"You may gimme E then, William; a sandy sile caves in more or less and costs for repairs."

"All right; set your name down here, John, under E. Now, if you don't mind payin' me your share of the $14, John, while we're on the business, everything's fixed."

After some higgling and sharp bargaining, the money was paid, and John bade his brother good night and took his leave. There was silence for some moments; then a soft chuckle welled up from the lonely William and he muttered: "I declare for't, if I haven't made a mistake! It's D that's mostly loom, not E. And John's booked for sandy sile after all."

There was another soft chuckle, and William departed to his rest also.

This anecdote is an excerpt from the beginning of an article entitled "Some Rambling Notes of an Idle Excursion," which is reprinted in its entirety in *Sketches & Tales* (308-42). The article also narrates the rest of the pleasure trip Twain and Twichell made to Bermuda.

25 September (Tuesday)
"Amusements"; p. 4

> The laughable sketch of the *Pink Domino*, as given by the Allen Combination, is enough to provoke the risibles of a graven image, or to make Mark Twain's deaf and dumb man laugh.

See 29 June 1874 for the joke that spawned this particular allusion. *Pink Dominos,* adapted from the French farce *Les Dominos Roses,* was a vaudeville entertainment especially popular in the West. A New York *Times* critic, however, was less enthusiastic about the drama: "Its material is old, the characters are commonplace. . . . On purely aesthetic grounds it is a . . . disagreeable achievement" (10 August 1877).

24 October (Wednesday)
"News of the Day"; p. 3

> There is said to be a lawsuit pending in Australia that is more peculiar than the famous one Mark Twain describes as having grown out of a landslide which piled one farm on top of the other.

Twain's story, originally written for the San Francisco *Daily Call* and later incorporated into *Roughing It*, narrates a joke played upon a lawyer asked to represent a man whose farm has been covered by a landslide. The final version of the story is reprinted in *Collected Tales I* (345-49), while *Landslide Case* prints all three known versions.

20 December (Thursday)
"Our Spice Box"; p. 2

> Booksellers report a marked wane in the sale of Mark Twain's writings.

Although *The Innocents Abroad* (1869) and *Roughing It* (1872) remained popular and continued to sell, sales of Twain's other books—*The Gilded Age* (1873), *Sketches, New and Old* (1875), and *The Adventures of Tom Sawyer* (1876)—were poor. In fact, if it were not for the phenomenal success of his play *Colonel Sellers* and the wealth of his wife, Twain might well have had to resume a lecturing and/or journalism career to support his lavish lifestyle.

28 December (Friday)
"Personal"; p. 2

Mark Twain's after-dinner speech at the banquet for Whittier was received coldly, and it is said to have even given offense on account of its coarseness.

The text of his controversial speech, which burlesqued the poetry of Ralph Waldo Emerson, Oliver Wendell Holmes, and Henry Wadsworth Longfellow and managed to offend nearly everyone at the banquet, is reprinted in *Collected Tales I* (695-99). At this Boston dinner to honor the poet John Greenleaf Whittier on 17 December 1877, Twain told a tall tale in which three impostors assume the identities of Emerson, Holmes, and Longfellow in order to steal from a miner kind enough to offer them shelter. The speech caused Twain to be ostracized from Boston society, although he apologized soon afterward for any offense he had caused (*Mr. Clemens & MT* 209-11). See 18 January 1878 for a report of his apology.

1878

17 January (Thursday)
"Post Pencilings"; p. 2

Had Mark Twain lived at that early day he would have made the apostles appear ridiculous at the last supper.

18 January (Friday)
"Post Pencilings"; p. 2

If Mark Twain has apologized for his Whittier speech in the abject manner reported, or, indeed, if he has apologized at all, it will not be necessary to apologize for him. They say, for instance, that he is a victim of emotional insanity.

29 March (Friday)
"Post Pencilings"; p. 2

A person oppressed with thickness of tongue speaks of a new church book: *The Guild Adage*, by Clemuel L. Samens and Charles Wudley Darner.

24 April (Wednesday)
"Post Pencilings"; p. 2

Mark Twain called his dog Joe Cook because he could not understand him.

This joke refers to the Rev. Flavius Josephus ("Joe") Cook (1838-1901), a moral lecturer and writer opposed to Darwinism. He had great appeal with the public but was often mocked by newspapers for his lack of education.

3 May (Friday)
"Post Pencilings"; p. 2

Mark Twain told a newspaper reporter that he was going abroad in order to find a quiet place to write, where he would not be disturbed once a day. It is singular that it never occurred to him to remain at home and secure a desk in a store that does not advertise.

13 May (Monday)
"Post Pencilings"; p. 2

It is now rumored by his enemies that that cruel and ferocious brigand Mark Twain, who recently sailed ostensibly for England, will fit out a privateer. He will issue the "letters of Mark" himself.

Twain and his family sailed for Europe on 11 April 1878 for a leisurely tour of Germany and France.

20 July (Saturday)
"Post Pencilings"; p. 2

Mark Twain has written home for his clergyman to visit him in Germany at his (Mark's) expense. It is strongly suspected that Twain is wrestling with a new humorous effort and desires his minister to pray for him—to ask Divine forgiveness for the awful thing he is about to do. This surmise may be wrong, however. The popular humorist may simply want a traveling companion who knows how to play a good game of euchre or "old sledge."

In fact, Twain wanted Twichell to join him in Europe for his company and because his friend's observations about the geography and people would help to inspire his pen. Twain's purpose was fulfilled, for after Twichell's arrival on 1 August, the writing of *A Tramp Abroad* went much faster (*Mr. Clemens & MT* 212 and 217-18; *Nook Farm* 70-71). "Old Sledge" is a card game also known as Seven-Up.

30 November (Saturday)
"Captain Cowden and Mark Twain"; p. 4

That famous scientist Mark Twain must look to his laurels, for he has a Western rival who bids fair to outstrip him. Mark's scientific reputation rests entirely on two gigantic efforts. In his *Innocents Abroad*, he alludes to the agony of an Indian gentleman whose watch could not keep up with the ship's time. It was the best watch that he had ever owned. He had paid a high price for it and felt confident that it could run as fast as any watch ever made; and he did not attempt to conceal his chagrin that it was showing a daily incapacity to keep up with the time of the ship. He had about made up his mind that he had been swindled when Mark came to his relief by showing him that the tardiness of the watch was owing to the eastward progress of the vessel. Mark then closes by stating that they had traveled eastward at a rate just sufficient to keep the moon at its full during the entire passage. Only one scientist ventured to question the accuracy of this statement, Mr. Richard Proctor, the celebrated English astronomer. He showed conclusively that no matter how fast or slow a man might travel around the earth, either east or west, the moon would change all the same. But Englishmen are always carping at something American.

Mark next tried his scientific hand on the Mississippi River. He collated a lot of statistics showing the constant tendency of the river to grow shorter. He instanced a number of cut-offs to establish the average rate of shortening, and then demonstrated that about 150,000 years ago the mouth of the river was in the middle of the Gulf of Mexico and that the river stuck out over the gulf like a fishing pole. This splendid deduction has passed unchallenged.

Now comes one Capt. John Cowden of Memphis with a plan for "improving the Mississippi," and shows himself fully the equal of Mark as a man of science. He accounts for the eastward trend of the river from Baton Rouge to the gulf by ascribing it to the rotary motion of the earth from west to east. The river, in flowing southward, flows toward a constantly increasing motion of rotation, which it bears very patiently so long as it is confined within its bluffs. But after passing Baton Rouge it has fair play, and then it loses no time in showing that it can run faster than the force which propels it in that direction. No doubt some Englishman will attempt to show that the current of the river, having a slower rotary motion than the earth, ought to get behind the earth, that is to say, incline westward; nevertheless, Capt. Cowden's theory of its ability to outstrip its propelling force is fully equal to Mark Twain's fishing-pole generalization.

Again, Capt. Cowden, in order to strengthen his theory, says that the eastern rail of railroads running north and south is more abraded by the wheel-flanges than the western rail. If we grant that southward bound trains ought to get ahead of the earth's rotary motion and hug the eastern rail, we might claim that the northward bound trains, being subject to the reverse action of the same force of rotation, would get behind it and wear away the western rail. But we are not going to play the Englishman. This railroad discovery of Capt. Cowden's is not a whit inferior to Mark Twain's famous lunar essay. And whereas Mark Twain has occupied the whole of his long career in reaching his present high position as a scientist, while Capt. Cowden eclipses him with his initial effort; therefore, we say that it is proved that Capt. Cowden is as great a scientific genius as Mark Twain, and it will go near to be thought so shortly.

Twain discusses the watch—allegedly worth $150—that could not keep proper time aboard a ship at the beginning of chapter 5 of *The Innocents Abroad*; its owner, however, is not an Indian but a man from the "Far West." Professor Proctor (1837-88), the most famous astronomer of the day, would again be linked with Twain on 8 February 1884.

1879

18 January (Thursday)
no headline; p. 2

At one of the "New England dinners" in New York, Mark Twain, in answering to the toast of "New England Weather," proudly claimed for his native land a larger amount and variety of weather than was known in any other country; but this was because he had had no experience of the weather St. Louis has exhibited for the past month. It is very fortunate that an economic Congress cut down the appropriation for the weather maps, for any attempt to do justice to our weather on a chart would have broken down the whole bureau of storms and signals.

This editorial refers to a speech Twain gave on 22 December 1876 in which he claimed to have witnessed 136 different weather patterns on a single spring day in New England. The text of his speech is reprinted in *Collected Tales I* (673-76).

21 January (Tuesday)
"Gambetta-Fourtou: Mark Twain's Account of the Recent French Duel"; p. 3

Much as the modern French duel is ridiculed by certain smart people, it is in reality one of the most dangerous institutions of our day. Since it is always fought in the open air, the combatants are sure to catch cold. M. Paul de Cassagnac, the most inveterate of French duelists, has suffered so often in this way that he is at last a confirmed invalid; and the best physician in Paris has expressed the opinion that if he goes on dueling for 15 or 20 years more—unless he forms the habit of fighting in a comfortable room where damps and draughts cannot intrude—he will eventually endanger his life. This ought to moderate the talk of those people who are so stubborn in maintaining that the French duel is the most health-giving of recreations because of the open air exercise it affords. And it ought also to moderate that foolish talk about French duelists and socialist-hated monarchs being the only people who are immortal.

But it is time to get at my subject. As soon as I heard of the fiery outbreak between M. Gambetta and M. Fourtou in the French Assembly, I knew that trouble must follow. I knew it because a long personal friendship with M. Gambetta had revealed to me the desperate and implacable nature of the man. Vast as are his physical proportions, I knew that the thirst for revenge would penetrate to the remotest frontiers of his person.

I did not wait for him to call on me, but went at once to him. As I expected, I found the brave fellow steeped in a profound French calm. I say French calm, because French calmness and English calmness have points of difference. He was moving swiftly back and forth among the debris of his furniture, now and then staving chance fragments of it across the room with his foot; grinding a constant grist of curses through his set teeth; and halting every little while to deposit another handful of his hair on the pile which he had been building of it on the table.

He threw his arms around my neck, bent me over his stomach to his breast, kissed me on both checks, hugged me four or five times, and then placed me in his own armchair. As soon as I had got well again, we began business at once.

I said I supposed he would wish me to act as his second, and he said, "Of course." I said I must be allowed to act under a French name, so that I might be shielded from obloquy in my country, in case of fatal results. He winced here, probably at my suggestion that dueling was not regarded with respect in America. However, he agreed to my requirement. This accounts for the fact that in all the newspaper reports M. Gambetta's second was apparently a Frenchman.

First, we drew up my principal's will. I insisted on this, and stuck to my point. I said I had never heard of a man in his right mind going out to fight a duel without first making out his will. He said he had never heard of a man in his right mind doing anything of the kind. When we had finished the will, he wished to proceed to a choice of his "last words." He wanted to know how the following words, as a dying exclamation, struck me:

"I die for my God, for my country, for freedom of speech, for progress and the universal brotherhood of man!"

I objected that this would require too lingering a death; it was a good speech for a consumptive, but not suited to the exigencies of the field of honor. We wrangled over a good many ante-mortem outbursts, but I finally got him to cut his obituary down to this, which he copied into his memorandum book, purposing to get it by heart:

'I DIE THAT FRANCE MAY LIVE."

I said that this remark seemed to lack relevancy; but he said relevancy was a matter of no consequence in last words—what you wanted was thrill.

The next thing in order was the choice of weapons. My principal said he was not feeling well, and would leave that and the other details of the proposed meeting to me. Therefore, I wrote the following note and carried it to M. Fourtou's friend:

"Sir—

"M. Gambetta accepts M. Fourtou's challenge, and authorizes me to propose Plessis-Piquet as the place of meeting; tomorrow morning at daybreak as the time; and axes as the weapons. I am, sir, with great respect,

"Mark Twain."

M. Fourtou's friend read this note, and shuddered. Then he turned to me and said, with a suggestion of severity in his voice:

"Have you considered, sir, what would be the inevitable result of such a meeting as this?"

"Well, for instance, what *would* it be?"

"Bloodshed."

"That's about the size of it," I said. "Now, if it is a fair question, what was your side proposing to shed?"

I had him there. He saw he had made a blunder, so he hastened to explain it away. He said that he had spoken jestingly. Then he added that he and his principal would enjoy axes, and indeed would prefer them, but such weapons were barred by the French code, and so I must change my proposal.

I walked the floor, turning the thing over in my mind, and it finally occurred to me that Gatling guns at 15 paces would be a likely way to get a verdict on the field of honor. So I framed this idea into a proposition.

But it was not accepted. The code was in the way again. I proposed rifles; then, double-barreled shotguns; then, Colt's navy revolvers. These all being rejected, I reflected a while, and sarcastically suggested brick-bats at three-quarters of a mile. I always hate to fool away a humorous thing on a person who has no perception of humor; and it filled me with bitterness when this man went soberly away to submit this last proposition to his principal.

He came back presently, and said his principal was charmed with the idea of brick-bats at three-quarters of a mile, but must decline on account of the danger to disinterested parties passing between. Then I said:

"Well, I am at the end of my string, now. Perhaps you would be good enough to suggest a weapon? Perhaps you have even had one in your mind all the time?"

His countenance brightened, and he said with alacrity:

"Oh, without a doubt, Monsieur!"

So he fell to hunting in his pockets—pocket after pocket, and he had plenty of them—muttering all the while, "Now, what could I have done with them?"

At last he was successful. He fished out of his vest pocket a couple of little things which I carried to the light and discovered to be pistols. They were single-barreled and silver-mounted, and very dainty and pretty. I was not able to speak for emotion. I silently hung one of them on my watch-chain, and returned the other. My companion in crime now unrolled a postage stamp containing several cartridges, and gave me one of them. I asked if he meant to signify by this that our men were allowed but one shot apiece. He replied that the French code permitted no more. I then begged him to go on and suggest a distance, for my mind was growing weak and confused under the strain which had been put upon it. He named 65 yards. I nearly lost my patience. I said:

"Sixty-five yards, with these instruments? Pop-guns would be deadlier at 50. Consider, my friend, you and I are banded together to destroy life, not make it eternal."

But with all my persuasions, all my arguments, I was only able to get him to reduce the distance to 35 yards; and even this concession he made with reluctance, and said with a sigh:

"I wash my hands of this slaughter; on your head be it."

There was nothing for me to do but to go home to my old

lion-heart and tell my humiliating story. When I entered, M. Gambetta was laying his last lock of hair upon the altar. He sprang toward me, exclaiming:

"You have made the fatal arrangements—I see it in your eye!"

"I have."

His face paled a trifle, and he leaned upon the table for support. He breathed thick and heavily for a moment or two, so tumultuous were his feelings; then he hoarsely whispered:

"The weapon, the weapon! Quick! what is the weapon?"

"This," and I displayed that silver-mounted thing. He caught but one glimpse of it, then swooned ponderously to the floor.

When he came to, he said mournfully:

"The unnatural calm to which I have subjected myself has told upon my nerves. But away with weakness! I will confront my fate like a man and a Frenchman."

He rose to his feet, and assumed an attitude which for sublimity has never been approached by man, and has seldom been surpassed by statues. Then he said, in his deep bass tones:

"Behold, I am calm, I am ready; reveal to me the distance."

"Thirty-five yards."

I could not lift him up, of course; but I rolled him over and poured water down his back. He presently came to and said:

"Thirty-five yards—without a rest? But why ask? Since murder was that man's intention, why should he palter with small details? But mark you one thing: in my fall the world shall see how the chivalry of France meets death."

After a long silence, he asked:

"Was nothing said about that man's family standing up with him, as an offset to my bulk? But no matter; I would not stoop to make such a suggestion; if he is not noble enough to suggest it himself, he is welcome to this advantage, which no honorable man would take."

He now sank into a sort of stupor of reflection, which lasted some minutes; after which he broke silence with—

"The hour—what was the hour fixed for the collision?"

"Dawn, tomorrow."

He seemed greatly surprised and immediately said:

"Insanity! I never heard of such a thing. Nobody is abroad at such an hour."

"That is the reason I named it. Do you mean to say you want an audience?"

"It is no time to bandy words. I am astonished that M. Fourtou should ever have agreed to so strange an innovation. Go at once and require a later hour."

I ran downstairs, threw open the front door, and almost plunged into the arms of Mr. Fourtou's second. He said:

"I have the honor to say that my principal strenuously objects to the hour chosen, and begs that you will consent to change it to half-past nine."

"Any courtesy, sir, which it is in our power to extend is at the service of your excellent principal. We agree to the proposed change of time."

"I beg you to accept the thanks of my client." Then he turned to a person behind him and said, "You hear, M. Noir, the hour is altered to half-past nine." Whereupon M. Noir bowed, expressed his thanks, and went away. My accomplice continued:

"If agreeable to you, your chief surgeons and ours shall proceed to the field in the same carriage, as is customary."

"It is entirely agreeable to me, and I am obliged to you for mentioning the surgeons for I am afraid I should not have thought of them. How many shall I want? I suppose two or three will be enough?"

"Two is the customary number for each party. I refer to 'chief' surgeons; but considering the exalted positions occupied by our clients, it will be well and decorous that each of us appoint several consulting surgeons from among the highest in the profession. These will come in their own private carriages. Have you engaged a hearse?"

"Bless my stupidity, I never thought of it! I will attend to it right away. I must seem very ignorant to you; but you must try to overlook that, because I have never had any experience of such a swell duel as this before. I have had a good deal to do with duels on the Pacific coast but I see now that they were crude affairs. A hearse—sho! we used to leave the elected lying around loose and let anybody cord them up and cart them off that wanted to. Have you anything further to suggest?"

"Nothing, except that the head undertakers shall ride together, as is usual. The subordinates and mutes will go on foot, as is also usual. I will see you at eight o'clock in the morning, and we will then arrange the order of the procession. I have the honor to bid you a good day."

I returned to my client, who said, "Very well; at what hour is the engagement to begin?

"Half-past nine."

"Very good, indeed. Have you sent the fact to the newspapers?"

"Sir! If after our long and intimate friendship you can for a moment deem me capable of so base a treachery—"

"Tut, tut! What words are these, my dear friend? Have I wounded you? Ah, forgive me. I am overloading you with labor. Therefore, go on with other details, and drop this one from your list. The bloody-minded Fourtou will be sure to attend to it. Or I myself—yes, to make certain, I will drop a note to my journalistic friend, M. Noir—"

"Oh, come to think, you may save yourself the trouble; that other second has informed M. Noir."

"H'm! I might have known it. It is just like that Fourtou, who always wants to make a display."

At half-past nine in the morning the procession approached the field of Plessis-Piquet in the following order: First came our carriage, nobody in it but M. Gambetta and myself; then a carriage containing M. Fourtou and his second; then a coach containing two poet-orators who did not believe in God, and these had MS. funeral orations projecting from their breast pockets; then a carriage containing the head surgeons and their cases of instruments; then eight private carriages containing consulting surgeons; then a hack containing the coroner; then the two hearses; then a carriage containing the head undertakers; then a train of assistants and mutes on foot; and after these came plodding through the fog a long procession of camp followers, police, and citizens generally. It was a noble turnout, and would have made a fine display if we had had thinner weather. There was no conversation. I spoke several times to my principal, but I judge he was not aware of it for he always referred to his notebook, and muttered absently, "I die that France may live." Arrived on the field, my fellow-second and I paced off the 35 yards, and then drew lots for choice of position. This latter was but an ornamental ceremony, for all choices were alike in such weather. These preliminaries being ended, I went to my principal and asked him if he were ready. He spread himself out to his full width, and in a stern voice, "Ready! Let the batteries be charged."

The loading was done in the presence of duly constituted witnesses. We considered it best to perform this delicate service with the assistance of a lantern, on account of the state of the weather. We now placed our men.

At this point the police noticed the public had massed themselves together on the right and left of the field; they therefore begged a delay while they should put these poor people in a place of safety. The request was granted.

The police having ordered the two multitudes to take positions behind the duelists, we were once more ready. The weather growing still more opaque, it was agreed between myself and the other second that before giving the fatal signal we should each deliver a loud whoop to enable the combatants to ascertain each other's whereabouts.

I now returned to my principal and was distressed to observe that he had lost a good deal of his spirit. I tried my best to hearten him. I said:

"Indeed, sir, things are not as bad as they seem. Considering the character of the weapons, the limited number of shots allowed, the generous distance, the impenetrable solidity of the fog, and the added fact that one of the combatants is one-eyed and the other cross-eyed and near-sighted, it seems to me that this conflict need not necessarily be fatal. There are chances that both of you may survive. Therefore, cheer up; do not be down-hearted."

This speech had so good an effect that my principal immediately stretched forth his hand and said: "I am myself again, give me the weapon."

I laid it, all lonely and forlorn, in the center of the vast solitude of his palm. He gazed at it and shuddered. And still mournfully contemplating it, he murmured in a broken voice:

"Alas, it is not death I dread, but mutilation."

I heartened him once more, and with such success that he presently said:

"Let the tragedy begin. Stand at my back; do not desert me in this solemn hour, my friend."

I gave my promise. I now assisted him to point his pistol

toward the spot where I judged his adversary to be standing and cautioned him to listen well and further guide himself by my fellow-second's whoop. Then I propped myself against M. Gambetta's back and raised a rousing "Whoop-ee!" This was answered out in the far distances of the fog, and I immediately shouted:

"One, two, three—fire!"

Two little sounds like spit! spit! broke upon my ear, and the same instant I was crushed to the earth under a mountain of flesh. Buried as I was, I was still able to catch a faint accent from above, to this affect:

"I die for—for—perdition take it, what is it I die for? Oh, yes—France! I die that France may live!"

The surgeons swarmed around with their probes in their hands, and applied their microscopes to the whole area of M. Gambetta's person, with the happy result in finding nothing in the nature of a wound. Then a scene ensued which was in every way gratifying and inspiriting.

The two gladiators fell upon each other's necks with floods of proud and happy tears; that other second embraced me; the surgeons, the orators, the undertakers, the police, everybody embraced, everybody congratulated, everybody cried, and the whole atmosphere was filled with praise and joy unspeakable.

It seemed to me then that I would rather be the hero of a French duel than a crowned and sceptered monarch.

When the commotion had somewhat subsided, the body of surgeons held a consultation, and after a good deal of debate decided with proper care and nursing there was reason to believe that I would survive my injuries. My internal hurts were deemed the most serious, since it was apparent that a broken rib had penetrated my left lung and that many of my organs had been pressed out so far to one side or the other of where they belonged that it was doubtful if they would ever learn to perform their functions in such remote and unaccustomed localities. They then set my left arm in two places, pulled my right hip into its socket again, and re-elevated my nose. I was an object of great interest, and even admiration, and many sincere and warm-hearted persons had themselves introduced to me and said they were proud to know the only man who had been hurt in a French duel for 40 years. I was placed in an ambulance at the very head of the procession;

and thus with gratifying *eclat* I was marched into Paris, the most conspicuous figure in that great spectacle, and deposited at the hospital. The cross of the Legion of Honor has been conferred upon me. However, few escape that distinction. Such is the true version of the most memorable private conflict of the age. My recovery is still doubtful, but there are hopes. I am able to dictate but there is no knowing when I shall be able to write. I have no complaints to make against anyone. I acted for myself, and I can stand the consequences. Without boasting, I think I may say that I am not afraid to stand before a modern French duelist, but I will never consent to stand behind one again.

Originally published in the *Atlantic*, this sketch later served as chapter 8 of *A Tramp Abroad*. On 18 November 1878, former Minister of the Interior Marie François Fourtou (1836-97) publicly called Léon Gambetta (1838-82), the primary spokesman for the Republic, a liar and demanded satisfaction for his injured reputation. The corpulent Gambetta agreed to meet Fourtou, who was indeed blind in one eye, at Plessis Piequet on 21 November to settle the matter in a duel. The New York *Times* of 22 November 1878 notes, however, that "men who fire at each other at a distance of 105 feet, with the miserable little pop-guns in use in France, cannot be bent on murder."

22 January (Wednesday)
"Pencilings"; p. 2
> Mark Twain claims to have been Gambetta's second in the recent duel. Well, Mark used to swing the lead himself, some years ago.

12 June (Thursday)
"Personal Notes; p. 2
> Mark Twain's brother the Rev. Orion Clemens, expelled from an Iowa church for heresy, was formerly an editor.

Although never a minister (but often a newspaper editor), Orion Clemens was indeed expelled from his church for a lecture he delivered entitled "Man, the Architect of Our Religion" (*Mr. Clemens & MT* 235).

14 June (Saturday)
"Personal Notes"; p. 5
> Mark Twain has the mumps, but that's not the worst of it. They have taken him for a United States Senator in Paris.

17 June (Tuesday)
"Rock Me to Sleep"; p. 2

Several years ago a man named Ball put in his claim as author of "Rock Me to Sleep." Mark Twain was a journalist then and he expressed the following opinion, which has been unearthed from a scrapbook by a correspondent of the Buffalo *Express*:

Backward, speed backward, O Ball in your flight!
Make not yourself an ass (just for to-night);
Pull the few silver threads out of your hair.
Fill up and varnish those furrows of care—
Care that was born of attempting fame's steep,
Which you couldn't climb, Ball, whom none rocked to
  sleep.
Oh, Bally, come back from the echoing shore!
Cease for a season the public to bore
With your infamous rhymes and your stupid complaint,
For you know you are claiming to be what you ain't.
Oh, drivel no more—don't snuffle, don't weep—
Hang up your lyre, Ball, I'll rock you to sleep.

"Rock Me to Sleep, Mother"—an immensely popular American song during the mid-19th century—was a poem set to music by Ernest Leslie. Periodically, as suggested by this item, a person would step forward to claim credit for the lyrics, but they were actually written by Florence Percy (1832-1911) who published them in the 9 June 1860 *Saturday Evening Post*. In 1869 Twain bought one-third interest in the Buffalo *Express* and became one of its chief editors. He made this investment primarily to have a steady income during the first years of his marriage to Livy Langdon, whom he married on 2 February 1870. By 1871, however, he had come to so despise Buffalo and the anxiety of owning a newspaper that he happily sold his interest in the *Express* for $15,000, taking a loss of $10,000 on the investment (*Mr. Clemens & MT* 135).

20 June (Friday)
"Pencilings"; p. 2

Mark Twain has recovered from the mumps, but the mumps have not recovered from Mark Twain. They made a painful mistake in attacking his cheek.

1 September (Monday)
"Pencilings"; p. 2

Mark Twain has realized more money from his play of

The Gilded Age than Shakespeare did from all of his dramas. It is not Shakespeare's fault, however. If Mark Twain had produced his plays in Shakespeare's time, and Shakespeare had deferred writing his plays until the present age, we wager that he could have "seen" Mark Twain's pile, and "go him a few hundred thousand better," as old Aristotle would say.

Colonel Sellers was indeed a huge financial success for Twain. During the peak of its popularity in 1875, for instance, it brought him an estimated $400 to $900 a week; by the summer of 1876, it had paid Twain $23,000 in royalties (*MT & the Theatre* 48, 56).

3 September (Wednesday)
"Pencilings"; p. 2

Mark Twain is expected home from Europe every day. When he gets here and finds that every respectable newspaper has its own "funny man," he will linger long enough to read their scintillations, and then double on his track by the next steamer. And in all human probability that will be the last we will ever see of Mark Twain.

5 September (Friday)
"Mark Twain's Return: The Great Humorist Delighted to be Home—How He passed His Time in Europe"; p. 3

Mr. Samuel L. Clemens (Mark Twain) arrived in this city yesterday, on the Cunard steamer *Gallia*, after a tour of 18 months through the principal countries of Europe. Mr. Clemens, who was accompanied by his wife and family, appeared in excellent health. "I enjoyed the trip greatly," he said to a *Herald* reporter, "and I learned a great deal that will serve me in after life."

"I am glad to find," said the reporter, "that after so many years of mental labor you at last enjoyed a long respite from your literary avocations."

"Respite!" he exclaimed with astonishment, and then, with a merry twinkle in his eye, he said in a confidential whisper, "You don't mean that."

"Why not?"

"If you are in earnest in your remark I can tell you just as earnestly I never spent a busier time in my life. I only wish I could show you the piles of manuscript that are lying in my trunks and then you would have some idea of the work in which I have been engaged."

As he spoke the custom house officers were rushing here and there along the wharf examining the baggage, and seeing them approach the place where his trunks lay he asked to be excused for a few minutes. When the inspection of what he termed his "cargo" was concluded he returned and resumed his conversation. "I feel a deep sense of relief," he said, "in returning to this, the dearest land to me in the world. Many a time"—

Here the conversation was interrupted by a visitor who abruptly remarked "Mr. Clemens, one moment."

With another apology, Mr. Clemens departed, but soon returned, and, taking his seat beside the reporter, said: "You desire to know how I was occupied during my travels. Well, I will tell you. I spent three months in Heidelberg. It is a delightful place. I spent three more in Paris. These were six months taken out of my trip. To tell you briefly, I traveled for the comfort of my family, and wherever I found they could enjoy the attractions and the scenes, there I settled down. I was not traveling in the ordinary sense of running from place to place.

"Do you intend to give a history of your travels through the public journals?"

"Oh, no; nothing will appear concerning my travels till my book is published. I have spent much time and labor on it, and I do not propose to anticipate its publication. It would not be fair to expect that after—

"See, there goes the Earl of Dunraven," he said suddenly, snapping the thread of his topic, "we have had aristocracy in abundance in company with us on our return trip. The earl is fast becoming Americanized."

"How?"

"Well, you see he has been so often in this country before that he has got a great deal of that aristocratic idea rubbed off him," and the last three words were delivered with an emphasis and a knowing wink that showed how the humorist was engaged in studying character during the voyage. "We had two other lords among the passengers—Lord Caleden and Rodney—but as I had not previously formed their acquaintance I cannot offer any opinion concerning them as representatives of the English aristocracy."

"What will be the title of your new book? asked the reporter.

"I cannot tell that now," was the reply, "it will take me some time for consideration on that point after I have arranged my manuscript. I have written more and torn up more manuscript after it was written than you can imagine. But it will not take me long to prepare the work for publication."

Mr. Clemens concluded by saying that after remaining a few days in this city he would return to his home in Hartford and there settle down for a few months to the completion of his book.

Originally printed in the New York *Herald*, this interview was reprinted by the *Post-Dispatch*. Although he returned to the United States on 3 September, Twain did not complete work on *A Tramp Abroad* for a number of months. It was finally published in March of 1880 to generally good reviews.

29 October (Wednesday)
"Pencilings'; p. 2

About the funniest thing in connection with Mark Twain's recent speech was the fact that several persons in the audience laughed.

Presumably, this comment is about Twain's political speech in Elmira, N. Y., on 16 October 1879. Its text is reprinted in *Mark Twain Speaking* (128-29).

18 November (Tuesday)
"Twain's Best Joke: How the Great Humorist Once Caught Himself Helping on His Own Boom"; p. 2

That quaint and original genius, Samuel L. Clemens— Mark Twain—told a story at his own expense while breakfasting with a journalistic friend on Thursday morning, which is too good to be lost, and which, by his consent is now published for the first time. There had been some talk at the table about the Grant banquet when Mr. Clemens remarked with a smile and his peculiar drawl:

"Speaking of banquets reminds me of a rather amusing incident that occurred to me during my stop in smoky, dirty, grand old London. I received an invitation to attend a banquet there, and I went. It was one of those tremendous dinners where there are from 800 to 900 invited guests. I hadn't been used to that sort of thing, and I didn't feel quite at home. When we took our seats at the tables I noticed that at each plate was a little plan of the hall, with the position of each guest numbered, so that one could see at a glance where a friend was seated by learning his number. Just before we fell to, someone—the Lord Mayor, or whoever was bossing the occasion—arose and began to read a list of those present— No. 1, lord So-and-so, No. 2, the duke of something-or-other, and so on. When this individual read the name of some prominent political character or literary celebrity, it would be greeted with more or less applause. The individual who was reading the names did so in so monotonous a manner that I became somewhat tired, and began looking about for something to engage my attention. I found the gentleman next to me on the right a well-informed personage, and I entered into conversation with him. I had never seen him before, but he was a good talker and I enjoyed it. Suddenly, just as he was giving me his view upon the future religious aspect of Great Britain, our ears were assailed by a deafening storm of applause. Such a clapping of hands I had never heard before. It sent the blood to my head with a rush, and I got terribly excited. I straightened up and commenced clapping my hands with all my might. I moved about excitedly in my chair, and clapped harder and harder. 'Who is it?' I asked the gentleman on my right. 'Whose name did he read?'

"'Samuel L. Clemens,' he answered.

"I stopped applauding. I didn't clap anymore. It kind of took the life out of me, and I sat there like a mummy and didn't even get up and bow. It was one of the most distressing fixes I ever got into, and it will be many a day before I forget it."

On 13 November 1879 at the Thirteenth Reunion Banquet for the Army of the Tennessee in Chicago honoring Gen. Grant, Twain delivered one of his most famous humorous speeches, "The Babies," which is reprinted in *Mark Twain Speaking* (131-34). It told about the troubles babies can cause their fathers, even when they are battle-hardened veterans of the Civil War.

1 December (Monday)
"Mark Twain in Trouble: He Protests Against What He Calls the New Postal Barbarism"; p. 6

The new postal regulation adds quite perceptibly to my daily burden of work. Needlessly, too—as I think. A day or two ago I made a note of the addresses which I had put upon letters that day, and then ciphered up to see how many words the additional particularities of the new ruling had cost me. It was 72. That amounts to just a page of my manuscript, exactly. If it were stuff that a magazine would enjoy, I could sell it, and gradually get rich as time rolled on—as it isn't I lose the time and the ink. I don't get a cent for it, the government grows no wealthier, I grow poorer, nobody in the world is benefited. Seventy-two words utterly wasted—and mind you, when a man is paid by the word (at least by the page, which is the same thing), this sort of thing hurts. Here are one or two specimens from those addresses—with the necessary additions in italics:

Editor, Atlantic Monthly,
Care, Messrs. Houghton, Osgood, & Co.
Windthrop Square,
Boston,
Mass.

Nine words wasted—I use only the first line and the word "Boston" and until the letter-carriers lose their minds the additional nine words can never become necessary.

Messrs. Arnold, Constable, & Co.
Cor. 19th & B'way.
New York
N. Y.

Six unnecessary words.

Gilsey House,
Cor. 29th & B'way
New York
N. Y.

Six unnecessary words.

Even the dead people in Boston and New York could tell a letter-carrier how to find those prominent houses. That same day I wrote a letter to a friend at the Windsor Hotel, New York—surely that house is prominent enough, ain't it? But I could not precisely name the side streets, neither did I know the name of the back street, nor the head cook's name. So that letter would have gone to the Dead Letter Office sure, if I hadn't covered it all over with an appeal to Mr. James to take it under his personal official protection, and let it go to that man at the Windsor just this once, and I would not offend any more.

Now, you know yourself that there is no need of an official decree to compel a man to make a letter-address full and elaborate where it is all necessary—for the writer is more anxious that his letter go through than the Postmaster-General can be. And when the writer cannot supply those minute details from lack of knowledge, the decree cannot help him in the least. So what is the use of the decree? As for those common mistakes, the mis-directing of letters, the leaving off the county, state, etc.—do you think an official decree can do away with that? You know yourself that heedless, absent-minded people are bound to make these mistakes, and that no decree can knock the disposition out of them.

Observe this—I have been ciphering, and I know that the following facts are correct. The new law will compel 18,000 great mercantile houses to employ three extra correspondents at $1,000 a year—$54,000—smaller establishments in proportion. It will compel 30,000,000 of our people to write a daily average of 10 words apiece—300,000,000 unnecessary words: most of these people are slow—the average will be half a minute consumed on each 10 words—15,000,000 minutes of this nation's time fooled away every day—say 247,400 hours, which amounts to about 25,000 working days of 10 hours each; this makes 82 years of 200 working days each, counting out Sundays and sickness—82 years of this nation's time wholly thrown away every day! Value of the average man's time, say $1,000 a year—now you see?—$2,000 thrown away daily; in round numbers $25,000,000 yearly; in ten years, $250,000,000; in a hundred years, $2,500,000,000; in a million years—but I have not the nerve to go on; you can see for yourself what we are coming to. If this law continues in force, there will not be money enough in this country, by and by, to pay for its obituary—and, you mark my words, it will need one.

Now we come to the ink. No, let us forebear—in fancy I already see the fleets of the world sailing in it.

Isn't it odd that we should take a spasm, every now and then, and go spinning back into the dark ages once more, after having put in a world of time and money and work toiling up the high lights of modern progress?

For many years it has been England's boast that her postal system is so admirable that you can't so cripple the direction of a letter that the Post Office Department won't manage some way to find the person the missive is intended for. We could say that, too, once.   But we have retired 100 years within the last two months, and now it is our boast that only the brightest, and thoughtfulest, and knowingest men's letters will ever be permitted to reach their destinations, and that those of the mighty majority of the American people— the heedless, the unthinking, the illiterate—will be rudely shot by the shortest route to the Dead Letter Office, and destruction. It seems to me that this new decree is very decidedly un-American.

                                                        Mark Twain.
Hartford, Conn., Nov. 22.

Reprinted from the Hartford *Courant*, this letter to the editor shows very well how Twain could twist statistics for humorous effect. As he argues in *Autobiography I*, "Figures often beguile me, particularly when I have the arranging of them myself; in which case the remark attributed to Disraeli would often apply with justice and force: 'There are three kinds of lies: lies, damned lies, and statistics'" (246). The "Mr. James" to whom Twain appeals for mercy was Thomas Lemuel James (1831-1916), current postmaster of New York City and later postmaster general for the United States. One wonders what Twain would say in this day of nine-digit zipcodes.

1880

2 February (Monday)
"Personal"; p. 2

Mark Twain wants to go to Congress, but he would be in the way there. Congress wants comic men and clowns, not humorists.

This report that Twain had an interest in political office is false.

6 August (Friday)
"Personal"; p. 4

It is said that Mark Twain sometimes writes all day and then throws away the manuscript. Poets will please paste this item in their hats.

9 August (Monday)
"Personal"; p. 4

Mark Twain's poet in *The Innocents Abroad*, Bloodworth [sic] H. Cutter, is dead. He survived long enough to write lines "On Noticing the Ladies' [sic] Hats at the Little Neck Festival" and "On Seeing a Black Mother and Her Baby at the Baby Show," but, so far as known, he died a natural death.

Bloodgood H. Cutter (1817-92), who Twain dubbed the "Poet Larriat," was a 50-year-old farmer/poet from Little Neck, Long Island, whose trite verses annoyed nearly everyone aboard the *Quaker City* cruise (*MT Abroad* 41). When the *Quaker City* pilgrims were about to meet the Czar of Russia, Twain states in chapter 37 of *The Innocents Abroad* that Cutter "rained ineffable bosh" until his fellow passengers threatened to have him confined to his quarters. This report of his death, however, was greatly exaggerated. In fact, Cutter's family would also have to deny that he had died in early August 1880, as many newspapers reported (New York *Times*, 9 August 1880). Twelve years later, though, his death could not be denied. He left an estate of $1 million, about half of which was willed to the Bible Society. Predictably, his heirs challenged the will and succeeded in having the amount reduced (*Times*, 6 December 1906).

20 August (Friday)
"Giblets"; p. 2
   Mark Twain sometimes writes all day and then destroys his manuscript at night. Thanks.

24 August (Tuesday)
"John Raymond's Failure"; p. 2
   Mr. Raymond, as you will doubtless learn by the cable, has brought his representations of Col. Sellers at the Gaiety to a close and sails for home by next week's White Star steamer, leaving on Thursday. He thus severs his season in the middle, as otherwise it would have run three weeks longer, making six weeks in all. I think on the whole, though, that he has come to a wise determination. There was nothing for him to gain by carrying forward a season which was admitted to be unsuccessful, and he has already received all that it was possible for him to elicit, handicapped as he was by a play that had been effectually damned and by members of a company which in the main was ill-suited to its representation, because being English they could not "change their spots." To see a Southern Negro played by an Englishman, for example, is like beholding a Connecticut Yankee struggling with the peculiarities of the London costermonger. Personally, Mr. Raymond made an unequivocal artistic success; every newspaper in London, from the *Times* down, acknowledged that he was a comedian of noteworthy gifts. The Prince of Wales, who came down with the Princess, sent for and complimented him; the Duke and Duchess of Cannaught came the night after their royal relatives had been at the Gaiety and seemed equally well pleased, and the cleverest men and women in London sent him congratulations. Moreover, the public laughed immoderately over certain scenes—albeit they could not quite grasp quite all the points about Congress, etc.—and have recalled him every night at the conclusion of the performance amid shouts of bravo. During the second week the attendance improved and it was thought that "business" would "work up," but such has not been the case. The press had so unanimously damned the play (and this means

more in London than New York) that, taken in connection with the fact that the season is over and the fashionable world out of town, it became apparent that Mark Twain's "dramatic sketch" was doomed. Mr. Hollingshed proposed that Mr. Raymond should play something else, and there was some thought of *My Son*, but the comedian finally asked to be released from filling the remainder of his engagement. All has been amicable and "star" and manager part on the best of terms. Mr. Raymond hastens back to the States to arrange for his fall and winter campaign. When he gets a good piece he may again present himself before a London audience, from whom he is always sure of a welcome. He bears what must be a disappointment so manfully and cheerily as to deepen the esteem everyone feels for him.

This article is attributed to the London correspondent of the Philadelphia *Times*.

26 August (Thursday)
"Personal"; p. 4

    Col. Sellers had a grand time in London, off the stage.

27 August (Friday)
"King Ludwig's Encore: He Would Have the Real Water in His Rain"; p. 7

    I am told that in a German concert or opera they hardly ever encore a song; that, though they may be dying to hear it again, their good breeding usually preserves them against requiring the repetition. Kings may encore; that is quite another matter; it delights everybody to see that the King is pleased, and, as to the actor encored, his pride and gratification are simply boundless. Still, there are circumstances in which even a royal encore—but it is better to illustrate. The King of Bavaria is a poet and has a poet's eccentricities, with the advantage over all other poets of being able to gratify them, no matter what form they may take. He is fond of opera, but not fond of sitting in the presence of an audience; therefore, it has sometimes occurred in Munich that when an opera has been concluded and the players are getting off their paint and finery, a command has come to get their paint and finery on again. Presently, the King would arrive solitary and alone, and the players would begin at the beginning and do the entire opera over again with only that one individual in that vast, solemn theater for an audience. Once he took an odd freak in his head. High up and out of sight over the prodigious stage of the Court Theatre is a maze of interlacing water pipes, so pierced that in case of fire innumerable little thread-like streams of water can be caused to descend and, in case of need, this discharge can be augmented to a pouring flood. American managers might make a note of that. The King was the sole audience. The opera proceeded. It was a piece with a storm in it; the mimic thunder began to mutter, the mimic wind began to wail and sough, and the mimic rain to patter. The King's interest rose higher and higher; it developed into enthusiasm. He cried out:

"It is good, very good, indeed! But I will have real rain. Turn on the water."

The manager pleaded for reversal of the command, said it would ruin the costly scenery and the splendid costumes, but the King cried:

"No matter, no matter, I will have real rain! Turn on the water!"

So the real rain was turned on and began to descend in gossamer lances to the mimic flower beds and gravel walks of the stage. The richly dressed actresses and actors tripped about, singing bravely and pretending not to mind it. The King was delighted; his enthusiasm grew higher. He cried out:

"Bravo, bravo! More thunder! More lightning! Turn on more rain!"

The thunder boomed, the lightning glared, the storm winds raged, the deluge poured down. The mimic royalty of the stage, with their soaked satins clinging to their bodies, slopped around ankle-deep in water, warbling their sweetest and best, the fiddlers under the eaves of the stage sawed away for dear life, with the cold overflow spouting down the backs of their necks, and the dry and happy King sat in his lofty box and wore his gloves to ribbons applauding.

"More yet!" cried the King, "More yet; let loose all the thunder, turn on all the water. I will hang the man who raises an umbrella!"

When the most tremendous and effective storm that had ever been produced in any theater was at last over, the King's approbation was measureless. He cried:

"Magnificent, magnificent! Encore! Do it again!"

But the management succeeded in persuading him to recall the encore, and said the company would feel sufficiently rewarded and complimented in the mere fact that the encore was demanded by his Majesty without fatiguing him with a repetition to gratify their own vanity.

During the remainder of the act the lucky performers were those whose parts required changes of dress; the others were a soaked, bedraggled and uncomfortable lot, but in the last degree, picturesque. The stage scenery was ruined, trap doors were so swollen they wouldn't work for a week afterward, the fine costumes were spoiled and no end of minor damages were done by the remarkable storm.

It was a royal idea—that storm—and royally carried out. But observe the moderation of the King. He did not insist upon his encore. If he had been a gladsome, unreflecting American opera audience he probably would have had his storm repeated until he drowned all those people.

This story, an excerpt from chapter 10 of *A Tramp Abroad*, may very well be true. King Louis II of Bavaria (1845-86) had a well-known love for spectacular opera and had formed a close friendship with Richard Wagner in the 1860s. By the late 1870s, however, Louis showed increasing signs of mental illness; consequently, he was removed from power 8 June 1886 and confined to his quarters. He was found drowned five days later. The aside to American theater managers for them to take note of the sprinkler system is a reference to a fire at the Brooklyn Theatre on 4 December 1876 which killed more than 300 patrons.

9 September (Thursday)
"An Enthusiastic Collector"; p. 4

Mark Twain's man who went into the collection of echoes has a serious competitor in no less illustrious a person than Sardou, who has just purchased the door through which Charlotte Corday passed to kill Marat. Enthusiasm in bric-a-brac could go but little further.

Victorien Sardou (1831-1908), an eccentric French playwright, wrote three plays about the French Revolution, which explains his interest in Marat's door.

11 September (Saturday)
no headline; p. 4

Mr. John T. Raymond, the clever American comedian, begins an engagement at Pope's Theater next week. The brutal manner in which the British public recently sat down upon Mr. Raymond and his play will prove an advantage to the gentleman in the end. Having received for himself and play the unanimous endorsement of the American people, his bad treatment in London was no less than a reflection on our national taste. After all the bad acting we have had to put up with on the part of English players, it would have only been a matter of good taste for John Bull to at least endure *Colonel Sellers*. His refusal to do so puts the onus on us, so to speak, and we are compelled, a proud, sensitive nation, to stand by Raymond. It wouldn't surprise us if Pope's Theater would be too small for the crowds next week.

15 September (Wednesday)

"Col. Mulberry Sellers: A Chatty Talk with John T. Raymond in his Dressing Room"; p. 7

Last evening a representative of the *Post-Dispatch*, between the acts of *My Son*, visited Mr. John T. Raymond in his dressing room behind the stage and received a warm reception from Col. Mulberry Sellers. Quite a chatty talk followed, enlivened by a good deal of gossip, and the conversation suspended at the termination of one act was resumed at its close. Mr. Raymond is in excellent health and spirits, mercurial, lighthearted and generous as ever. He possesses a happy, magnetic flow of animal spirits, and any company of which he may be the member always feels the effect of his exhilarating presence. The conversation last evening drifted to the subject of Raymond's trip to England and the failure of *The Gilded Age* at the Gaiety Theatre, London.

"Is it true, Mr. Raymond, that our English cousins failed to appreciate the humor of Col. Sellers—that they couldn't see the points?"

"No; that is not so. The English readily seized upon the salient features of Col. Sellers' character, and almost every point told. There were one or two notable exceptions, such as the turnip and stove business. No, Col. Sellers was a complete success—that is, the characters. My reception personally was of the warmest, most hospitable kind. My acting of Col. Sellers received the highest praise from the critics. What damned the whole thing was the play itself. Now the Florences have made a success. They are upon the stage in *The*

Mighty Dollar nearly the whole time. There, the bright surroundings are dressy and bright, picnic scenes and so forth.
Now the setting of *The Gilded Age* is sombre and heavy and
Col. Sellers is frequently off the boards for a long time. I
don't think the attack upon the trial scene was exactly justified. I told Hollingshead, the manager of the Olympic, in reference to it that I had been a few nights before to the Lyceum
to see Irving as Shylock and I saw there a far more absurd
thing in the trial scene. I mean, for instance, Gratiano, who
taunts and curses the Jew before the royal tribunal. Certainly,
that is as ridiculous as anything in the *Col. Sellers* trial scene.
But the one is Shakespeare's; the other is Mark Twain's. The
character of Col. Sellers was highly appreciated and relished
by the British public, but they couldn't stand the play. Then I
had the disadvantage of following a disastrous season of the
French Vaudeville Company, and the theatrical season
proper was over. The Prince of Wales said to me: 'Raymond,
if you had put this on during the fashionable season I think
Col. Sellers would have carried the play through.' 'In fact,'
said the Prince, 'John, if you had put your blooming play on
when all the boys were in town you would have knocked
them silly.'"
    "Do you think you would have done better if you had had
a company of American artists?"
    "No, not at all. Nothing could have saved the play. Personally, my reception was highly flattering and satisfactory to
me. They wanted me to appear as Icabod Crane in *Wolfert's
Roost*, but I would not do it."

Sir Henry Irving (1838-1905), the most celebrated British actor of his
day, appeared in many productions of Shakespeare's plays. His version of *The Merchant of Venice*, revived in 1879, featured an interpretation of Shylock as a tragic character wronged by a vengeful society.
W. J. Florence (1831-91), an American actor, was noted for being
equally adept in comic or tragic roles. Beginning in September 1875, he
regularly appeared with his wife in a popular comedy by Benjamin
Edward Woolf entitled *The Mighty Dollar*.

18 September (Saturday)
"Mark Twain: The Funny Man's Latest Excruciating Joke"; p. 3
    I have just seen your dispatch from San Francisco in Saturday's *Evening's Post* about "Gold in Solution in Calistoga
Springs," and about the proprietor having extracted $1,060 in

gold of the utmost fineness from 10 barrels of water during the last fortnight by a process known only to himself. This will surprise many of your readers, but it does not surprise me for I once owned those springs myself. What does surprise me, however, is the falling off in the richness of the water. In my time the yield was a dollar a dipperful. I am not saying this to injure the property in case a sale is contemplated. I am saying this in the interest of history. It may be that this hotel proprietor's process is an inferior one. Yes, that may be the fault. Mine was to take my uncle. I had an extra uncle at that time on account of his parents dying and leaving him on my hands. I filled him up and let him stand for 15 minutes to give the water a chance to settle. Well, then I inserted him in an exhausted receiver, which had the effect of sucking gold out through his pores. I have taken more than $11,000 out of that old man in a day and a half. I should have held on to those springs but for the badness of the roads and difficulty of getting the gold to market. I consider that gold-yielding water in many respects remarkable, and yet no more remarkable than the gold-bearing air of Cat-Gut Canon up there toward the head of the auriferous range. This air, or the wind (for it is a kind of trade wind which blows steadily down through 600 miles of rich quartz croppings during an hour and a quarter every day except Sundays), is heavily charged with exquisitely fine, impalpable gold. Nothing precipitates and solidifies this gold so readily as contact with human flesh heated by passion. The time that William Abrams was disappointed in love he used to step outdoors when the wind was blowing and come in again and begin to sigh, and I would extract over a dollar and half out of every sigh. He sighed right along. And the time that John Harbison and Aleck Norton quarreled about Harbison's dog, they stood there swearing at each other all they knew how, and what they didn't know about swearing they couldn't learn from you and me, not by a good deal, and at the end of three or four minutes they had to stop and make a dividend. If they didn't, their jaws would clog up so that they couldn't get big, nine-syllabled ones out at all, and when the wind was done blowing they cleaned up just a little over $1,600 apiece. I know these facts to be absolutely true, because I got them from a man whose mother I knew personally. I do not suppose a person could buy the water privileges at Calistoga now at any price, but several good locations along the course of Cat-Gut Canon gold-bearing trade wind are for sale. They are going to be stocked for the New York market, and they will sell, too. People will swarm for them as thick as Hancock veterans in the South.

Originally printed on 16 September 1880 as a letter to the editor of the New York *Evening Post*, this tall tale was subsequently reprinted by the *Post-Dispatch*. Calistoga Springs, a popular resort in the 1880s, is located approximately 30 miles north of Oakland, Ca. The last line of the piece jokes about the Union veterans who enthusiastically supported the presidential candidacy of Maj. Gen. Winfield Scott Hancock (1824-86).

8 November (Monday)
"Gems of Thought"; p. 1

The time has arrived that Mulberry Sellers predicted, when "hogs" would become jewelry, for they are now shown in bracelets, rings, charms, and scarf pins in both gold and silver.

1881

3 January (Monday)
"Mark Twain at Home"; p. 2

The pleasantest view I had of Hartford was from the cosy fireside in that wonderful home of Mr. S. L. Clemens, who was my host during my stay in Hartford. I am not a man addicted to cold weather. I am not sufficiently "British" to wander through December and January in a short checker coat and no ulster. I am given to much wrapping up when I do go out in the snow, and to very little going out in the snow at all. I begin to shiver with the first frost; and I keep it up until the following April. And so when I can sit down before a bright wood fire and burn up cigars while somebody entertains me, I love the icy winter. I think I have never been in a home more beautifully home-like than this palace of the king of the humorists. The surroundings of the house are beautiful, and its quaint architecture, broad East India porticos, and Greek patterns in mosaic in the dark-red brick walls attract and charm the attention and good taste of the passerby, for the home, inside and out, is the perfection of exquisite taste and harmony. But with all its architectual beauty and originality, the elegance of its interior finish and decorations, the greatest charm about the house is the atmosphere of "home-likeness" that pervades it. Charmingly as he can entertain thousands of people at a time from the platform, Mr. Clemens is even a more perfect entertainer in his home. The brightest and best sides of his nature shine out at his fireside. The humor and drollery that sparkle in his conversation are as utterly unaffected and natural as sunlight. Indeed, I don't believe he knows or thinks that most of his talk before the sparkling fire, up in the pleasant retirement of his billiard-room study, is marketable merchandise worth so much a page to the publishers; but it is. And it is not all drollery and humor. He is so earnest that his earnestness charms you fully as much as his brighter flashes, and once in a while there is in his voice an inflection of wonderful pathos, so touched with melancholy that you look into the kind, earnest eyes to see what thought has touched his voice. And he has a heart as big as his body; I believe there does not live a man more thoroughly unselfish and self-forgetful. Two little girls and a boy baby, bright-eyed, good-tempered, and with a head full of hair as brown as his father's, assist Mrs. Clemens to fill the heart of the reigning humorist, and they do it most completely. Personally, Mr. Clemens is perhaps a little above the medium height, of good symmetrical physique; brown hair, scarcely touched with gray, that curls over a high, white forehead; friendship is in his eyes; hearty cordiality in the grasp of a well-shaped white hand, strong enough and heavy enough to be a manly hand; his age is 40-something, and he looks 35; in the evening, "after the lamps are lighted," his face has a wonderful boyish look; and he loves a good cigar even better than Grant does.

This look at Twain by humorist Bob Burdette (1844-1914) was originally published in the Burlington (Iowa) *Hawkeye*. Burdette mistakes Twain's six-month-old daughter Jean for a son; Twain's other two daughters—Susy and Clara—were nine- and seven-years-old.

21 May (Saturday)
"American Literature"; p. 2

In an article reprinted from the London *News*, an anonymous critic summarizes the contributions American authors have made to the English language. The article mentions Twain in one paragraph:

From a writer much less frivolous than he is commonly thought to be, Mark Twain, we have derived not only bywords but opportunities for that indistinguishable laughter which seems to refresh and renew the whole system. If Mark Twain had written nothing but the account of his purchase of the celebrated Mexican plug and the account of how he had increased the circulation of an agricultural newspaper, he would have made his mark among the humorists that have used the English language.

The text of "A Genuine Mexican Plug," a ferocious horse that Twain could not ride, is reprinted in *Sketches & Tales* (209-13); it was also incorporated into chapter 24 of *Roughing It*. See 4 April 1876 for Twain's account of editing an agricultural newspaper.

1 June (Wednesday)
"Mark Twain's Luck: A Good Story That Lost a Good Claim in the Diggins"; p. 2

Mark Twain's narrow escape from becoming a pocket miner has never been told. It is worth recording, as it gave him the story of the "Jumping Frog" and sent him off along the line of the literary lode and set him to searching therein for "pockets" of fun. In 1865, Mark, weary of Bohemian life in San Francisco, went up to the mining regions of Tuolumne County to rusticate with some old friends, Steve, Jim, and Billy Gillis. Jim Gillis was and is one of the most expert pocket miners in California. Although educated with a view of eventually fighting the battle of life as a physician, and though still finding solace in his leisure moments in the works of Latin and Greek authors that repose on their shelves in his cabin, he is booked for life as a pocket miner. The business has charms for him that bind him to it in chains of gold—chains that bind him more firmly than iron or steel. Show him a particle of quartz gold on the side of a mountain, and if came to where it was found through the processes of accidents of nature, undisturbed in any way by the interference of man, he will as unerringly trace it to its golden source as the bee-hunter will follow the bee to its hoard of sweets.

Mark Twain found the Bohemian style of mining practiced by the Gillis brothers to be very attractive. He and Jim Gillis took to the hills in search of golden pockets and spent some days in hunting for the undisturbed trail of an undisturbed deposit. Finally, they struck a golden bee-line. They were two or three days in following it up, as it was necessary to carry each sample of dirt a considerable distance to a small stream in the bed of a canyon in order to pan it out. Each step made sure by golden grains, they at last came to the pocket. It was a cold, dreary, drizzling day when the home deposit was found. The first samples carried to the stream and washed yielded but a few cents. Although the right vein had been discovered, they had as yet found the tail of the pocket. Returning to the vein, they dug a sample from a new place, and were about to carry it down the ravine and test it, when the rain began to pour down heavily, and Mark, with chattering teeth, declared he would remain no longer.

He said there was no sense in freezing to death as in a day or two, when it was bright and warm, they could return and pursue their investigations in comfort. Yielding to Mark's entreaties, backed as they were by his blue nose, humped back, and generally miserable and dejected appearance, Jim emptied the sack of dirt upon the ground, first having written and posted up a notice of their claim to a certain number of feet on the vein, which notice would be good for 30 days. Angel's Camp being at no great distance, while their cabin was some miles away, Mark and Jim struck out for that place. The only hotel in the little mining camp was kept by Coon Drayton, an old Mississippi River pilot, and at his house the half-drowned pocket miners found shelter. Mark, having for some years followed the business of pilot on the Mississippi, and Coon were soon great friends and swapped scores of yarns. It continued to rain for three days, and until the weather cleared up Mark and Jim remained at Coon's hotel.

Among the yarns told Mark by Coon was that of the "Jumping Frog," and it struck him as being so comical that he determined to write it up in good shape; and when he returned to the Gillis cabin Mark set to work upon it. He also wrote some sketches of life in the mines for the San Francisco *Morning Call*. Mark did not think as much of the frog story as he did when he first heard it. He gave some other sketches the preference and sent them to the *Call* and other papers. Steve Gillis, however, declared it was the best thing he had written and advised him to save and publish it in a book of sketches that was talked of. A literary turn having thus been given to the thoughts of the inmates of the Gillis cabin, a month passed without a return to the business of pocket mining.

While the days were passed by Mark and his friends in discussing the merits of the "Jumping Frog," other prospectors were not idle. A trio of Austrian miners who were out in search of gold-bearing quartz happened upon the spot where Mark and Jim had dug into their ledge. It was but a few days after they had retreated from the spot in the pouring rain. The Austrian prospectors were not a little astonished at seeing the grounds literally glittering with gold. Where the dirt emptied from the sack had been dissolved and washed away by the rain lay some three ounces of bright quartz gold. The Austrians were not long in gathering this, but the speedy discovery of the notice forbade their delving into the deposit whence it came.

They could only wait and watch and pray in the hope that the parties who put up the notice would not return while it still held good. The sun that rose on the morning of the day after the Twain-Gillis claim expired saw the Austrians in possession of the ground, with a notice of their own conspicuously and defiantly posted. The newcomers cleaned out the pocket containing a little over $7,500 in a few days. Had Mark Twain's backbone held out a little longer the sack of dirt would have been washed and the grand discovery made. He would not then have gone to Angel's Camp, and would never have heard of or written up the story of "Jumping Frog"—the story which gave him his first "boost" in the literary world. Had Mark found that gold he would have settled down as a jumping miner. He would never have given up the chase and to this day, when gray as a badger, he would have been pounding quartz as Jim Gillis's "pard" in the Sierra Nevada Mountains.

This article by an anonymous reporter from the New York *Tribune* conflates two different stories about Twain, although it sounds as if Twain was the reporter's source. At any rate, the time that Twain lost a fortune because a claim was not worked took place in 1862 when he was partners with Calvin H. Higbie, a close friend to whom he dedicated *Roughing It*. According to chapters 40 and 41 of that book, Twain and Higbie discovered a "blind lead"—a vein of gold that does not appear above ground but instead is found by sinking a shaft where the prospectors suspect it runs. The two men promptly staked out the claim as their own and had, according to Nevada law, 10 days to work the claim before it would be forfeited. The next day, after they had made their preparations for the dig, Twain went into town, where he learned that Capt. John Nye, brother to the territorial governor and a friend of his brother Orion Clemens, was ill at a mining camp and needed attention. Twain then wrote a note to Higbie telling him he needed to leave to care for Nye and reminding him to be certain to work the claim. Higbie, however, had already left town to explore another mine and never saw the note. Neither man worked the claim, and a fortune was lost. Some scholars have argued that this story from *Roughing It* is apocryphal, but *MT: Bachelor* makes an excellent case for its authenticity (177-79). If it is in fact true, Twain lost considerably more than $7,500; he states in *Roughing It* that the blind lead would have made millionaires of both men. It would not be until early 1865, however, that Twain visited Jackass Gulch in California to pocket mine with Jim Gillis, older brother of one of his friends, Steve Gillis. (See 10 April 1876 for an account of Steve serving as Twain's second in a proposed duel.) Pocket mining, which was not nearly as lucrative as finding a blind lead, involved a great deal of backbreaking labor, as suggested in the *Tribune* article. Essentially, Twain points out in chapter 60 of *Roughing It*, a miner took a shovelful of dirt from a promising spot on hill and washed it out. If there was gold at the bottom of the pan, he then worked his way up the hill—moving left and right to find where the gold was thickest—until he found where the pocket of gold was located. According to *MT: Bachelor*, Twain arrived at Angel's Camp, Calaveras County, in late January 1865, but neither Gillis nor Twain had found a promising location before the rains began that forced them to take shelter at Ross Coon's hotel (263-64). There, the two men swapped yarns with Coon and other miners, and in the exchange Twain heard the "jumping frog" tale from Coon. After the weather cleared, Twain and Gillis left to pocket mine, but a few weeks of arduous labor proved to be enough for Twain; he left in late February for San Francisco where eight months later he wrote "The Celebrated Jumping Frog of Calaveras County." It would be published under the title of "Jim Smiley and His Jumping Frog" in the New York *Saturday Press* on 18 November 1865 and subsequently be reprinted in newspapers all across the country.

11 June (Saturday)
"The Art of War: Mark Twain's Speech to the Army of the Potomac Society"; p. 2

At the banquet given to the Society of the Army of the Potomac this evening Mr. Samuel L. Clemens (Mark Twain) responded to the toast "The Benefit of Judicious Training." He said that he had been to West Point and had loaded up with military information, and in what he said he was backed by the highest military authority. He added:

"To begin, gentlemen, when an engagement is meditated, it is best to feel the enemy first, that is if it is night, for, as one of the cadets explained to me, you do not have to feel him in the daytime because you can see him then. I should never have thought of that, but it is true, perfectly true. In the daytime the methods of procedure are various, but the best, it seems to me, is one which was introduced by Gen. Grant. Gen. Grant always sent an active young man redoubt to reconnoitre and get the enemy's bearings. I got this from a high officer at the Point, who told me he used to be a redoubt

on Gen. Grant's staff, and had done it often. When the hour
for battle is come, move to the field with celerity—fool away
no time. Under this head, I was told of a favorite maxim of
Gen. Sheridan's. Gen. Sheridan always said: 'If the siege train
isn't ready, don't wait—go by any trains that are handy. To
get there is the main thing.' Now, the correct idea—as you
approach the field it is better to get out and walk. This gives
you a better chance to dispose of your forces judiciously for
the assault. Get your artillery in position and throw out
stragglers to the right and left to hold your lines of communication against surprise, see that every hod carrier connected
with a mortar battery is at his post. They told me at the Point
that Napoleon despised mortar batteries and never would
use them. He said that for real efficiency he wouldn't give a
hatful of bricks for a ton of mortar. However, that is all he
knew about it.

"Everything being ready for the assault, you want to enter
the field with your baggage to the front. This idea was invented by our renowned guest, Gen. Sherman. They told me
that Gen. Sherman said that the trunks and baggage make a
good protection for the soldiers, but that chiefly they attract
the attention and rivet the interest of the enemy, and this
gives you the opportunity to whirl the other end of the column around and attack him in the rear. I have given a good
deal of study to this tactic since I learned about it, and it appears to me that it is a rattling good idea. Never fetch on
your reserves at the start. This was Napoleon's first mistake
at Waterloo. Next, he assaulted with his bombproofs and
ambulances and embrasures when he ought to have used a
heavier artillery. Thirdly, he retired his right to Ricochet—
which uncovered his pickets—when his only possibility of
success lay in doubling up his center flank by flank and
throwing out his *chevaux de frise* by the left oblique to
relieve the skirmish line and confuse the enemy, if such
a maneuver would confuse him, and at West Point they
said it would. It was about this time that the Emperor had
two horses shot under him. How often you see the remark
that Gen. So-and-So in such and such a battle had two or
three horses shot under him. Gen. Burnside and many great
European military men, as I was informed by a high military
officer at West Point, have justly characterized this as a
wanton waste of projectiles, and he impressed upon me a

conversation in the tent of the Prussian chiefs at Gravelotte, in the course of which our honored guest just referred to— Gen. Burnside—observed that if you can't aim a horse so as to hit a general with it, shoot it over him and you may bag something on the other side; whereas a horse shot under a general does no sort of damage. I agree cordially with Gen. Burnside, and heaven knows I shall rejoice to see artillerists of this land and all lands cease from this wicked and idiotic custom.

"At West Point they told me of another mistake at Waterloo, namely that the French were under fire from the beginning of the fight till the end—which was plainly a most effeminate and ill-timed attention to comfort and a foolish division of military strength, for it probably took as many men to keep up the fires as it did to do the fighting. It would have been much better to have had a small fire in the rear and let the men go there in detachments and get warm and not try to warm up the whole army at once. All the cadets said that an assault along the whole line was the one thing which could have restored Napoleon's advantage at this juncture, and he was actually rising up in his stirrups to order it when a sutler burst in at his side and covered him with dirt and debris, and before he could recover Wellington opened a tremendous and devastating fire upon him from a monstrous battery of vivandiers, and the star of the great Captain's glory set to rise no more. The cadet wept while he told me these mournful particulars.

"When you leave a battlefield always leave it in good order, remove the wreck and rubbish and tidy up the place. However, in the case of a drawn battle, it is neither party's business to tidy up anything. You can leave the field looking as if the city government of New York had bossed the fight. When you are traversing the enemy's country, in order to destroy his supplies and cripple his resources, you want to take along plenty of camp followers. The more the better. They are a tremendously effective arm of the service, and they inspire in the foe the liveliest dread. A West Point professor told me the wisdom of this was recognized as far back as Scripture times. He quoted the verse. He said it was from the new revision and was a little different from the way it reads in the old one. I do not recollect the exact wording of it now, but I remember that it wound up with something about such and such a devastating agent being as 'terrible as an army with bummers.' I believe I have nothing further to add but this: The West Pointers said a private should preserve a respectful attitude toward his superiors and should seldom, or never, proceed so far as to offer suggestions to his general in the field. If the battle is not being conducted to suit him, it is better for him to resign. By the etiquette of war, it is permitted to none below the rank of newspaper correspondent to dictate to the general in the field."

This speech, reported by the Hartford correspondent of the New York *Sun*, was delivered in Hartford on 8 June 1881 to the 12th Annual Reunion of the Army of the Potomac. Twain had visited West Point in February of that year.

13 June (Monday)
no headline; p. 4

Since Mark Twain developed his wonderful genius for military criticism before the Society of the Army of the Potomac, Mr. Romeo Reed, the modern Jomini of the Cincinnati *Gazette*, has observed a discreet silence. That Mark has not wasted his time is evidenced by the following extract from his address:

"Never fetch on your reserves at the start. This was Napoleon's first mistake at Waterloo. Next, he assaulted with his bombproofs and ambulances and embrasures when he ought to have used a heavier artillery. Thirdly, he retired his right by Ricochet—which uncovered his pickets—when his only possibility of success lay in doubling up his center flank by flank and throwing out his *chevaux de frise* by the left oblique to relieve the skirmish line and confuse the enemy, if such a maneuver would confuse him, and at West Point they said it would."

The thing that Mr. Reed blames Gen. McClellan for is that at the Battle of the Seven Pines he did not shove his sappers and miners under the Chickahomony with instructions to blow up the enemy's light cavalry, while the pioneers *en chellon* played on the commissary department of the rebels with battle-axes and grubbing hoes.

Baron Antoine Henri Jomini (1779-1869), a Swiss national, was one of the most famous generals in 19th-century Europe, first serving Napoleon but later switching his allegiance to Czar Alexander. He wrote many influential treatises about military strategy. Gen. George

B. McClellan (1826-85), popular with his troops but disliked by Pres. Lincoln, had a reputation for excessive caution in his attacks upon the Confederate Army. After his removal from command, McClellan ran for the presidency against Lincoln in 1864.

15 June (Wednesday)
no headline; p. 4

We used to think that Mark Twain was a licensed funny man, but the Louisville *Post* declares that he is an imbecile and vulgarian and "out of place in the East among men of culture." This would convey the idea indirectly that Mr. Clemens would be more at home in the West. We emphatically object. Let him stay where he is. Imbeciles and vulgarians are so scarce in the East that the people can afford to treat them as curiosities and take good care of them.

7 July (Thursday)
"Sam Clemens: A Gambler's Story about the Humorist's Life in Nevada"; p. 4

Mining camp journalism is crowded with experiences the city newspaperman knows not of. He of the mining camp journal knows nothing of "details," "beats," "scoops," "watches," early or late; or of "boiling," "amplifying," "shooting rot," and many other exigencies, requirements, and necessities connected with the lot of the city newspaperman. Talking with a member of his fraternity from the auriferous regions, a *Chronicle* reporter the other evening heard the following story about two well-known Nevada characters:

I met them in Aurora, Nev., about three years ago when that mining camp was in the first flush of its second attack of the quartz fever. Long Bill, I had learned, was a well-disposed and amiable citizen who dealt in faro in good times and inducted the guileless Paiutes in the mysteries of poker and other ethics of a higher civilization in the interims, in return wherefor they supplied his larder with quail and rabbit and his purse with such scarce coins as they could steal. Hearing, also, that he had "cabined" with Mark Twain when that self-accused humorist was a luckless prospector in the hills of Nevada, I was pleased to find him my companion one day on the outside seat of the Bodie stage.

"You knew Mark Twain?" I suggested to my companion

when we had left the town and the horses had settled into their dreary, between-station jog.

"Sam Clemens?"

"Yes, I believe he was called that then."

"Wasn't that his name?"

"So it was."

"Yes, I knew Sam. Cabined with him in '62, or mebbe, '3."

"I suppose Mark—"

"Sam?"

"Sam was very popular here; jolly and all that, eh?"

"Well, no I can't say Sam was very popular with the boys here, though he did cabin with me. He kinder had a way of forgetting the boys who staked him; that didn't wash well. Sam was the means, though, and it was rather curious, too, of making the most unpopular man in town popular."

"How was that?"

"Well, you see Cluggage, he owned the stage line between here'n Carson, and he played it rather low down on the boys; brought 'em here for $25 and charged 'em $75 to return. When the boys got broke, which they mostly did, for they would play agin the bank, it was a pretty tough game to get out of town. Well, Sam, he wanted to go back to some of his folks in Carson, but somehow he couldn't see Cluggage's limit. That was the state of the game when it was given out one night that Cluggage had presented Sam with a free pass to Carson. You never saw anything like the way Cluggage rose in favor that night, and the next morning half the town was down at the stage office and gave the driver a big cheer when the stage, with Sam inside, pulled out."

We rode on in silence for some time after that while I considered Bill's story in its various points of view until just as we entered a broad portion of the canyon, dignified by the name of "Sunshine Valley," when Bill asked me: "You are the new editor, ain't you?"

I glowed a little and blushed becomingly, I trust, for I was not unwilling to officially announce that I was no longer a reporter.

"I am the new editor."

Bill was again silent until we reached the center of the "valley," when, pointing to a little clump of bushes, he slowly remarked:

"We killed the last editor over there."

I ceased to glow and no longer blushed. I recovered enough to make a desperate attempt to faceticiousness and asked:

"Where was the one before him killed?"

"Oh, he was killed back in town in a barroom fight; but the one before him, who was the first, wasn't killed."

"That was too bad."

"Yes, the fellow he offended meant well, but only shot him through the ankle. Some do say as how he died from the shot, but as he lived four months and took in considerable whisky all the time, I say it's giving too much credit to the buckshot to say he died from the wound."

This anonymous article, which may or may not have a grain of truth in it, is reprinted from the San Francisco *Chronicle*.

29 July (Friday)
"Personal"; p. 2

"Mark Twain is summering at Indian Neck," says a paragraph. This is bad for the poor Indian.

23 August (Tuesday)
"The Genesis of Slang"; p. 2

This long article about how phrases from literature came into everyday use cites one example from Twain:

"There's millions in it," comes from Mark Twain's novel *The Gilded Age*.

10 September (Saturday)
no headline; p. 4

Mark Twain has a new book in press. As a rule, Mark Twain has a new book in press about once a year. It is becoming periodic with him and if quinine and whisky will do anything a subscription could easily be arranged. This country is getting very weary of Mr. Samuel C. [sic] Clemens. He was a second-class pilot on the western rivers and went into humor because the pay was better and the work not so exhausting. His style is bad, his matter bad, and his humor was worn out three years ago. His later books are simply a rehash of the earlier ones. He adapts a lot of matter which everybody read long ago, to a new story, and palms it off on the people as a new book. As a matter of fact, Mr. Saml. C. Clemens is a standing monument to the success which will always attend literary dishonesty.

This editorial refers to *The Prince and the Pauper*, published December 1881. Since it was a serious romance, however, it would be a very different book from what the *Post-Dispatch* and Twain's other critics expected. Over the next year, most reviews were favorable and sales reasonably good.

12 September (Monday)
"Authors' Profits"; p. 2

In a long article, a correspondent from the Cincinnati *Gazette* speculates about the financial affairs of American writers. He said this about Twain:

Clemens, the humorist better known as Mark Twain, has done better than any man at his train of labor. He has been 15 years before the public and during that time has become rich enough to live on his income. His property in Hartford is worth more than $80,000.

6 December (Tuesday)
"Personal"; p. 4

Mark Twain's new book *The Prince and the Pauper* has been published in London in advance of its American issue. The author is temporarily residing in Canada, and will superintend the Canadian copyright edition to be published soon.

Twain was in Canada in an attempt to claim Canadian residency for copyright protection; his claim would be denied. *The Prince and the Pauper* would subsequently be pirated by unscrupulous Canadian booksellers who failed to pay any royalties on the novel. See 12 and 21 December for two articles about this problem.

12 December (Monday)
"Mark Twain in Canada"; p. 2

The citizens of Montreal entertained Mark Twain at a sumptuous dinner this evening. The attendance was very large and influential. Hon. L. Huntingdon, M.P., presided and had the guests on his right. After a few preliminary toasts, Mark's health was drunk, and on rising he received an ovation. He commenced by acknowledging his gratitude for the kind reception he had met with since coming here. He then paid a high compliment to Canada's poet, who had, he said, been the first foreigner crowned by the French Academy as its laureate. He thought this was honor enough for Canada in one decade. He next launched into humorous hits at the weather, which had been miserably wet since he came here and anything but what the Canada prophet had predicted. He would not criticize the weather of Canada, which bore so good a reputation, only he was among friends who would not let his observations go further. He was of opinion, however, that honor and loyalty on the part of the prophet should have made him furnish better weather. If, however, the weather was bad, Montreal made up for it by having so many means of grace within its limits. A boy could scarely throw a stone without breaking a pane of glass in a church window. He had heard they were going to build another, which he admitted was a good scheme; but where would they get a good site unless they built it on top of another church and used an elevator?

He next adverted to being driven by cabmen perpendicularly up a mountain at Quebec to the Plains of Abraham. He did not see the old gentleman, but the cabman pointed him out in a snowstorm, which he could have seen as well as from the hotel windows. A literary gas man, he said, never went out with a cabman that he did not make an ass of himself, and it had always been so in his case. The cabby got the best of him, however, on the Heights of Abraham. He saw the site where Wolfe said he would rather be author of Gray's "Elegy" than to take Quebec. No doubt, he said, the gallant soldier thought there was going to be an international copyright. This brought down the house, as the speaker is here for the special purpose of copyrighting his new work. After a great many more pleasant allusions, in which he mixed up Canadian history past and present, combined with many funny local bits, he concluded by saying that the only two conspicuous industries he saw mentioned in the local press were burglaries and elections. These were to his taste and he intended taking a hand at both.

He kept the audience in a roar of laughter from beginning to end.

This article, which summarizes a speech delivered by Twain on 8 December, was a "Montreal Special Dispatch" to the *Post-Dispatch*. The full text of Twain's speech is included in *Collected Tales I* (776-80). The poet laureate referred to is Louis Honoré Fréchette (1839-1908), brother-in-law to Twain's friend William Dean Howells. The most decisive battle of the French and Indian War took place on the Plains of Abraham on 13 September 1759. British General James Wolfe (1727-59) led his troops into the battle and, although he was soon killed, they won a great victory over the French.

21 December (Wednesday)
"No Copyright for Mark Twain"; p. 14
    Mark Twain's application for a Canadian copyright of his new book, *The Prince and the Pauper*, has been refused, the authorities deciding that two weeks in Montreal is not a legal domiciliation. The action is really extraordinary, for although everybody sees at once that such a sojourn is a mere fiction of residence, it has nevertheless repeatedly been accepted by the Dominion and copyrights granted accordingly. Mrs. Burnett, for instance, is an American author who did just what Mr. Clemens has done for a copyright, and got it. The secret of it must lie in his speeches at that banquet. Twain either too honestly stripped the tenuous veil from his object in visiting Montreal—for an open secret should be kept as secret as a close one—or he made too many bad jokes about Montreal cabmen, Toronto publishers, and other choice Canadian institutions. Twain should beware of his tongue—it has proved a very embarrassing organ before now.

This editorial, reprinted from the Springfield (Mass.) *Republican*, angered Twain, who subsequently responded to it with a letter to the newspaper on 25 December 1881. In his letter, reprinted in *MT Speaks for Himself*, Twain argues incorrectly that he had in fact received a copyright for *The Prince and the Pauper* (129-34). Throughout the 1880s Twain fought for authors to have international copyright protection; he appeared before the U. S. Congress as an expert in the matter and read from his works at authors' readings to publicize the problem of literary works being pirated. See 28 January 1886 for an example of the former activity, and 1 April and 11 December 1887 for the latter. The "Mrs. Burnett" referred to was Francis Eliza Burnett (1849-1924), author of *Little Lord Fauntleroy* (1886) and *The Secret Garden* (1909).

1882

4 January (Wednesday)
"Fortunate Authors"; p. 3

In a story about a number of popular authors, an anonymous *Post-Dispatch* editorialist says this about Twain:

> Mark Twain (Clemens) has met with phenomenal success, and no book published in the last 25 years has met with such a ready sale as his *Innocents Abroad*. Mark ought to have reaped a large fortune from this work, but, although a joker himself, the joke in this case is with his publishers, who allowed him but five percent of the sales. Still, from this source Twain has managed to lay by quite a sum.

In 1868 when he signed his contract with the American Publishing Company of Hartford, Twain considered his royalty of five percent to be excellent; it would not be until later in his life that he thought it was too low. As this item points out, however, Twain was still able to become quite wealthy from sales of *The Innocents Abroad*.

26 January (Thursday)
no headline; p. 4

> Mark Twain's jokes are the result of a plain, chemical formula; given a man with a chair, a dark night and a tumble, a grammar school boy could construct a witticism which Mr. Clemens would swear was his own.

8 May (Monday)
"Personal"; p. 4

> Mark Twain is a dangerous man. He travels with a private stenographer.

9 May (Tuesday)
"Mark Twain: How Young Clemens Became a Mississippi Pilot";
p. 3

It is reasonable to suppose that everyone who knows anything about American literature has heard of Mark Twain,
and heartily laughed at the quaint humor which fills his
books. There are, however, few, if any, persons outside of the
circle of intimate friends who are acquainted with his early
history, or the manner in which he introduced himself to the
steamboat fraternity of antebellum days.

In order to obtain an account of how Mark Twain became
a pilot, a *T-D* reporter yesterday made inquiries among old
steamboatmen and was rewarded by receiving information to
the effect that the great humorist had first served as a pilot
under Capt. H. E. Bixby, who is now the popular commander
of the Anchor Line steamer *City of Baton Rouge*.

As soon as the reporter heard this he turned his footsteps
in the direction of the levee, and boarding the *City of Baton
Rouge*, found Capt. Bixby seated on the boiler-deck with his
little blue-eyed daughter in his lap, and engaged in assisting
her to arrange a number of picture blocks which were scattered over the bottom of a chair.

When the reporter approached and stated the object of his
visit the old captain's eyes brightened with the recollection of
former days.

"Well, sir," he said, "the first time that I met Mark Twain,
or knew that such a person existed, was in 1857. At that time
I was the chief pilot on the *Paul Jones*, a boat that made occasional trips from Pittsburg to New Orleans. One day, while
we were coming down the Mississippi, a long angular,
hoosier-like young fellow, whose limbs appeared to be fas-
tened with leather hinges, entered the pilothouse and in a
peculiar, drawling voice said: 'Good mawnin', sir. Don't you
want to take er pert young fellow and teach'im how to be er
pilot.'

"'No sir, there is more bother about it than it's worth.'

"'I wish you would, mister. I'm er printer by trade, but it
don't 'pear to 'gree with me, and I'm on my way to Central
America for my health. I believe I'll make 'er tolerable good
pilot 'cause I like the river.'

"'What makes you pull your words that way?'

"'I don't know, mister, you'll have to ask my ma. She

pull hern, too. Ain't there some way we can fix it so that you'll teach me how to be'er pilot?'

"'The only way is for money.'

"'How much are you going to charge?'

"'Well, I'll teach you the river for $500.'

"'Geewhilikeers! he! he! I ain't got $500, but I've got five lots in Keokuk, Iowa and 2,000 acres of land in Tennessee that is worth two bits an acre any time. You can have that if you want it.'"

"I told him that I did not care for his land, and after talking awhile he agreed to pay $100 in cash, $150 in 12 months and the balance when he became a pilot. He was with me a long time, but sometimes took occasional trips with other pilots. At the breaking out of the war he was a regular pilot on the *Alonzo Childs*, and remained on that boat until she was turned into a Confederate ram, when he got through the lines, and going to Hannibal, Mo., his native town, enlisted as a three month's volunteer in the Confederate army under Gen. Price. At the expiration of the time of his enlistment he went out to Nevada, where his brother Orion Clemens was filling the position of Secretary of the Territory. Out there he drifted into journalism and gradually developed the humor that has since made him famous."

"Did you ever hear from him after he went out West?" inquired the reporter.

"Yes, he used to write and let me know of his whereabouts. On his return from the Holy Land, he sent me a letter which contained his wedding card. The wording of the letter, as far as I can remember, was as follows: 'Thirty tons of paper have been used in publishing my book *Innocents Abroad*. It has met with greater sale than any book ever published except *Uncle Tom's Cabin*. The volumes sell from $3 to $5, according to finish, and I get one-half the profit. Not so bad for a scrub pilot, is it? How do you run Plum Point—a son-of-a-gun of a place? I would rather be a pilot than anything I ever tried.'"

"Meeting him in this city gave you considerable pleasure, did it not?"

"Yes; I had not seen him in 15 years, and when I met him it brought back old days."

"Has he changed much?"

"No, very little. His hair, it is true, is somewhat silvered, and his face has a few more wrinkles in it, but he has the same light in his eye, the same nose, which always appears as if it was expecting to smell something bad, and the same rick-etty swing of his limb he had when I first met him in the pi-lothouse of the *Paul Jones* 25 years ago.

"Did he betray much humor as a cub pilot?"

"Yes; he was always drawling out dry jokes, but then we did not pay much attention to him. I was talking to him yes-terday about the river, and he told me that on his down trip to this city he did not recognize a single point on the river as everything had changed since he left."

At the termination of the interview, and after the reporter had thanked Capt. Bixby for his information, his little daugh-ter looked up with a winsome smile and said: "Mr. Reporter, are you going to put my papa's name in the paper?" The scribe answered in the affirmative. "Well, then, I want you to say my papa is the best captain on the river." The reporter promised to do so, and at the same time mentally resolved to say that the little girl was the sweetest and prettiest little girl on the river.

Twain's odd drawl was frequently alluded to at this time in his career; he may have indeed inherited his speech from his mother. As *Sam Clemens* points out, "His most striking mannerism was the soft-spo-ken drawl borrowed from his mother, which she called 'Sammy's long talk.' It lent a whimisical turn to what he said, amusing his playmates even as it diverted audiences in later years. . . ." (124). Bixby's account of charging Twain $500 to teach him the river squares with Twain's own memories about being Bixby's apprentice (*Autobiography* 98).

12 May (Friday)

"An 'Innocent' Interviewed: Mark Twain Pays a Visit to St. Louis"; p. 2

Samuel L. Clemens, Hartford, Conn., registered at the Southern this morning. He did not want a room, and the clerk tossed him off in the usual nonchalant way and paid no attention to him. By and by, a New Yorker dropped in, cast his eye over the register, and said:

"Hello! you've got Mark Twain here, I see."

"Where?" said both clerks, rushing to the register pell-mell.

"Why, here. Sam Clemens," said the wise informer, pointing to the name.

"Him?" said clerk Harvey Willard, with a disdainful smile. "Is that the funny man? Why, he don't look half as funny as I do."

It was Mark all the same, and in his usual good humor. He has not been here since 1864, so that most of the people do not know how he looks. Imagine a middle-sized, stout-built man in a common suit of gray, with coat cut sack-style. A careless, wide-brimmed hat is thrown recklessly over his hair, which is full and long and rather gray. A countenance which shows good living, a pair of gray eyes, and a face entirely smooth, save a rakish gray moustache that gives a slight devil-may-care appearance to the man. He certainly does not look at "all funny," as the clerks put it, and would be mistaken for a serious, matter-of-fact gentleman who would not waste his time on anecdotes and would look down upon a joke with lofty contempt. The most curious thing about him is a reckless, rolling gait, which he probably caught when, as a cub pilot, he swaggered on the upper deck of the *Mary Amanda Jane* on the lower Mississippi. The aforesaid gait has stuck to him so persistently that it would make a sensitive man seasick to sit and look at Mark meander across the corridor of even so solid a hotel as the Southern.

He also has remarkable drawling way of speaking, which he most dislikes to see mimicked in print, and which adds quite a charm to his conversation. A *Post-Dispatch* reporter met him in the rotunda of the hotel and was received very cordially. It was only when the possibility of an interview was broached that Mr. Clemens grew slightly restive.

"I guess I haven't got time," he said. "The fact is you can say anything you like if you put it in your own words, but don't quote me saying anything. No man can get me right unless he takes it down in shorthand, very particularly, too."

"You don't love the interviewer, I see, Mr. Clemens."

"No; I don't. I have never yet met a man who attempted to interview me whose report of the process did not try very hard to make me out an idiot, and did not amply succeed, in my mind, in making him a thorough one. They try to imitate my manner of speech, and not being artists, they never succeed, you see. No, I want to fight shy of that class of people."

The reader can imagine the position of a reporter whose fate was fixed that he should write himself down as an idiot, but Twain was assured that no attempt would be made to exhibit his style of conversation, that the present interviewer's weekly rate of compensation did not warrant him to make such flights, and that he was a plain, cheap man used for doing easy police work, meetings of the Board of Public Improvements and elections among the school directors. Mr. Clemens melted a little and said:

"I have not been out here since 1864, I think, and I had intended on remaining some time in the city. But I waited too long at New Orleans to catch the *Baton Rouge*, the commander of which was my old master, and in consequence will have to leave tonight."

"You ought not to be in such a hurry. The newspapers represent you as being fabulously wealthy and in living in great splendor at Hartford."

"Oh, there is quite an amount of fiction in that statement. Of course I'm living at Hartford, and I had a house when I left there, but I have not gone into competition with Vanderbilt yet, and I don't think that I'll do so."

"What about the statement that humorous writing is not paying now as it did formerly?"

"That is fictional, too, I think. Is the writing that does not pay really humorous? I'm not talking about myself, but in my opinion good writing of any kind pays always."

"How is it in your case?'

"Well, I don't think that any kind of books will ever yield quite as well as the Bible and indecent works—I might say other indecent works, but that might get the church people down on me. Don't put that in, now."

"No; but, really, is there not a rich harvest in your line?"

"Now, I don't want to make an assignment, and why should I prepare a statement of my assets? I am preparing to try the public again, and my shorthand secretary accompanies me on this trip."

"What is the nature of the new work?"

"I have been writing a series of articles in the *Atlantic Monthly* on subjects connected with the Mississippi, and I found that I had got my distances a little mixed. I took this trip for the purpose of making observations on this subject. I was getting a little rusty about it."

"The new book will treat of your early life on the river?"

"Yes; altogether of that subject."

"When will it be finished?"

"In about nine months."

"And what will you call it?"

"Oh, that is the last thing to be thought about. I never write a title until I finish a book, and then I frequently don't know what to call it. I usually write out anywhere from a half dozen to dozen and a half titles, and the publisher casts his experienced eye over them and guides me largely in the selection. That's what I did in the case of *Roughing It*, and, in fact, it has always been my practice."

"You have come a little late," said the reporter, changing the conversation. "You should have been here in time for the banquet of the Army of the Tennessee."

"I came very near to jumping on the cars at Cairo yesterday and slipping in on that occasion. As a general thing I dislike banquets, if I am down for a speech. The sense of responsibility weighs me down and destroys all the enjoyment until I have gotten the confounded speech out of my system. But I really had something that I would like to have said last night—a matter that I am really interested in."

"What was that?" asked the reporter. "Why can't you say it now? Gen. Sherman and all the members of the Army of the Tennessee are regular subscribers to the *Post-Dispatch*. Make your speech to them through its columns."

"I wanted to talk to them about Arctic expeditions. I wished to say that, in my humble judgment, we have spent too much money on these trips. Too many valuable lives have been immolated in this search. Even if it is finally successful, what is the good result of it? We could not borrow any money in the North Pole, and I don't think it would become fashionable as a summer resort. Now, I am full of an expedition of another kind. I want the next set of explorers sent in another direction. We have got some doubts to the exact location of hell, and I was very desirous to suggest to the assembled warriors last night, and through them to the government and the American people, that the next expedition go in search of the place I have mentioned. If we ever locate that region, we can make some practical use of it. I had sketched a plan, which is shadowy yet, but I thought it might grow real and practical under the potent influence of champagne."

"Had you any people to suggest as leaders of this trip?"

"Yes, that part could be easily arranged. Of course, I would give my friends all the places of trust. For instance, I would insist on putting Talmage in command of the fleet, with full and absolute control over all arrangements. He knows as much about the route as anybody I could think of, and I assure you I have given the matter some thought. The other officers could be easily selected."

"Would it be strictly in accordance with the fitness of things if the expedition, like those to the Arctic regions, should get stranded and lost, and those who sailed in it should never reach their destination?"

Mr. Clemens smiled broadly and declared that he was not being interviewed and that he really would not answer leading questions. Then his private secretary and a couple of friends got hold of him. He put on his overcoat, tucked his umbrella under his arm and started out to do the town. He leaves here at 4 o'clock this afternoon for Hannibal, the place where he was born, where he intends to make a visit. From that point, he will run up the river to St. Paul and then back East. He says that he never expects to get so far from home again.

Mr. J. H. Carter (Commodore Rollingpin), an old friend of Mr. Clemens, went down the river to meet him last night, escorted him to the hotel, and looked after his comfort during his stay in the city.

Twain gives his memories about this visit to St. Louis in chapters 51 and 52 of *Life on the Mississippi*. Thomas DeWitt Talmage (1832-1902) was a prominent clergyman and lecturer who Twain disliked intensely, while "Commodore Rollingpin" was the pseudonym of John H. Carter, a popular cartoonist and satirist of the time. The *Post-Dispatch's* primary competitor, *The Globe-Democrat*, also published an interview with Twain; see the appendix for 13 May 1882.

15 May (Monday)
no headline; p. 4

It is said Mark Twain visited the historical encampment at the Armory last week for the fell purpose of writing it up humorously. It is to be hoped that his friends will induce him to pause and reflect before he does anything rash in this regard. Twain is gradually acquiring a solid reputation for gravity and stupidity which this sort of thing is calculated to wreck. Even Twain at his worst could not write a chapter about the encampment without making it funny, and a chapter of fun in any of Twain's late works would be a shock which few of his regular readers are prepared for. Now that it is all over, we presume it is fair to say that the encampment was certainly the funniest thing we have had in St. Louis for years. The humor was unconscious, but it was there. There was an ingenious unfitness between the character of the representer and the character of the represented which sometimes amounted to inspiration. In a great many instances the clothes did not fit; in a great many of these instances it was a mercy that they did not. The most violently diverse colors were made to abide side by side in the tents. One could hear the blues and reds and yellows swearing at each other in a subdued tone all the time. Brunette ladies suffered from the stiffling propinquity of blonde costumes, their only offset being the knowledge that they were retaliating in the deadliest manner possible.

This editorial refers to the Army of the Tennessee's reunion in St. Louis the previous week.

19 May (Friday)
"Personal"; p. 4

They welcomed Mark Twain down south as a patriot who had served three months in the army under Gen. Sterling Price. This is a bit of an episode in Mr. Twain's career upon which he has not expatiated lovingly to his northern friends.

20 June (Tuesday)
"Personal"; p. 4

A recent visitor to Mark Twain describes once more his sluggish speech, every word being deliberately uttered, "not as though it were weighted before delivery, but rather as though it had come a great distance and was tired."

24 July (Monday)
no headline; p. 4

Cameron finds it necessary to do a little 'possuming in Pennsylvania. His candidate, Gen. Beaver, declares that he is not a Cameron man, and that there is no understanding or alliance between himself and Simon's son. If this strategm succeeds we shall have Cameronism reformed in the Keystone State about as well as Mark Twain says the favorite vice

of the natives was reformed by the missionaries in the Sandwich Islands—so thoroughly that it has since existed in reality only, and not in name.

Simon Cameron (1799-1889), "boss" of Pennsylvania politics, fixed the
1877 U. S. Senate election to ensure his son would succeed him in national politics; both men were known to be corrupt. Twain jokes in
chapter 66 of *Roughing It* about how the missionaries failed to teach
chastity to the natives of Hawaii.

4 November (Saturday)
"Mark Twain's Speech"; p. 3

A militia regiment from Worcester being upon a visit to
Hartford, Mark Twain's home, he was put forward as the
spokesman to welcome, officially, the soldier guests of the
city.

This is what Mark Twain said: "His Honor, the mayor,
deputes me to speak for him in answer to the toast to the City
of Hartford. He is in politics, a delicate situation at all times,
where exceeding caution is necessary. I admire his prudence
as much as I admire my own intrepidity because, although he
is not willing to answer for and endorse Hartford, I am. I will
back up Hartford in everything else if he will be responsible
for the weather. Now, as I am talking for Hartford, I will talk
earnestly but modestly.

"There is much here to see—the State House, Colt's factory, and where the Charter Oak was. And we have an antiquity here—the East Hartford bridge. Now, let me beseech
you, don't go away without seeing that tunnel on stilts. You
may think it a trifle, but go on and see it! Think what it may
be to your posterity, generations hence, who come here and
say: 'There's that same old bridge.' It is coeval with the flood,
and will be coexistent with the millennium. Hartford has a
larger population than any other city excepting Worcester,
and it is the honestest city in the world. Well, that will do for
Hartford. I will rest my case there.

"When asked to respond I said I would be glad to; but
there were reasons why I could not make a speech. But I said
I would talk. I never make a speech without getting together
a lot of statistics and being instructive. The man who starts
in on a speech without preparation enters upon a sea of infe-
licities and troubles. I had thought of a great many things
that I had intended to say. In fact, nearly all of these things

that I have heard said here tonight I had thought of. Get a
man way down here on the list and he starts out empty. I
was going to say something about prominent people, and
about the Foot Guards, who had seen everything that has
happened for 111 years. Five years they fought for King
George and 106 for liberty. They fought for 111 years and
never lost a man. And the enemy never lost a man. What I
mean is to compliment the Foot Guards, and I hope I have
done so. One reason I didn't like to come here to make a
prepared speech was because I had sworn off. I have reformed. I would not make a prepared speech without statistics and philosophy. The advantage of a prepared speech is
that you start when you are ready and stop when you get
through. If unprepared, you are all at sea, you don't know
where you are. I thought to achieve brevity but I was mistaken. A man never hangs on so long on his hind legs as
when he don't know when to stop.

   "I once heard of a man who tried to be reformed. He tried
to be brief. A number of strangers sat in a hotel parlor. One
sat off to one side and said nothing. Finally all went out except one man and this dummy. Then the dummy touched
this man on the shoulder and said:

   "'I think I have s-s-s-e (whistles) een you before.'

   "'What makes you whistle? asked the other man.

   "'I used to s-s-s-s-tammer, and the d-d-d-d- (whistles) octor
told me when I w-w-w-w-w- (whistles) wanted t-t-t-o speak
and st-t-t-tammered to whistle. I d-d-d-d-d (whistle) id w-
whistle, and it c-c-c-ured me.'

   "So it is with a man who makes an unprepared speech.
He tries to be brief and it takes him longer. I won't detain
you. We welcome you with cordial hospitality, and if you
remain we will try to furnish better weather tomorrow."

The *Post-Dispatch* reprinted this account of Twain's speech from the
Worcester *Spy*. In *Autobiography*, Twain describes his futile attempts
to teach this favorite anecdote about a stammering patient to his family's doctor (196-97).

16 November (Thursday)
"Personal"; p. 4

   Mark Twain is supposed by many sober-minded people to
be a crank.

7 December (Thursday)
"McWilliams' Burglar Alarm: Mark Twain in the Christmas
Harper's"; p. 7

The conversation drifted smoothly and pleasantly along
from weather to crops, from crops to literature, from literature to scandal, from scandal to religion; then took a random
jump, and landed on the subject of burglar alarms. And now
for the first time Mr. McWilliams showed feeling. Whenever I perceive this sign on this man's dial I comprehend it
and lapse into silence and give him opportunity to unload
his heart. Said he, with but ill-controlled emotion:

"I do not go one single cent on burglar alarms, Mr.
Twain—not a single cent—and I will tell you why. When we
were finishing our house, we found we had a little cash left
over, on account of the plumber not knowing it. I was for en-
lightening the heathen with it, for I was always unaccount-
ably down on the heathen somehow; but Mrs. McWilliams
said no, let's have a burglar alarm. I agreed to this compromise. I will explain that whenever I want a thing, and Mrs.
McWilliams wants another thing, and we decide upon the
thing that Mrs. McWilliams wants—as we always do—she
calls that a compromise. Very well; the man came up from
New York and put in the alarm, and charged $325 for it, and
said we could sleep without uneasiness now. So we did for
awhile—say a month. Then one night we smelled smoke,
and I was advised to get up and see what the matter was. I lit
a candle and started toward the stairs, and met a burglar coming out of a room with a basketful of tinware, which he had
mistaken for solid silver in the dark. He was smoking a pipe.
I said: 'My friend, we do not allow smoking in this room.'
He said he was a stranger and could not be expected to know
the rules of the house; said he had been in many houses just
as good as this one, and it had never been objected to before.
He added that, as far as his experience went, such rules had
never been considered to apply to burglars anyway.

"I said, 'Smoke along, then, if it is the custom, though I
think that the conceding of a privilege to a burglar which is
denied to a bishop is a conspicuous sign of the looseness of
the times. But waiving all that, what business have you to be
entering this house in this furtive and clandestine way, without ringing the burglar alarm?'

"He looked confused and ashamed and said with embarrassment: 'I beg a thousand pardons. I did not know you had a burglar alarm, else I would have rung it. I beg you will not mention it where my parents may hear of it, for they are old and feeble and such a seeming wanton breach of the hallowed conventionalities of our Christian civilization might all too rudely sunder the frail bridge which hangs darkling between the pale and evanescent present and the solemn great deeps of the eternities. May I trouble you for a match?'

"I said, 'Your sentiments do you honor, but if you allow me to say it, metaphor is not your best hold. Spare your thigh; this kind light only on the box, and seldom there, in fact; my experience may be trusted. But to return to business; how did you get in here?'

"'Through a second-story window.'

"It was even so. I redeemed the tinware at pawnbroker's rates, less cost of advertising, bade the burglar good night, closed the window after him and retired to headquarters to report. Next morning we sent for the burglar-alarm man, and he came up and explained that the reason the alarm did not go off was that no part of the house but the first floor was attached to the alarm. This was simply idiotic; one might as well have no armor at all in battle as have it only on his legs. The expert now put the whole second story on the alarm, charged $300 for it and went his way. By and by, one night I found a burglar in the third story about to start down the ladder with a lot of miscellaneous property. My first impulse was to crack his head with a billiard-cue, but my second was to refrain from this intention, because he was between me and the cue-rack. The second impulse was plainly the soundest, so I refrained and proceeded to compromise. I redeemed the property at former rates, after deducting 10 percent for use of the ladder, it being my ladder, and next day we went down for the expert once more, and had the third story added to the alarm for $300.

"By this time the 'annunciator' had grown to formidable dimensions. It had 47 tags on it, marked with the names of various rooms and chimneys, and it occupied the space of an ordinary wardrobe. The gong was the size of a wash-bowl and was placed above the head of our bed. There was a wire from the house to the coachman's quarters in the stable, and a noble gong alongside his pillow.

"We should have been comfortable now but for one defect. Every morning at five the cook opened the kitchen door, in the way of business, and rip went that gong! The first time this happened I thought the last day was come sure. I didn't think it in bed—no, but out of it—for the first effect of that frightful gong is to hurl you across the house and slam you against the wall, and then curl you up and squirm you like a spider on a stove-lid, till somebody shuts that kitchen door. In solid fact, there is no clamor that is even remotely comparable to the dire clamor which that gong makes. Well, this catastrophe happened every morning regularly at five o'clock, and lost us three hour's sleep; for, mind you, when that thing wakes you, it doesn't merely wake you in spots; it wakes you all over, conscience and all, and you are good for 18 hours of wide-awakedness subsequently—18 hours of the most inconceivable wide-awakedness that you ever experienced in your life. A stranger died on our hands once, and we vacated and left him in our room overnight. Did that stranger wait for the general judgment? No, sir; he got up at five the next morning in the most prompt and unostentatious way. I knew he would; I knew it mighty well. He collected his life insurance and lived happily ever after, for there was plenty of proof as to the perfect squareness of his death.

"Well, we were gradually fading away toward a better land on account of our daily loss of sleep, so we finally had the expert again and he ran a wire to the outside of our door and placed a switch there, whereby Thomas, the butler, could take off and put on the alarm; but Thomas always made one little mistake—he switched the alarm off at night when he went to bed, and switched it on again at daybreak in the morning, just in time for the cook to open the kitchen door and enable that gong to slam us across the house, sometimes breaking a window with one or other of us. At the end of a week we recognized that this switch business was a delusion and a snare. We also discovered that a band of burglars had been lodging in the house the whole time—not exactly to steal, for there wasn't much left now, but to hide from the police for they were hot pressed and they shrewdly judged that the detectives would never think of a tribe of burglars taking sanctuary in a house notoriously protected by the most imposing and elaborate burglar alarm in America.

"Sent down for the expert again, and this time he struck a

most dazzling idea—he fixed the thing so that opening the kitchen door would take off the alarm. It was a noble idea and he charged accordingly. But you already foresee the result. I switched on the alarm every night at bedtime, no longer trusting to Thomas's frail memory; and as soon as the lights went out the burglars walked in at the kitchen door, thus taking the alarm off without waiting for the cook to do it in the morning. You see how aggravatingly we were situated. For months we couldn't have any company. Not a spare bed in the house; all occupied by burglars.

"Finally, I got up a cure of my own. The expert answered my call and ran another underground wire to the stable and established a switch there, so that the coachman could put on and take off the alarm. That worked first-rate, and a season of peace ensued, during which we got to inviting company once more and enjoying life.

"But by and by the irrepressible alarm invented a new kink. One winter's night we were flung out of bed by the sudden music of that awful gong, and when we hobbled to the annunciator, turned up the gas and saw the word 'Nursery' exposed, Mrs. McWilliams fainted dead away, and I came precious near to doing the same thing myself. I seized my shotgun and stood timing the coachman while that appalling buzzing went on. I knew that his gong had flung him out, too, and that he would be along with his gun as soon as he could jump into his clothes. When I judged that the time was ripe, I crept to the room next to the nursery, glanced through the window and saw the dim outline of the coachman in the yard below, standing at present arms and waiting for a chance. Then I hopped into the nursery and fired, and at the same instant the coachman fired at the red flash of my gun. Both of us were successful. I crippled a nurse and he shot off all of my back hair. We turned up the gas and telephoned for a surgeon. There was not a sign of a burglar and no window had been raised. One glass was absent, but that was where the coachman's charge had come through. Here was a fine mystery—a burglar alarm 'going off' at midnight of its own accord and not a burglar in the neighborhood.

"The expert answered the usual call, and explained that it was a 'false alarm.' Said it was easily fixed. So he overhauled the nursery window, charged a remunerative figure for it, and departed.

"What we suffered from false alarms for the next three years no stylographic pen can describe. During the first few months I always flew to the room indicated, and the coachman always sallied forth with his battery to support me. But there was never anything to shoot at—windows all tight and secure. We always sent down for the expert the next day, and he fixed those particular windows so they would keep quiet a week or so, and always remembered to send a bill about like this:

Wire	$2.15
Nipple	75
Two hour's of labor	1.50
Wax	47
Tape	34
Screws	15
Recharging battery	98
Three hour's labor	2.25
String	02
Lard	66
Pond's Extract	1.25
Springs, 4 at 50	2.00
Railroad fares	7.25
Total	$19.77

"At length a perfectly natural thing came about—after we had answered 300 or 400 false alarms—to wit, we stopped answering them. Yes, I simply rose up calmly, when slammed across the house by the alarm, calmly inspected the annunciator, took note of the room indicated, and then calmly disconnected that room from the alarm and went back to bed as if nothing had happened. Moreover, I left that room off permanently and did not send for the expert. Well, it goes without saying that in the course of time all the rooms were taken off and the entire machine was out of service.

"It was at this unprotected time that the heaviest clamity of all happened. The burglars walked in one night and carried off the burglar alarm! Yes, sir; every hide and hair of it; ripped it out tooth and toenail; springs, bells, gongs, battery and all; they took 150 miles of copper wire; they just cleaned her out, bag and baggage, and never left us a vestige of her to swear at—swear by, I mean.

"We had a time of it to get her back, but we accomplished it finally, for money. Then the alarm firm said that what we needed now was to have her put in right—with their new patent springs in the windows to make false alarms impossible, and their new patent clock attachment to take off and put on the alarm morning and night without human assistance. That seemed a good scheme. They promised to have the whole thing finished in 10 days. They began work and we left for the summer. They worked a couple of days; then they left for the summer. After which the burglars moved in and began their summer vacation. When we returned in the fall the house was as empty as a beer closet in premises where painters have been at work. We refurnished and then sent down to hurry up the expert. He came up to finish the job and said: 'Now this clock is set to put on the alarm every night at 10, and take it off every morning at 5:45. All you've got to do is to wind her up every week and then leave her alone—she will take care of the alarm herself.'

"After that we had the most tranquil season during three months. The bill was prodigious, of course, and I had said I would not pay it until the new machinery had proved itself to be flawless. The time stipulated was three months. So I paid the bill, and the very next day the alarm went to buzzing like 10,000 bee-swarms at 10 o'clock in the morning. I turned the hands around twelve hours, according to instructions, and this took off the alarm; but there was another hitch at night, and I had to set her ahead twelve hours once more to get her on the alarm again. That sort of nonsense went on a week or two; then the expert came up and put in a new clock. He came up every three months during the next three years and put in a new clock. But it was always a failure. His clocks all had the same perverse defect. They would put the alarm on in the day time, and they would not put it on at night; and if you forced it on yourself, they would take it off again the minute your back was turned.

"Now, there is the history of that burglar alarm—everything just as it happened; nothing extenuated and naught set down in malice. Yes, sir; and when I had slept nine years with burglars, and maintained an expensive burglar alarm the whole time, for their protection, not mine, and at my sole cost—not a d—d cent could I get them to contribute—I said to Mrs. McWilliams that I had had enough of that kind of pie; so with her full consent I took the whole thing out and traded it off for a dog, and shot the dog. I don't know what you think about it, Mr. Twain; but I think those things are made solely in the interests of the burglars. Yes, sir, a burglar alarm combines in its person all that is objectionable about a fire, a riot and harem, and at the same time it has none of the compensating advantages of one sort or other that customarily belong with that combination. Goodbye; I get off here."

So saying, Mr. McWilliams gathered up his satchel and umbrella, and bowed himself out of the train.

Originally printed in *Harper's Christmas* for 1882, this story echoes Twain's own difficulties with burglar alarms. As he points out in *Autobiography*, the alarm in his Hartford house "led a gay and careless life and had no principles," which means it had the annoying habit of going off for no apparent reason (204-08). Twain wrote two other stories about the McWilliams family, "Experience of the McWilliamses with Membranous Croup" and "Mrs. McWilliams and the Lightning," both of which are reprinted in *Collected Tales I*. All three McWilliams stories, narrated by the much-harried Mr. McWilliams, tell about events the Twain family itself experienced in their Hartford house. Twain presumably borrows the name "McWilliams" from a young couple—John James and Esther Keeler Norton McWilliams—he met in Buffalo soon after he bought one-third interest in the Buffalo *Express*. The couple lived at 39 Swan Street, where Twain also took lodgings. In a 1879 letter to W. D. Howells, Twain—pestered as usual through the mails by people requesting his autograph—asked his friend if he would have his children sign for him: "Will you ask Winnie or John to write on the postal cards & ship them. Let both be dated Hartford, & signed 'S. L. Clemens—Per J. L. McWilliams'" (*MT & Howells* 137). Evidently, Twain had an understandable admiration and fondness for the name "McWilliams."

29 December (Friday)
"Personal"; p. 4

Mark Twain failed to answer a letter written to him by Sergeant Ballantine. After waiting a reasonable time the latter was so exasperated at not receiving an answer that he mailed Twain a sheet of paper and a postage stamp as a gentle reminder. Mr. Clemens wrote back on a postal: "Paper and stamp received; please send an envelope."

"Sergeant Ballantine," an "eminent English barrister" according to the 16 December 1882 New York *Times*, delivered a number of popular lectures about the English legal system during a visit to the United States. A "sergeant," also spelled "serjeant," belonged to a high order of barristers (*OED*).

1883

9 January (Tuesday)
no headline; p. 4

A Chicago judge has rendered a decision that Mr. Samuel L. Clemens does not enjoy any exclusive privilege to what is called the "nommy de plumy" of "Mark Twain." If this decision shall enable Mr. Clemens to repudiate a great many utterances which have been recently attributed to him, it will greatly elevate him in the opinion of the great American public.

26 January (Friday)
"Personal Points"; p. 4

Mark Twain's new book is in the hands of the publishers. It may be funnier than his New England dinner speech.

Twain's book was *Life on the Mississippi*, published in May 1883, and his dinner speech was an address entitled "Woman—God Bless Her" that he delivered to the New England Society of New York on 22 December 1882. Although the speech lapses into occasional sarcasm, especially regarding women and clothing, underneath its surface Twain's genuine appreciation for women is clear. Its text is reprinted in *Collected Tales I* (834-36).

14 February (Wednesday)
"The Original Col. Sellers: The Operations of Old Bill Muldrow in the Wilds of Missouri"; p. 7

The writer has seen several sketches purporting to be of the original Col. Sellers. Having been reared near the birthplace of Mark Twain and the home of the celebrated Col. Mulberry, he takes the liberty of saying that, although some of the peculiarities ascribed may have been obtained from the aforesaid originals, yet the original Col. Sellers has never been written up. He was William Muldrow, commonly known as Bill Muldrow. He was a farmer and speculator near Philadelphia, Mo. Philadelphia was then a village of few inhabitants and is still a mere post-office.

Bill Muldrow was the first man who conceived the idea of a railroad connecting the valley of the Mississippi with the Pacific slope. By some course of reasoning known only to him, he reached the conclusion that Philadelphia could be made the future great city of the West, if not of the world, and with this end in view he perfected his plans for the building of a railway that was to have San Francisco for its western terminus and for its eastern terminus Marion City, a boat landing on the Mississippi, about 15 miles east of Philadelphia. Fully persuaded that there were "millions in it," he went East and confided to a few capitalists his plans for buying up corner lots by the acre and selling at $2,000 per front foot in connection with his railroad scheme.

What sort of a talker he was, and how well he succeeded in imbuing these capitalists with his own enthusiasm, may be imagined when we state that the sound of the hammer and saw and the steady tramp of the hod-carrier in the lanes of Philadelphia soon succeeded the musical tinkle of the sheep bell. A fine brick hotel climbed story by story towards the clouds. Blocks of buildings rose faster than men could or would flock to occupy them. A wharf was erected at Marion City, and the embankment that was to reach from the Mississippi west to the great city of Philadelphia, and still west to the golden gate of the Pacific, was begun. Things were booming, but it was a surface boom. Deeper down there was a heavy undertow.

Large sums of money were required. Muldrow's backers, beginning to mistrust the financial success of the scheme, became more niggardly in their advances. As the expenses became heavier the money with which to meet them grew less, and as, little by little, they fell behind, the array of brick-layers, the horde of laborers on the embankment, and the pile-drivers and bridge builders of Marion City, for like Venice it was on the water, became more clamorous for their pay.

The crash came, as in such cases it inevitably must come. Bill Muldrow was ruined financially, but, as he soon had occasion to demonstrate, not intellectually. The sheriff, preparatory to making a levy, called on him for an inventory of his real estate. Bill was equal to the occasion. He gave in not only his own land, but interspersed between tracts much that was not his own. Now, Muldrow, like many other unfortunate men, was blessed with sons-in-law, and to these he confided his scheme and asked their assistance. He described his own land minutely and told them when to bid.

The sale came off. The first tract offered did not belong to Bill, and this soon became whispered around. The result was that the bidding was very slow, and the sale was about paralyzed. The sons-in-law scooped in the bonafide tract for a palty sum.

Having saved his farm, Bill went to California where he engaged in some kind of land speculation, and where his fondness for lawsuits became proverbial. A 10-minutes' conversation with him invariably resulted in a suit of law. Failing to retrieve his fortunes in the West, he returned in his old age to the scene of his former triumph, and his ashes now rest in the country churchyard near his old home.

Philadelphia still stands, a relic, not of what it was, but of what it might have been. The hotel looms up, gray and grand in its utter desolation. The window glass is broken, the walls are cracked, the ceilings are mildewed, and the very bricks seem crumbling back to the dust from whence they came.

Marion City found a grave 'mid the swirling waters of the Mississippi in the great flood of '81, but the embankment and old rock bridge still fight their share of the battle that always end in oblivion.

Attributed to the Withers' Mill correspondent of the New York *Sun*, who otherwise remains anonymous, this piece accurately describes Bill Muldrow as an eccentric character of the region, and it is likely that Twain knew of him since Philadelphia is only 10-15 miles northwest of Hannibal and Muldrow's efforts to make Marion City a great commercial center were legendary (*Sam Clemens* 51 and 54-55). Twain himself, however, states in *Autobiography* that his source for "Col. Sellers" was his uncle James Lampton, noted by many for his eternal optimism that he would someday strike it rich (19-21).

19 June (Tuesday)
no headline; p. 4

A Mark Twain interview has involved the New York *Times* in a libel suit, brought by Shipping Commissioner C. C. Duncan, whose official accounts have recently been the subject of much unfavorable comment. Twain and the *Times* seem to have known that the interview was loaded, and it will probably be found that they have on hand enough reserve ammunition to make the libel suit more entertaining than profitable to Mr. Duncan.

Twain considered Charles C. Duncan (1821-98), captain of the *Quaker City* steamer which attained fame through *The Innocents Abroad*, to be a hypocrite because he professed strong Christian beliefs yet failed to show charity toward others. He also lacked a sense of humor, which was a cardinal sin according to Twain. Duncan, on the other hand, disliked Twain because of the humorist's fondness for liquor and jokes (*Mr. Clemens & MT* 27-28, 204). In the *Times* interview, published 10 June 1883 on page 1, Twain denounces Duncan as a crook. Twain's later claims of being misquoted, however, led to his exoneration from the charge of libel. Although the *Times* eventually lost the lawsuit, the court awarded Duncan minimal damages of 12¢ (*MT Abroad* 302). On 14 May 1884, Duncan was removed from office because of new allegations of financial misconduct.

13 July (Friday)
"Mark Twain's Birthdays"; p. 7

Mr. and Mrs. Samuel L. Clemens, who are now the parents of three children, have signalized their natal days in a manner at once substantial, ornamental, and useful. The monuments consist of three granite watering troughs, those being placed at convenient intervals along the side of the road leading past Theodore W. Crane's "Quarry Farm" on East Hill. On each trough, chiseled deep, is the name and date of birth of one of the children. It was a happy and original thought of the genial and well-known father.

Twain's first child, a son named Langdon, was born 7 November 1871. Always sickly, he died from diphtheria on 2 June 1872; Twain blamed himself for his son's fatal illness because he forgot to keep the infant warm during a carriage ride on a chilly morning (*Autobiography* 190). Twain's other children were Olivia Susan (Susy), born 19 March 1872 and died 18 August 1896 from spinal meningitis; Clara Langdon, born 8 June 1874 and died 19 November 1962 of old age; and Jane Lampton (Jean), born 26 July 1880 and died 24 December 1909 from heart failure

during an epileptic seizure. After the bustle of a social season in Hartford, the Twain family enjoyed many quiet summers at Quarry Farm,
located on a hill overlooking Elmira, N.Y. Twain's sister-in-law
owned the estate and had an outdoor study, one resembling an octag-
onal steamboat pilothouse, built 100 yards from the main house for
Twain to use during his visits (*Mr. Clemens & MT* 178-81). This
study—in which Twain worked from morning to dusk, often without
a lunch break—sparked his memories of Hannibal and fired his cre-
ative imagination; in it, he wrote substantial parts of *Tom Sawyer* and
Huckleberry Finn. *MT Himself* prints six photographs of Twain at
work in his study (146-47).

9 November (Friday)
"An Unpublished Letter: What Mark Twain Wrote to Garfield
in the Interest of Fred Douglass"; p. 7
    A Sunday paper says: The following letter written by Mark
Twain, endorsing Fred Douglass, has never been published,
but it is in the best vein of the great humorist:
                                                "Hartford, Jan. 12, 1881
"Gen. Garfield:
    "Dear Sir—Several times since your election people want-
ing office have asked me to use my influence with you in
their behalf. To word it in that way was such a pleasant compliment to me that I never complied. I could not without ex-
posing the fact that I hadn't any influence with you, and that
was a thing which I had no mind to do. It seems to me that it
is better to have a good man's flattering estimate of my influence—and keep it—than to fool it away trying to get him an
office. But when my brother, on my wife's side, Mr. Charles
J. Langdon, late of the Chicago Convention, desires me to
speak a word for Mr. Frederick Douglass, I am not asked 'to
use my influence.' Consequently I am not risking anything.
So I am writing this as a simple citizen. I am not drawing on
my fund of influence at all. A simple citizen may express a
desire with all propriety in the matter of a recommendation
to office, and so I beg permission to hope that you will retain
Mr. Douglass in his present office of marshall of the District
of Columbia, if such a course will not clash with your own
preferences or with the expedience and interests of your ad-
ministration. I offer this petition with peculiar pleasure and
strong desire, because I so honor the man's high and blem-
ishless character and so admire his brave, long crusade for the
liberties and elevation of his race. He is a personal friend of

mine, but that is nothing to the point, for his history would move me to say these things without that, and I feel them, too.

"With great respect, General, yours truly.

"(Signed)   S. L. Clemens."

Originally printed in the Boston *Globe*, it is not known whether or not this letter influenced Garfield, but the president did later name Douglass to be recorder of deeds for Washington D.C. Twain met Douglass in 1869 and afterward expressed his admiration for the black leader's commitment to liberty and economic emancipation for the freed slaves. The Langdons—long-time abolitionists—had formed an even earlier friendship with Douglass when they sheltered him in 1842 as he escaped slavery through the Underground Railroad (*Mr. Clemens & MT* 77). According to *Autobiography*, soon after he had befriended Charles Jervis Langdon (1849-1916) while they sailed on the *Quaker City* cruise, Twain saw a miniature portrait of Livy Langdon and immediately fell in love with her. Upon the steamer's return to America, Charles invited the humorist to spend the Christmas season of 1867 with the Langdons. Twain, after being formally introduced to Livy, then began his long courtship of her.

27 November (Tuesday)
"Mark Twain's Roughing It"; p. 5

    Leadville, Co.—

    The *Chronicle* says: Of all the hardships and privations endured by the Argonauts of '49 while "roughing it," none was greater than the absence of St. Jacob's Oil, the great cure for pain.

This advertisement, masquerading as a news story, suggests that Twain endorsed the product. Other ads for St. Jacob's Oil claimed that it was the "Great German Remedy for Pain," curing everything from a sore throat to rheumatism. It sold for 50¢ a bottle.

14 December (Friday)
"Mark Twain Aggrieved: Why a Statue of Liberty When We Have Adam?"; p. 7

    Mark Twain was asked to contribute to the album of artists' sketches and autograph letters, to be raffled at the Bartholdi Pedestal Fund Art Loan Exhibition, and this is his response, which accompanied his contribution:

    "You know my weakness for Adam and you know how I have struggled to get him a monument and failed. Now, it seems to me, here is my chance. What do we care for a statue of liberty when we've got the thing itself in its wildest sublimity? What you want of a monument is to keep you in mind of something you haven't got—something you've lost. Very well; we haven't lost liberty; we've lost Adam.

"Another thing: What has liberty done for us? Nothing in particular that I know of. What have we done for her? Everything. We've given her a home, and a good home, too. And if she knows anything, she knows it's the first time she ever struck that novelty. She knows that when we took her in she had been a mere tramp for 6,000 years, Biblical measure. Yes, and we not only ended her troubles and made things soft for her permanently, but we've made her respectable—and that she hadn't ever been before. And now, after we've poured out these Atlantics of benefits upon this aged outcast, lo! and behold you, we are asked to come forward and set up a monument to her! Go to. Let her set up a monument to us if she wants to do the clean thing.

"But suppose your statue represented her old, bent, clothed in rags, downcast, shame-faced, with the insults and humiliations of 6,000 years, imploring a crust and an hour's rest for God's sake at our backdoor?—come, now you're shouting! That's the aspect of her which we need to be reminded of, lest we forget it—not this proposed one, where she's hearty and well-fed, and holds up her head and flourishes her hospitable schooner of flame, and appears to be inviting all the rest of the tramps to come over. O, go to—this is the very insolence of prosperity.

"But on the other hand—look at Adam. What have we done for Adam? Nothing. What has Adam done for us? Everything. He gave us life, he gave us death, he gave us heaven, he gave us hell. These are inestimable privileges, and remember, not one of them should we have had without Adam. Well, then, he ought to have a monument, for Evolution is steadily and surely abolishing him; and we must get up a monument, and be quick about it, or our children's children will grow up ignorant that there ever was an Adam. With trifling alterations, this present statue will answer very well for Adam. You can turn that blanket into an ulster without any trouble, part the hair on one side, or conceal the sex of the head with a fire helmet, and at once he's a man; put a harp and a halo and a palm branch in the left hand to symbolize a part of what Adam did for us, and leave the fire-basket just where it is, to symbolize the rest. My friend, the father of life and death and taxes has been neglected long enough. Shall this infamy be allowed to go on, or shall it stop right here?

"Is it but a question of finance? Behold the enclosed (paid bank) checks. Use them as freely as they are freely contributed. Heaven knows I would there were a ton of them; I would send them all to you, for my heart is in this sublime work.

"S. L. C."

Eventually, more than $350,000 was contributed to the fund through various fundraising activities; President Cleveland officially dedicated the statue and its pedestal on 28 October 1886. In 1879, Twain had helped to organize a petition to build a monument to Adam—which would then be located in Elmira—but by 1881 the petition drive had died (*MT Speaks* 135). One can only assume that Twain considered the idea a monumental joke.

1884

15 January (Tuesday)
"Men of Mark"; p. 4

    R. J. Burdette is 40, Bret Harte is 45, Mark Twain is 45, W. D. Howells is 46, Thomas Bailey Aldrich is 45, Joaquin Miller is 42, James Russell Lowell is 64 and John G. Saxe is 68.

7 February (Thursday)
"Men of Mark"; p. 4

    Mr. Cable, the New Orleans novelist, has chills and fever at Mark Twain's.

Although initially sympathetic, Twain grew exasperated by Cable's three-week illness and was elated when he finally felt well enough to leave in mid-February. Twain subsequently blamed him for the mumps epidemic that struck the household shortly afterward (*Mr. Clemens & MT* 254-55). But this impatience with Cable was not strong enough for Twain to cancel an upcoming reading tour with him. Cable (1844-1925), author of many novels that attacked the poor treatment of freed slaves, remained one of Twain's favorite authors and social critics. Friction between the two men during the tour, however, strained their friendship. See 18 May 1885 for a *Post-Dispatch* account of their feud.

8 February (Friday)
"Men of Mark"; p. 4

    Professor Proctor, the famous astronomer, is married to the niece of Broadus Thompson, the original of Mark Twain's "Colonel Sellers," made so famous by John T. Raymond.

The "original" of Colonel Sellers was Twain's uncle James Lampton; see 14 February 1883.

9 February (Saturday)
"Aunt Rachel's Story"; p. 11

It was summer time and twilight. We were sitting on the porch of the farmhouse on the summit of the hill, and "Aunt Rachel" was sitting respectfully below our level on the steps, for she was our servant and colored. She was of mighty frame and stature; she was 60 years old, but her eye was undimmed and her strength unabated. She was a cheerful, hearty soul, and it was no more trouble for her to laugh than it is for a bird to sing. She was under fire now, as usual when the day was done. That is to say, she was being chaffed without mercy and was enjoying it. She would let off peal after peal of laughter and then sit with her face in her hands and shake with throes of enjoyment which she could no longer get breath enough to express. At such a moment as this a thought occurred to me and I said:

"Aunt Rachel, how is it that you've lived 60 years and never had any trouble?"

She stopped quaking. She paused and there was a moment of silence. She turned her face over her shoulder toward me and said, without even a smile in her voice:

"Misto C—, is you in 'arnest?"

It surprised me a good deal; and it sobered my manner and speech, too. I said:

"Why, I thought—that is, I meant—why, you can't have any trouble. I've never heard you sigh and never seen your eye when there wasn't a laugh in it."

She faced fairly around now and was full of earnestness.

"Has I had any trouble? Misto C—, I's gwyne to tell you, den I leave it to you. I was bawn down 'mongst de slaves; I knows all 'bout slavery, 'case I been one of 'em my own se'f. Well, sah, my ole man—that's my husban'—he was lovin' an' kind to me, jist as kind as you is to yo' own wife. An' we had chil'en—seven chil'en—an' we loved dem chil'en jis de same as you loves yo' chil'en. Dey was black, but de Lord can't make no chil'en so black but what dey mother loves 'em, and wouldn't give 'em up, no, not for anything dat's in de whole world.

"Well, sah, I was raised in ole Fo'ginny, but my mother, she was raised in Maryland; an' my souls! she was turrible when she'd git started. My lan'! but she'd make de fur fly. When she'd git into dem tantrums she always had one word dat she said. She'd straighten herse'f up an' put her fists in her hips an' say, 'I want you to understan' dat I wasn't bawn in de mash to be fool'd by trash. I'se one o' de ole Blue Hen's Chickens, I is.' 'Ca'se, you see, dat's what folks dat's bawn in Maryland call deyselves, an' deys proud of it. Well, dat was her word. I don't ever forget it, beca'se she said it so much, and beca'se she said it one day when my little Henry tore his wris' and most busted his head right up at de top of his forehead, an' de niggers didn't fly aroun' fas' enough to tend to him. An' when dey talk back at her, she up an' says, 'Lookaheah,' she says, 'I want you niggers to understan' that I wan't bawn in de mash to be fool' by trash! I'se one o' de ole Blue Hen's Chickens, I is!' and den she clar' dat kitchen an' bandage' up de chile herse'f. So I says dat word, too, when I'se riled.

"Well, bymeby, my ole mistis, she's broke, an' she got to sell all de niggers on de place. An' when I hea dat dey gwine to sell us all at auction in Richmon', oh, de good gracious! I knew whet dat me'an."

Aunt Rachel had gradually risen while she warmed to her subject, and now she towered above us, black against the stars.

"Dey put chains on us an' put us on a stan' as high as dis porch—20 foot high—an' all de people stood aroun', crowds an' crowds. An' dey'd come up dah an' look at us all roun', an' squeeze our arm, an' make us git up an' walk, an' den say, 'Dis one too ole,' or 'Dis one lame,' or 'Dis one don't amount to much.' An' dey sole my ole man an' took him away, an' dey begin to sell my chil'en an' take dem away, an' I begin to cry, an' de man say, 'Shet up yo dam blubberin', 'an' hit me on de mouf wid his han'. An' when de las' one was gone but my little Henry, I grab him close up to my breast, so, an' I ris' up an' says, 'You shan't take him away.' I says: 'I'll kill de man dat tetches him,' I says. But my little Henry whisper an' say, 'I'm gwyne to run away, an' den I work an' buy yo' freedom.' Oh, bless de chile, he always so good! But dey got him—dey got him, de men did; but I took an' tear de clo'es most off'em and beat 'em over de head wid my chain, and dey give it to me, too, but I didn't min' dat.

"Well, dah was my ole man gone, an' all my chil'en, all my seven chil'en—an' six o' dem I hain't set eyes on ag'in to dis day, an' dat's 22 year ago last Easter. De man dat bought me b'long in Newbern, an' he took me dah. Well, bymeby, de years roll on an' de waw come. My marster, he was a Confererit colonel, an' I was his family's cook. So when de Unions tooks dat town, dey all run away an' lef me all by myse'f wid de other niggers in dat mons'us big house. So de big Union officers move in dah, an' dey ask me would I cook for dem. 'Lord bless you,' I says, 'dat's what I's for.'

"Dey wa'nt no small-fry officers, mine you, dey was de biggest dey is; an' de way dey made dem sojers mosey 'roun'! De gen'l he tole me to boss dat kitchen; an' he say, 'If anybody come meddlin' wid you, you jist make 'em walk chalk; don't you be afeared,' he says, 'you's 'mong frens now.'

"Well, I thinks to myse'f, if my little Henry ever got a chance to run away, he'd make to de Norf, o' course. So one day I comes in dah whar de big officers was in de parlor, an' I drops a kurtchy, so, an' I up an' tole 'em 'bout my Henry, dey a'listenin' to my troubles jist de same as if I was white folks, an' I says, 'What I come for is bec'ase if he got away and got up Norf whar you gemmen comes from, you might a'seen him, maybe, an' could tell me so I could fine him ag'in; he was very little, an' he had a sk-yar on his lef' wris', an' at de top of his forehead.' Den dey look mournful, an' de gen'l say, 'How long since you los' him?' an' I say, 'Thirteen year.' Den de gen'l say, 'He wouldn't be little no mo', now—he's a man!'

"I never thought o' dat befo'! He was only dat little feller to me yit. I never thought 'bout him growin' up an' bein' big. But I see it den. None of the gemmen had run acrost him, so dey couldn't do nothin' for me. But all dat time, do' I didn't know it, my Henry was run off to de Norf, years an' years, an' he was a barber, too, an' worked for hisse'f An' bymeby, when de waw come, he ups an' he says: 'I's done barberin',' he says, 'I's gywne to fin' old mammy, less'n she's dead.' So he sole out an' went to whar dey was recruitin' and hired hisse'f out to de colonel for his servant, an' den he went all from de battles everywhar, huntin' for his ole mammy; yes, indeedy, he'd hire to fust one officer an' den another, till he'd ransacked de whole Souf; but you see I didn't know nuffin' 'bout dis. How was I gwyne to know it?'

"Well, one night we had a big sojer ball; de sojers dah at Newbern was always havin' balls an' carryn' on. Dey had 'em in my kitchen, heaps o' times, 'case it was so big. Mine you, I was down on sich doin's; beca'se my place was wid de officers, and it rasp me to have dem common sojers cavoortin' 'roun my kitchen like dat. But I alway' stood roun' an' kep' things straight, I did; an' sometimes dey git my dander up, an' den I'd make 'em clar dat kitchen, mine I tell you!

"Well, one night—it was a Friday night—dey comes a whole platoon f'm a nigger ridgment dat was on guard at de house—de house was headquarters, you know—an' den I was jist a'bilin'! Mad? I was jist a-boomin'! I swelled aroun', and swelled aroun'; I was jist a-itchin' for 'em to do somefin' for to start me. An' dey was a-waltzing and a-dancin'! My! but dey was havin' a time! An' I jist a-swellin' an' a-swellin' up! Pooty soon, 'long come sich a spruce young nigger a-sailin' down de room with a yaller wench roun' de wais'; an' roun' an' roun' an roun' dey went enough to make a body drunk to look at 'em; an' when dey get abreas' of me, dey went to kin' o' balancin' aroun' fust on one leg an' den on t'other, an' smilin' at my big red turban, an' makin' fun, an' I up an' says, 'Git along wid you!—rubbage!' De young man's face kin' o' changed, all of a sudden for 'bout a second, but den he went to smilin' ag'in, same as he was befo'. Well, 'bout dis time, in comes some niggers dat played music an' b'long to de ban', an' dey never could git along without puttin' on airs. An' de very fust air dey put on dat night, I lit into 'em! Dey laughed, an' dat made me wuss. De res' o' de niggers got to laughin', and den my soul alive but I was hot! My eye was jist a'blazin'! I jist straightened myse'f up, so—jist as I is now, plum to de ceilin', mos'—an' I digs my fists into my hips, an' I says, 'Look a-heah!' I says, 'I want you niggers to understan' dat I wa'nt bawn in de mash to be fool' by trash! I's one o' de ole Blue Hen's Chickens, I is!' An' den I see dat young man stan' a-starin' and stiff, lookin' kin' o' up at de ceilin' like he forgot somethin', and couldn't 'member it no mo'. Well, I jist march on dem niggers—so, lookin' like a gen'l—an' dey jist cave' away befor' me an' out at de do'. An' as dis young man was a-goin' out I hear him say to another nigger, 'Jim,' he says, 'you go 'long an' tell de cap'n I be on han' 'bout 8 o'clock in de mawnin'; dey's somethin' on my mine,' he says. 'I don't sleep no mo' dis night. You go 'long,' he says, 'an' leave me by my own se'l.'

"Dis was 'bout 1 o'clock in the mawnin'. Well, 'bout 7 I was up all on han' gettin' de officers' breakfast. I was a-stoopin' down by de stove—jist so, same as if yo' foot was de stove—an' I opened de stove do' wid my right han'—so, pushin' it back, jist as I pushes you' foot—an' I'd jist got de pan o' hot biscuits in my han' an' was 'bout to raise up when I see a black face comin' roun' under mine, an' see eyes a-lookin' up into mine, jist as I's a-lookin' up clost under yo' face now; an' I jist stopped right dah, an' never budged!, jist gazed, an' gazed so; an' de pan begin to tremble, an' all of a suden I knowd! De pan drop' on the flo' an' I grab his lef' han' an' shove back his sleeve—jist so, as I's doin' to you—an' den I goes for his forehead an' push de ha'r back, so, an' 'Boy!' I says, 'if you ain't my Henry, what is you doin' wid dis welt on you' wris' an' dat sk'ar on yo' forehead? De Lord God ob heaben be praise', an' I got my own agin!'

"Oh, Misto C—. I hain't hab no trouble. An' no joy!"

Originally printed in the November 1874 *Atlantic* under the title "A True Story," this narrative, which Twain heard from a cook at Quarry Farm, confused his readers since they had expected a joke at its conclusion. It was one of W. D. Howells's favorite pieces, however. He argues that its "'rugged truth . . . leaves all other stories of slave life infinitely far behind, and reveals a gift in the author for the simple, dramatic report of reality which we have seen equalled in no other American writer'" (qtd. in *Mr. Clemens & MT* 180-81).

18 March (Tuesday)
"Men of Mark"; p. 4

Samuel L. Clemens (Mark Twain) is at work in his house at Hartford trying to dramatize his story *The Prince and the Pauper*, hoping to make it as profitable as *Colonel Sellers*.

Although Twain eventually finished the play—he applied for a copyright in February 1884—this version was never acted professionally (*Mr. Clemens & MT* 257). Amateur productions, however, were occasionally staged in Hartford; often, Twain's daughter Susy played the role of the prince (*MT Himself* 137-38). A second adaptation of the novel would later involve Twain in a lawsuit; see 9 March 1890.

10 April (Thursday)
"Mark Twain's Autograph: How Geo. W. Cable Played a Joke on the Humorist"; p. 4

New York, April 10—

George Washington Cable sat in his room yesterday when a *Post-Dispatch* correspondent called and asked him the result of the practical joke played upon Mark Twain April 1, of which Mr. Cable was the author. Mr. Cable said that he had kept out of Mark's way since that time and really could not tell how Mark took it, and he was not anxious to know if he would have to meet Mark face to face. "During the winter I was lying ill at Mr. Twain's house," said Mr. Cable, "and as I improved he and I used to attend to our correspondence together. Occasionally I would open a letter containing an application for my autograph, and he would open another asking for his. One day when he had an unusually large mail, I remarked that those autograph applicants were insufferable bores. I left his house on February 18 and started over to Philadelphia. While lecturing there, the idea of playing on my friend Clemens a joke occurred to me. Now, I am not a practical joker; in fact, I have always considered myself incapable of perpetrating a joke with any kind of a point to it. Therefore, when this suggestion occurred to me, I flattered myself that I had struck something rich. Henry Ward Beecher was in Philadelphia lecturing in the Academy, and I was reading in Association Hall. We were both stopping at the Lafayette. In all the fullness of a simple and guileless heart I revealed my plot to Mr. Beecher and he was charmed with it. I had previously mentioned it to Johnson of the *Century*, and when I met him again he reminded me of my proposed joke and insisted upon my working it up. Even then I did not fully make up my mind to do it and I went off West on a tour. About the 26th of March my manager, Major Pond, reminded me again of the proposed joke and stated that Beecher and Johnson were ripe for it. I immediately sat down and wrote out a circular. These I had printed and sent all over the country. The circular asked Mark for his autograph. I also forwarded some to J. R. Osgood, asking him to pass them along, but he was away at the time and did not receive them until too late. Mr. Beecher was tickled with the idea. He loves a joke better than a girl loves ice cream. There were only 100 circulars printed, but the word was passed among Clemens' friends and the result was that about the first of the month he was confronted with appalling piles of mail from every quarter containing applications for his autograph from authors, publishers, bankers, merchants, actors and actresses, editors, and society ladies.   Occasionally, Clemens, when otherwise engaged, puts aside his mail for a day or so, and to prevent our joke from being spoiled by such a circumstance, I wrote to the Rev. Joe Twichell to go over to Clemens' house and make him take his medicine. I went off on the road, going as far West as Madison, Wis., and as far East as New Bedford. I came here from the East, but took special pains to come by another route than that touching at Hartford. I am, however, inclined to think that he was a mad man about the first of the month, but I don't see what he has particularly to growl about. If he don't want his collection I'll take it."

28 April (Monday)
"Men of Mark"; p. 4

Mark Twain now proposes to plague the inventors of the autograph April-Fool hoax by publishing in a pamphlet all the requests, with caricature portraits of the sender and brief biographical essays, for which the sharp pen of Twain will be dipped in a mixture of vitriol and vinegar.

17 May (Saturday)
"The Mississippi Pilot"; p. 3

The steamer left Vicksburg about 10 o'clock at night, and it was a night as black as the inside of a tar kettle. After we were well under way I went up into the pilothouse to see some fine work. According to Mark Twain, the pilot would be steering by the barking of a dog, the feel of current, or some convenient intuition that kept him in mid-channel. I had been up there about five minutes, and had just started off to wonder how on earth and Gen. Jackson he could see the river when I couldn't see down on the deck, when there came a bump and we were ashore.

The pilot he cussed, and the mate he ripped, and the captain he swore, and after a half an hour of hard work we got off and went on our way. The night seemed to grow blacker. Now was the time for a dog to bark, and lo! we hadn't gone half a mile when the sound reached us. The pilot heaved a sigh of relief. He was all right. He pulled the wheel over to hold dead for the dog, but his chuckle hadn't died away before grind! rasp! bump! and we were ashore on an island. The dog which used to bark for Mark Twain to steer by was probably dead, and this was an animal barking for his own amusement.

Then the pilot he wrenched himself, and the mate he tore things apart, and the captain he knocked things endways, and after a delay of 20 minutes we were again afloat.

I made up my mind that the pilot would now feel the current, and I was right. He shoved the boat out for the middle of the river, and his hands gripped the spokes as if he were dead sure of his route for the next 10 miles. Now he is feeling on the port side—now on the starboard side—now dead ahead. A push or a pull of the wheel carries us straight down the channel. It is wonderful. If Mark Twain hadn't written it in his book, no man would believe that this pilot could tell to a foot where the channel banks are. He is holding us in the very center of the mighty river when—. Well, we were not in the center. We were fast ashore in Louisiana, and after the pilot and the mate and the captain had cussed all the cusswords ever heard of in any known language, we concluded to stop right there until next morning.

This report by an anonymous writer is from the Detroit *Free Press*.

17 May (Saturday)
"Josh Billings on Humorists"; p. 14

In a long interview originally printed in the New York *Mail and Express*, Josh Billings discusses the state of American humor. After defining humor as a "mixture of truth and pathos," and consequently criticizing purposeless comedy, Billings judges the living humorists and says this about Mark Twain:

Nothing ever equaled the humor of Mark Twain's descriptions. He is, in fact, the greatest descriptive humorist America has produced.

Billings states later in the interview that "[h]umorists are the saddest and soberest of fellows. . . . Mark Twain does not know how to laugh and Nasby has never laughed in his life." Josh Billings (1818-85) and Petroleum Vesuvius Nasby (1833-88), very popular humorists of the 1880s, have now passed into obscurity. Twain was friends with both; a photograph of the three men on tour together in 1869 is in *Mr. Clemens & MT*.

21 May (Wednesday)
"About Humorists"; p. 7

In a recent interview with a reporter of the New York *Mail and Express*, Mr. Joshua Billings reinterates the popular notion that "humorists are the saddest and soberest of fellows." Then he goes on to say that Mark Twain does not know how to laugh and Nasby never laughed in his life. Bah! Mark Twain does his share of laughing, and don't you forget it. It isn't fair to judge Mark Twain or Nasby or any other professional humorist when he is on dress parade, for a professional humorist knows very well that when he is on dress parade he is expected to look melancholy, and accordingly he looks so. But in their private lives you will find these humorists as sociable and merry as other men.

This editorial by Eugene Field also relates a few anecdotes about Nasby and Bob Burdette but says nothing more about Twain. Field (1850-95) wrote the popular "Sharps and Flats" column for the Chicago *Daily News* for more than 20 years.

29 May (Thursday)
"She Hadn't Thought of That"; p. 7

Mark Twain tells this story of Mr. Bergh: A lady was talking with Mr. Bergh one day and chanced to speak of a friend of hers who had been traveling out West. In crossing the frontier it became necessary that her father, mother and three children should cross a somewhat swollen ford. Their only beast of burden was a mule. So the father placed two of his children on its back, then plunged in and led the beast in with him. It swam obediently behind him, and all reached the other shore in safety. At the man's bidding the intelligent mule returned to where the mother and child were waiting to cross. The mother, fearing to put too heavy a burden on the already tired animal, put only the child on its back, bade him hold fast, and with a prayer, led the animal to the water edge. They plunged in, swam bravely for a time, then were seen to struggle and go down. "Oh, think, Mr. Bergh," said the excited and pitying lady, "just think what must have been the feelings of that mother as she saw her darling child lost in the depths of that black water!" "True! oh, too true," sighed Mr. Bergh. "But what must have been the feelings of that mule!"

Henry Bergh (1823-88), a prominent animal-rights advocate and founder of the ASPCA, was frequently the butt of jokes in the 1880s.

13 June (Friday)
"Authors Popular on the Continent"; p. 2

Baron Christian Bernard von Tauchnitz, in a story reprinted from the Pall Mall *Gazette*, mentions that "Mark Twain and Bret Harte have a great vogue" in Europe. He also briefly discusses W. D. Howells, Henry James, and other American authors. Tauchnitz (1816-95) founded a Leipzig publishing firm in 1837, which later published German editions of Twain's works. He was one of the few scrupulous foreign publishers of Twain since he usually paid him a royalty.

17 June (Tuesday)
"Men of Mark"; p. 4

Mr. Clemens, better known as Mark Twain, has several blank forms pinned over the table on which he writes. One is a formal declination to an invitation to dinner, another is for declinations to give opinions (otherwise compliments, Clemens phrases it) on literary productions, and another is a blank for declining to send articles solicited by this and that journal.

10 July (Thursday)
"Answers to Correspondents"; p. 4

I. G.—Mark Twain's real name is Samuel L. Clemens.

This regular column in the *Post-Dispatch* printed answers to questions from its readers.

14 July (Monday)
"Men of Mark"; p. 4

We learn from a London society paper, the *Ladies' Pictoral*, that Bret Harte squints; that Mark Twain stammers; that Howells has an iron gray moustache and "careless dark hair"; that Henry James is like the Prince of Wales, and that Mr. George William Curtis wears a glass eye.

24 July (Thursday)
"Men of Mark"; p. 4

S. L. Clemens and George W. Cable will give readings the coming season. They will give the evening's entertainment by each reading from his own published works and contributing original sketches prepared especially for the occasion.

This notice announced the beginning of one of Twain's most celebrated tours of the country. The two writers—the self-dubbed "Twins of Genius"—gave more than 100 performances throughout the United States to enthusiastic audiences in sold-out halls; they appeared in St. Louis on 9 January 1885. Twain discusses how he prepared his material for the tour in *Autobiography* (174-83). See *Twins of Genius* for more information about the tour.

1 October (Wednesday)
"Sellers' Ghost: John T. Raymond Haunted by His Great Character"; p. 5

In the course of a long interview with Raymond, a *Post-Dispatch* reporter asked about the actor's feelings toward his most famous role, that of Col. Sellers:

Mr. Raymond then branched off on the difficulty in the way of a man who has created a character and made a name in it attempting to change to something else.

"Why, people think," he said, "that I never existed before Col. Mulberry Sellers, and was born with my hand in the air. I had played nearly all the comedy characters before I ever heard of Sellers, but it clings to me like a ban. It is the same way with Joe Jefferson and *Rip Van Winkle*. He is always Rip to the public, no matter what else he may be playing and with what consummate art he may take the character. We all have our peculiarities of gesture, action, and modulation, but it is not so with the tragedians. Booth or any of them say 'to be or not to be,' this way," the comedian mimicked the tragedian, "and they all clap and cry out 'how grand!' Then again in *Othello*, 'most potent, grave, and reverend seignors' with exactly the same modulation and action, and it is 'how magnificent!' They don't say 'that is Booth for Hamlet' but it is always 'Raymond is Raymond,' or, 'Egad, he is Sellers!' Why, in *Fresh*, I strike out from the shoulder thus, exactly opposite from the Sellers gesture and it's, 'Egad, he can't help being Sellers.' If I should appear on the stage as a driveling old man, they would say, 'It is just like Sellers.' I tried *My Son*, a very pathetic play, once. And I saw two men looking at my lithograph. I heard one of them say, 'We'll go and have a good laugh.' I thought to myself, my boy, you'll be mistaken. Well, the next day I saw the very same men standing before this picture, cursing it because they had gone to have a laugh and got a cry. I took the night off. Why, in the garret scene, when the old man says, 'No, I am [the next word or two is illegible] up in the world,' the audience changed from tears to laughter at once. And I never did get anyone to understand that the effect was intended, and was only an illustration of pathos in humor and of the intimate connection between tears and laughter. They persistently thought it was Sellers cropping out in me. By the way, Twain and Howells are writing a new Sellers play, a sort of continuation of the old one.

MT Himself reproduces a playbill from *Colonel Sellers* which shows Raymond with his hand in the air, acting the part of the ever-optimistic colonel (175). Joseph Jefferson (1829-1905) found renown in 1865 when he played the title role in *Rip Van Winkle*; the acclaim was so great that he never played another role afterward. Edwin Thomas Booth (1833-93), brother of Abraham Lincoln's assassin, was the most noted American Shakespearean actor of his day. His subtle performances of Hamlet, Macbeth, and Othello captivated audiences in the United States and Europe. Twain and W. D. Howells completed *Colonel Sellers as a Scientist*, a sequel to *Colonel Sellers*, in late 1883, but Raymond rejected it as too slight (*MT & the Theatre* 67-72). Although Howells eventually distanced himself from the play, Twain revised it into *The American Claimant*. See 19 June 1886 for an account of its aborted production.

8 October (Monday)
"Men of Mark"; p. 4

Mark Twain is the richest humorist in America. Besides his own large earnings and savings he married a lady worth several hundred thousand dollars.

Livy's father, Jervis Langdon, made his fortune through a coal and iron monopoly in upstate New York; his daughter did indeed inherit a great deal of money from his estate upon his death in 1871.

20 October (Monday)
"Men of Mark"; p. 4

The humorous Mark Twain must feel that the Italians have got the best of him just once. A Florence publisher announces the works of Marco Duo, further translated as Samuel Langhorne Clemensini.

24 October (Friday)
"Men of Mark"; p. 4

Mark Twain, who has been an ardent Republican all his life, has come out for Cleveland. He is one of the signers of the stirring address issued by the Independent Republicans of Connecticut. Mr. Blaine will not be able to see anything funny in this performance of Mr. Twain.

Like many other Republicans dubbed the "Mugwumps," Twain believed his party's nominee for the presidency, James G. Blaine (1830-93), to be corrupt. Consequently, he worked to elect Grover Cleveland (1837-1908) president. At a political meeting in Hartford in October, Twain gave a speech entitled "Turncoats" about why Republicans with a conscience should desert their party; its text is reprinted in *Collected Tales I* (849-51).

27 October (Monday)
"Men of Mark"; p. 4

Mr. Clements [sic] (Mark Twain) is speaking in Connecticut for Cleveland.

30 October (Thursday)
"Men of Mark"; p. 4

Col. Sellers took clever advertising of the campaign excitement in Cleveland, Oh., by parading in a Blaine procession, [with] men carrying transparencies bearing the legend: "For Congress—John T. Raymond."

3 November (Monday)
"Men of Mark"; p. 4

Mark Twain has deferred his proposed humorous course with Creole Cable till after the election, alleging more serious duty in doing all he can, publically and privately, to assist in carrying Connecticut for Cleveland.

5 November (Wednesday)
"Men of Mark"; p. 4

Since Mark Twain took the stump for Cleveland his Republican friends don't find him so immensely amusing as he used to be.

14 November (Friday)
"Hoaxing the Humorists: Mark Twain and Geo. W. Cable Have a Funny Experience in Boston"; p. 2

Boston, November 14—

Mark Twain and George W. Cable, who were to give readings in Music Hall last night, had a funny experience yesterday. They called early in the afternoon upon W. D. Howells in Beacon Street, and, while sitting at his window, saw a young woman jump in the Back Bay from the end of Arlington Street. They hurried out, but she had been rescued when they got there. As she gave evidence of a desire to repeat the performance, they took her in charge and walked up Beacon Street with her, one on each side. Her dripping garments and excited manner attracted a great deal of attention in the usually quiet neighborhood of the elite. The famous men were often the center of gaping groups, but nobody recognized them. Finally they found a policeman, who took the woman in charge. They followed her to the station house. The officer said she was drunk, and, when they said she was not, the captain bluntly told them to "shut up." He was quietly writing up his record books and kept them standing outside the rail about 50 minutes. When he was through he booked the woman, who belonged to a respectable family and turned out to be insane, and gave the Creole author and the funny man to understand there was no further need for them there. They accordingly left and agreed to keep their own counsel, but Mark last night divulged it to a reporter.

This anecdote, relayed by telegraph to the *Post-Dispatch*, is presumably by the same correspondent who conducted the 20 November interview with Twain and filed the 27 November story about *Adventures of Huckleberry Finn*. It seems likely that a *Post-Dispatch* reporter was among the many journalists who followed Twain from town to town on this particular lecture tour.

20 November (Thursday)
"Talking About Fun: Mark Twain Discourses Seriously on How to Amuse Audiences"; p. 1

New York, November 20—

Mark Twain, in dress suit, received the correspondent of the *Post-Dispatch* yesterday in a waiting room at Chickering Hall. Mr. George W. Cable was giving his recital of Creole life.

"Ah, you are cruel," he said, with an air of utter sadness, "to attempt to interview a man just at the moment when he needs to feel good. You've got to feel good, you know, in order to make the audience feel the same way, but to try to be funny after you've been interviewed"—the thought seemed to overpower him.

"I did not know it was such a physical strain to deliver a humorous lecture."

"Ah, you have never attempted it; you don't know. On a day like this, when we give two performances, I feel like I'm all burnt out after the first performance. As soon as I get back to the hotel, I go to bed. I must get some sleep, somehow. If I don't, I will not be able to go through with the evening performance the way I want to. It's the same thing when you're traveling. The audiences, intelligent newspaper-reading audiences, are responsive enough. They quickly catch the point you are trying to make; often times they anticipate it. Then you are put on your mettle to give a sudden turn to the story so as to bring out a new and unexpected point. If these things don't happen, don't blame the audience; it is yourself who is at fault. The traveling has exhausted you, and, as I said before, you're not feeling good."

"All this you can judge of by the effect you produce on the audience?"

"Oh, yes. If you hear a rustle here or there, or see a particularly stolid face, you can tell that there is something wrong with yourself. The effect, of course, is not general. Heaven forbid! You would then have to stop right off. Audiences have their peculiarities, you know. It is a great inspiration to find a particular individual fairly respond to you as if you were in telegraphic communication with him. You are tempted to address yourself solely to him. I've tried that experiment. Sometimes it is dangerous. Laughter is very infectious, and when you see a man give one great big guffaw, you begin to laugh with him in spite of yourself. Now, it would not do for the lecturer to laugh. His is a grave and serious business, however it might strike the audience. His demeanor should be grave and serious. He should not ever smile."

"You have had ample opportunity to average your audiences on their respective faculties for fun."

"Audiences are much the same everywhere. I have been

delighted with all before whom I have had the honor of appearing. In Boston, where Mr. Cable and I appeared before coming here, the audiences were delighted with our efforts to please them. You should have witnessed the enthusiasm last evening. Oh, I have nothing to complain of my audiences; perhaps they cannot say the same of me. Our entertainment lasts one hour and three quarters. The fact that Mr. Cable and I alternate makes us able to extend it to that length. Were I lecturing alone, one hour and five minutes is as much as I would dare impose on the audience. The strain on them in the humorous direction would be too much. But now Mr. Cable gently soothes them, then I excite them to laughter, or try to, at least. Then Mr. Cable has his turn and so the change is very healthful and beneficial."

"Your tour will be an extended one?"

"Our agent has booked us to the end of January. I should like to go to California, if I can manage it. You know this is my farewell performance. I so intimated to the audience last evening. I told them that I had not practically appeared on the platform for nine years, and that when this term was over I would not appear again—at least, not for nine years. It will do me good; it will do my hearers good. Yet, I've known people to give farewell performances for 50 years in succession."

A burst of applause at this juncture announced the conclusion of Mr. Cable's recital and that the time had come for Mark Twain to appear on the stage. As the reporter passed out he heard an outburst of laughter. The humorist had made a point.

Like the story six days earlier, this was relayed by telegraph to the *Post-Dispatch*. The New York City newspapers had mixed reactions to Twain's three performances in that city; the *Times*, for example, was "supercilious and cool" about Twain's tales, while the *Sun* found his storytelling to be powerful and compelling (*Twins of Genius* 19-22).

27 November (Thursday)
"Men of Mark"; p. 4

Cable and Twain are the Robson and Crane of the lecture platform.

W. H. Crane (1845-1928) and Stuart Robson (1836-1903) were a noted acting duo of the period. Not long after this line appeared in the *Post-Dispatch*, they performed *As You Like It* in St. Louis.

27 November (Thursday)
"*Huckleberry Finn*: How Mark Twain's Latest Work was Nearly Ruined"; p. 1

Hartford, Conn., November 27—

Huckleberry Finn, Mark Twain's new book, was completed last March, but owing to complications and differences with his publishers it has not yet appeared, although it has been extensively announced, a prospectus of the story sent out, and the opening chapters recently published in the *Century*. When the book was finished last month, Mark Twain made a proposition in regard to its publication to the American Publishing Company of this city, which published his *Innocents Abroad* and his later works. From them, the company, which heretofore had been but a small concern, achieved a reputation and standing equal to any of the older established publishing houses of the country. Mark Twain, on his side, obtained royalties amounting in all to well over $408,000. When *Huckleberry Finn*, the sequel to *Tom Sawyer*, was completed, Twain again made a proposition to his publishers to produce the new work. Negotiations were commenced, but never completed. The parties could not come to terms. Evidently, Mark Twain considered that he had built up the American Publishing Company, while they seemed to think themselves the founders of his fame and fortune. Liberal royalties were offered Twain by the Publishing Company, but he refused to accept them. The final offer was that the profits should be divided, each of the parties to receive 50 percent of the proceeds from the sale of the new work. This proposition was not satisfactory to the author, who wanted 60 percent of the profits. This offer the company refused to accept and he determined on entering a new business, combining that of the publisher with that of author. Mark Twain had a nephew residing in New York in whose business ability he had great confidence. This man, whose name is Charles L. Webster, is engaged in the book publishing business at No. 658 Broadway. Twain entered into a partnership with his nephew to produce his new work and to supervise all the mechanical details of its production. The copy was all sent to him, and by him given to the printers. In order to properly embellish the book, the services of a leading metropolitan engraver were secured, and from this comes all the trouble which Hartford's popular author is now plunged.

The engravings, after having been cut on the plates, were sent to the electrotyper. One of the plates represented a man with a downcast head, standing in the foreground of a particularly striking illustration. In front of him was a ragged urchin with a look of dismay overspreading his countenance. In the background, and standing behind the boy, was an attractive-looking young girl whose face was enlivened by a broad grin. Something which the boy or man had said or done evidently amused her highly. The title of the cut was "In a dilemma. What shall I do?" When the plate was sent to the electrotyper a wicked spirit must have possessed him. The title was suggestive. A mere stroke of the awl would suffice to give to the cut an indecent character never intended by the author or engraver. It would make no difference in the surface of the plate that would be visible to the naked eye, but when printed would add to the engraving a characteristic which would be repudiated, not only by the author, but by all the respectable people of the country into whose hands the volume should fall. The work of the engraver was successful. It passed the eye of the inspector and was approved. A proof was taken and submitted. If the alteration of the plate was manifested in the proof, it was evidently attributed to a defect in the press and paper, which would be remedied when the volume was sent to the press. Now the work was ready for printing. In issuing books to be sold by "subscription only," the publishers first strike off a large number of prospectuses which are to be used by the agents when soliciting subscribers to the work. Some 3,000 of these prospectuses with the defective cut were presented and distributed to the different agents throughout the country. The entire work had passed the eyes of the various readers and inspectors and the glaring indecency of the cut had not been discovered. Throughout the country were hundreds of agents displaying the merits of the work and elaborating on the artistic work of the engravings. It was remarkable that while the defect was so palpable, none of the agents noticed it, or, if he did, he failed to report it to the publishers. Possibly, they might have considered the alteration intentional, as the title to the illustration was now doubly suggestive. At last came a letter from the Chicago agent, calling attention to the cut. Then there was consternation in the office of the publishers. Copies of the prospectus were hauled from the shelf and critically examined. Then, for the first time, it dawned on the publishers that such an illustration would condemn the work. Immediately all the agents were telegraphed to and the prospectuses were called in. The page containing the cut was torn from the book, a new and perfect illustration being substituted. Agents were supplied with the improved volumes and are now happy in canvassing for a work to which there can be no objection, while they smile at the prospects of heavy commissions. But the story leaked out. Several opposition publishers got hold of copies of the cut, however, and these now adorn their respective offices.

This article, like those of 14 November and 20 November, was telegraphed to the *Post-Dispatch* by a correspondent; it seems clear that either Twain or Webster served as a source for the story. In any case, the vandal who drew a crude picture of a penis on Silas Phelps in the illustration was never found, even though Webster offered a substantial award for his identification (*Mr. Clemens & MT* 263-64). Even with this setback, *Adventures of Huckleberry Finn* was published on 16 February 1885 and was an immediate financial success.

4 December (Thursday)
"Men of Mark"; p. 4
Mark Twain and his friend Mr. Cable carried away $1,000 apiece for their two readings in Washington.

5 December (Friday)
"Men of Mark"; p. 4
Mark Twain lies abed most of the day when on his lecture tours and is not traveling. He receives no cards and refuses to see anyone.

22 December (Monday)
"Men of Mark"; p. 4
When Mark Twain appeared before his Buffalo audience the other evening he scanned them carefully. He then said that he missed many faces that he knew 14 or 15 years ago. "They have gone," he added sadly, "to the tomb, to the gallows or to—the White House. All of us must go to one or the other of these destinations, and it behooves us to be wise and prepare for all."

25 December (Thursday)
"Mark Twain Talks About Humor"; p. 7

"Is the American taste for humor still growing in your opinion?"

"Yes, I think so. Humor is always popular, and especially so with Americans. It is born in every American and he can't help liking it."

"Is it true that the American style of humor is becoming very popular in England?"

"Yes, the liking for American humor over there has become immense. It awakens the people to a new life, and is supplanting the dry wit which formerly passed for humor. American humor wins its own way and does not need to be cultivated. The English come to like it naturally."

This excerpt from an interview was originally printed in the Detroit *Post*.

1885

7 January (Wednesday)
"Mark Twain's Overcoat"; p. 5

This advertisement, surely printed without Twain's approval, boasts that the humorist purchased a particularly fine coat from the F. W. Humphrey & Co. store in St. Louis. Alongside a caricature of a man in a rather foppish coat, this ad copy appears:

> The one he bought here some two years ago since, we mean. He strolled majestically into our store and asked for something warm—in the way of an overcoat. He was politely informed that all of our topcoats, being new, were warm. None of them were elderly; none of them had been brought over by "Christofo Columbo," or even by the Pilgrims. Mark selected the first coat shown him, although it was a world too large. The sleeves almost covered his fingers, and when his attention was drawn to the fact he very dryly re-MARK-ed that the extra length would answer for a muff, should he lose his mitts. The salesman made a great effort and said, "The coat is just the thing for 'Roughing It' among the 'Innocents,'"—when Twain interrupted him by loudly asking the price of the garment. It was told him; he paid for it, and quietly and gracefully walked out.

This advertisement also quotes prices ranging from $3 to $15 for coats.

8 January (Thursday)
"Men of Mark"; p. 4

> Mr. Cable eats chocolate ice cream at midnight after his readings, and still lives. His yoke-fellow, however, Mark Twain, hurls his bootjack at St. John and uncorks a bottle or so of Bass' pale ale.

9 January (Friday)
"Cable and Twain: The Author and the Humorist Arrive in the City Today"; p. 7

While Mr. J. B. Pond was this morning standing in the rotunda of the Southern Hotel with Samuel C. [sic] Clemens (Mark Twain) standing on one side of him and George W. Cable on the other, the *Post-Dispatch* reporter present was struck by the touching likeness which the group bore to that beautiful legend which provides a human being with two attendent spirits, one of them of diabolical mien always urging him on to commit felonies and misdemeanors, the other, of angelic aspect, constantly coaxing him to give up his criminal ways. Mark Twain's features, familiarized to the public by several brands of chewing tobacco, cigars, and cigarettes, are so well-known that it only becomes necessary to describe the appearance of his less Mephistophelian companion. Mr. Cable is, or rather, if he were a woman, would be what the society editors describe as a petite brunette. He is short and slender and dark of complexion, and, dressing in black, presents very much the appearance of a clerical gentleman of absolutely orthodox views. His most remarkable features are his eyes and his forehead, the former being very large and dark and intelligent, while the latter is high and broad and gifted with an intellectual bulge which makes him a much more imposing person when he takes his hat off than he previously appears. A long black beard and a still longer moustache, which would be of phenomenal beauty were the beard not allowed to take the wind out of its sails, complete a very interesting, though not particularly strong, face. After the tableau vivant had signed their names in the hotel register they were accompanied by the *Post-Dispatch* reporter to Mr. Clemens's room, where the conversation at once turned upon an accident which had happened to the train they were on just as it entered upon the first of the arches coming from the Illinois shore. Mr. Clemens undertook to supply the descriptive work and at once began as follows in his particular drone which, being a difficult matter to reproduce with the ordinary, copper-faced type as commonly in use among the high class of American newspapers, must be left for the imagination of the reader to supply:

"We had," he said, "just reached that portion of the bridge which overhangs the crystal waters of the Mississippi River when a misunderstanding arose between the forward and rear portions of the train. The engine conceived the intention of leaving the track upon which the rest of the train was and moving upon another one, while the remainder of the train decided to remain where it was. The result was that one of the forward passenger cars was switched diagonally across the track. If we had not been going very slowly at the time the whole train would have left the track."

"Personally, I suppose, you had no fears, being familiar with the river currents?"

"Not in the slightest. It would not have discommoded me in the least to have been tossed into the Mississippi. I know the river thoroughly. It was the other people I was thinking of."

"I noticed that you seemed very anxious about the other people," Mr. Cable remarked with a quiet smile.

"It's no wonder," Mr. Clemens resumed. "There was a continuous kind of jolting which became more and more ominous and suggestive as the train advanced. A sense of crumbling—something crumbling beneath us, where stability was of the highest importance to us all personally—became very prominent. I fully expected the bridge to break down—I have always done so when I crossed it—and my anxiety for the safety of the other passengers led me to leap quite hastily from my seat and make a rush for the nearest exit. I wanted to get out and see what was the matter so I could intelligently supply the required relief."

"And you got there?" the reporter asked.

"Yes, but unfortunately, too late to be of any service. The train had stopped of its own accord. There were not many people hurt in the accident."

"How were they injured?"

"They happened to be in the front when I was going out. I went out in a great deal of a hurry and they were in the way. I'm sorry that I cannot furnish you with a list of the wounded and a statement of where they came from and the nature of the injuries. I did think of getting up such a list and giving the name of prominent men, but it don't do, after all, to play a practical joke on a newspaper. There are so many people who don't understand a joke, however plain it may be, that the possibility of serious results stands in the way of their perpetration."

Turning the subject the reporter offered to sympathize with Mr. Clemens upon the atrocious character of the cuts which were being published of himself and Mr. Cable.

"They're bad; yes, they're very bad," he said, "but I am glad of it. I would rather have that kind of a picture in the newspapers, because, when people look at us after seeing the picture, we make a favorable impression by contrast. This is a new idea of pictoral advertising and it works admirably. Take the average theatrical chromo; it flatters the subject, and when the latter comes under the gaze of an audience the result is a certain amount of disappointment. If the people we go to see on the stage were as handsome as their portraits they could charge double prices. I think Cable's picture flatters him, but mine does not begin to do me justice."

So much time had already been wasted upon commonplaces that the reporter informed Mr. Twain that he had been entrusted to secure an interview and that if he had no objections—

"Not in the least," Mr. Clemens remarked as he groped nervously through his pockets and finally looked at his visitor with a glance of blank amazement. Then he called out to his partner in the next room: "Cable, have we entirely run out of our Friday interviews?"

"Completely," Cable answered.

"Too bad," Mr. Clemens remarked.

"Give me a Wednesday or a Saturday one," the reporter suggested.

"T'wouldn't do," Mr. Clemens said with a decisive shake of the head. "We can interchange the other days' interviews among themselves, but none of them are with the Friday one. They are too lively. Our Friday one is staid, sober, calm. Cable wrote it and we've had a run on them. They're all gone. Never mind, I'll hunt through my trunk and if I find one I'll bring it around to the office."

The reporter left, but up to the time of going to press neither the humorist nor the interview had arrived at the office.

The three-day visit to St. Louis was one of the more memorable stops on the long tour because it enabled Twain to visit with relatives and old friends as the city welcomed him enthusiastically; Cable was also warmly received (*Twins of Genius* 36-42). Although James B. Pond

(1838-1903)—an experienced promoter—was ostensibly Twain's manager, Twain himself directed the 15-week tour and made all the important decisions. He also earned the most money, an estimated $17,000 (*Mr. Clemens & MT* 259-60).

10 January (Saturday)
"Saturday Chat"; p. 4

I wonder if Mark Twain, in his prosperity and fame, when he can fill a hall on short notice, remembers the first lecture he delivered in St. Louis. It was a good many years ago, before Twain had made a national reputation. He was in St. Louis, having just come from California and was scarcely known to anyone. One day a young businessman, who was running a mission school in the northern part of the city, announced to his friends that he was going to have a good lecture at his school. They asked who was going to lecture, and he said Mark Twain. This was Hebrew to most of them. Twain had a lot of his usual style of posters printed announcing the lecture and stating that a lot of prizes would be given, among which were 10 smooth auger holes and others of a similar funny kind. The evening came and went and the young man's friends asked him how the lecture came off. "Oh, not very well," said he, "we had bad weather and the people somehow wouldn't come."

"How much did you take in, anyhow?"

"Only $8," was the mournful reply. Eight dollars was a bigger sum to the lecturer then than $800 is now.

Twain lectured twice for the mission school on the topic of his experiences in Nevada and California during his mining days; both lectures—25 and 26 March 1867—were successful, contrary to how this editorial remembers them (*MT: Bachelor* 323-24).

21 January (Wednesday)
"Men of Mark"; p. 4

"Bis-marck and Mark Twain mean the same," writes a philosophical humorist, who is altogether too smart for this world.

29 January (Thursday)
"Men of Mark"; p. 4

Mark Twain's mother and brother live in Keokuk, Iowa. Mrs. Clemens is 80 years of age.

Actually, Twain's mother (born 18 June 1803) was 81 on this date. See 7 April 1885 for an interview with her.

31 January (Saturday)
"A Valiant Soldier"; p. 10

Near the end of a column of miscellaneous gossip, an anonymous writer—the Chicago correspondent to the *Post-Dispatch*—adds this report:

Hearing Mark Twain read the other evening at Central Music Hall, I was reminded of a story which is told on him, but which had its real foundation, "so they say," in the experience of one of our best-known and best-liked Chicago journalists. Guy Magee is the man in question, and it is said of him that one night at least 100 years ago—when Guy was full of reportorial zeal—going home from the *Tribune* office he found a man lying dead on the sidewalk. Here was a sensation, but what to do with it was the question, for the newspaper had gone to press. It was plain that the "sensation" had to be saved until the next day; so Guy stowed it away under the sidewalk, and next morning discovered the corpse again and the *Tribune* came out with a magnificent double-headed "scoop" three columns long—"Appalling Discovery," etc., etc.

"Yes," said a friend to whom I had mentioned the anecdote, "I've heard the same yarn told about Mark Twain. It is not as good, however, as the story that one day out in San Francisco, being sadly out of news matter, he discovered some men hanging a fellow up to a lamp-post, whereupon he ran up to them with tears of gratitude in his eyes, and shook their hands and thanked them for furnishing him an item."

Mark Twain, it seems, is a very congenial, modest sort of fellow, and likes a convivial time with friends. A few years ago when he was here, a committee of newspapermen waited upon him and tendered some sort of entertainment on his behalf.

"Well," said he with his customary colloquial limp, "I've had a good deal of this sort of marble-palace and gilded-chandelier business, and I don't want any more, but if I could get together with the boys in a quiet, cozy place, where a fellow might smoke a cob-pipe and put his feet on the table if he wanted to, then I don't know but what I'd enjoy it."

The place was secured and the humorist sat with a pipe

and tobacco beside him and his hat on his head, and related yarns the whole night through to the edification of a score of fellow-scribblers.

6 February (Friday)
"Men of Mark"; p. 4
>Mark Twain smokes 20 cigars a day. Cable indulges in a glass of soda when business is particularly good.

17 March (Tuesday)
no headline; p. 4
>The directors of the Concord Public Library have joined in the general scheme to advertise Mark Twain's new book *Huckleberry Finn*. They have placed it on the *Index Expurgatorius*, and this will compel every citizen of Concord to read the book in order to see why the guardians of his morals prohibited it. Concord keeps up its recent reputation of being the home of speculative philosophy and of practical non-sense.

This editorial correctly predicts the response to Huck's banishment. In fact, Twain boasted in a press release that he felt assured the library's actions would help make his novel a huge financial success (*Mr. Clemens & MT* 267-70). See 7 April for another statement by Twain on this controversy.

18 March (Wednesday)
"Men of Mark"; p. 4
>Mark Twain now coolly declares that his recent reading tour with Creole Cable was solely for recreation, and as he netted $35,000 for his share a good many people would like to similarly recreate.

While he certainly did well on the tour, this estimate of Twain's share is too high. More likely, it was around $17,000.

7 April (Tuesday)
"Men of Mark"; p. 4
>Mr. Clemens, Mark Twain, writes to Frank A. Nicols of Concord, Mass., a letter expressing feelings of gratitude toward Massachusetts for various things, especially the recent advertisement of his *Huckleberry Finn* book, which "the moral icebergs of the Concord library committee" praised with faint damns.

7 April (Tuesday)
"Mark Twain's Boyhood: An Interview with Mrs. Jane Clemens"; p. 7

In an unpretentious two-story brick dwelling at the intersection of High and Seventh Streets, Keokuk, Iowa, lives Orion Clemens and his wife. The former is the eldest brother of the famous Mark Twain, and is a lawyer by profession. He is the personage who was the "Governor's Secretary" at Carson, Nev., and who gave Mark the subordinate position which resulted, with its attendant experiences, in the production of probably the most thrillingly realistic portrayal of frontier life ever given to the world—the book *Roughing It*. Mr. Orion Clemens now lives a very quiet and secluded life, being much given to literary pursuits in which he is assisted by his graceful and accomplished wife. They have no children.

With them resides Mr. Clemens' mother, who will be 82 years of age next June. The writer, being stranded in Keokuk for a few hours, improved the opportunity to make a call upon the venerable lady, and in the course of an hour's pleasant conversation which followed, received from her lips many anecdotes concerning her most noted son, which will be new to the generality of readers.

"Sam was always a good-hearted boy," said Mrs. Clemens, "but he was a very wild and mischievous one, and do what we would we could never make him go to school. This used to trouble his father and me dreadfully, and we were convinced that he would never amount to as much in the world as his brothers because he was not near so steady and sober-minded as they were."

"I suppose, Mrs. Clemens, that your son in his boyhood days somewhat resembled his own 'Tom Sawyer,' and that a fellow feeling is what made him so kind to the many hair-breadth escapades of that celebrated youth!"

"Ah, no," replied the old lady with a merry twinkle in her eye, "he was more like 'Huckleberry Finn' than 'Tom Sawyer.' Often his father would start him off to school and in a little while would follow him to ascertain his whereabouts. There was a large stump on the way to the school house, and Sam would take position behind that and as his father went past would gradually circle around it in such a way as to keep out of sight. Finally his father and the teacher said it was of no use to try to teach Sam anything, because he was determined not to learn. But I never gave up. He was always a great boy for history and could never get tired of that kind of reading, but he hadn't any use for school houses and textbooks."

"It must have been a great trial to you."

"Indeed it was," rejoined his mother, "and when Sam's father died, which occurred when Sam was 11 years of age, I thought then, if ever, was the proper time to make a lasting impression on the boy and work a change in him, so I took him by the hand and went with him into the room where the coffin was and in which his father lay, and with it between Sam and me I said to him that here in his presence I had some serious requests to make of him, and I knew his word once given was never broken. For Sam never told a falsehood. He turned his streaming eyes upon me and cried out, 'Oh mother, I will do anything, anything you ask of me except go to school; I can't do that!' That was the very request I was going to make. Well, we afterward had a sober talk, and I concluded to let him go into a printing office to learn the trade as I couldn't have him running wild. He did so, and has gradually picked up enough education to enable him to do about as well as those who were more studious in early life. He was about 20 years old when he went on the Mississippi as a pilot. I gave him up then, for I always thought steamboating was a wicked business and was sure he would meet bad associates. I asked him if he would promise me on the Bible not to touch intoxicating liquors nor swear, and he said: 'Yes, mother, I will.' He repeated the words after me, with my hand and his clasped on the holy book, and I believe he always kept that promise. But Sam has a good wife now who would soon bring him back if he was inclined to stray away from the right. He obtained for his brother Henry a place on the same boat as clerk, and soon after Sam left the river Henry was blown up with the boat by an explosion and killed."

The dear old lady gave the last reminiscences in a trembling voice and with eyes filled with tears, but in a moment recovered her wonted serenity of expression and told many more incidents and entertaining stories of the then embryo humorist of which my memory is not sufficiently accurate to enable me to reliably reproduce though the general idea will always remain in my mind as an indelible photograph of Mark Twain, not as the world knows him, but as he was and is to the mother whose idol he evidently is and whose strong good sense and wise counsel in his youth undoubtedly has contributed largely to his success. Mrs. Clemens, aside from a deafness, which necessitates the use of an ear trumpet, is well-preserved and sprightly for her years.

"Mark Twain inherited the humor and talents which have made him famous from his mother," stated the younger Mrs. Clemens. "He is all 'Lampton,' and resembles her as strongly in person as in mind. Tom Sawyer's Aunt Polly and Mrs. Hawkins in *Gilded Age* are direct portraits of his mother."

Mrs. Clemens was Miss Jane Lampton before her marriage, and was a native of Kentucky. Mr. Clemens was of the F. F. V.'s of Virginia. They did not accumulate property, and the father left the family at his death nothing but, in Mark's own words, "a sumptuous stock of pride and a good old name," which, it will be allowed, has proved in this case anyway a sufficient inheritance.

Originally printed in the Chicago *Inter-Ocean*, this interview gives a good portrait of Twain's mother, a sensitive woman who nevertheless did not lack a propensity for fun; she was her son's earliest influence and he did indeed immortalize her as "Aunt Polly" in *Tom Sawyer*. Twain's views of his mother and how important she was to him are in *Autobiography* (25-31). He loved to tell one particular anecdote about his mother: When he visited her a year or so before her death, he asked if his many illnesses as an infant had caused her a great deal of anxiety. Yes, was the reply, she had worried constantly. "Afraid I wouldn't live?" Twain asked. After a long pause, his mother answered, "No, afraid you would." *Jane Clemens* remains the best source for more information about Twain's mother. In 1859 Twain had found for his brother Henry (1838-58) a berth as a clerk aboard the *Pennsylvania*, a steamboat upon which he served as an apprentice pilot. Later that year, however, Twain left the boat after quarreling with the pilot and, shortly afterward, the *Pennsylvania* exploded; Henry, with his brother by his side, died in a make-shift Memphis hospital on 21 June (*MT: Bachelor* 122-29). Ironically, Twain wrote years later in *Autobiography*, only days before the explosion, he had dreamed of seeing Henry lying in a casket in St. Louis (98-102). Henry Clemens— along with his father, mother, and brother Orion—is buried in Mt. Olivet Cemetery in Hannibal.

8 April (Wednesday)

"Men of Mark"; p. 4

Mark Twain consoles himself with the reflection that the Concord Philosophers never would have called his books "flippant, irreverent, and trashy" had he not been conspicuous in the Connecticut Mugwump ranks last fall.

16 April (Thursday)

"Men of Mark"; p. 4

Mark Twain, when a boy, hated schools with an unremitting ardor.

This fact is certainly true, as the interview with his mother clearly shows. *MT: Bachelor* sums up Twain's school years by pointing out that "school was boyhood's heaviest burden" (51-52).

20 April (Monday)

"Men of Mark"; p. 4

Mark Twain says he set type in the Philadelphia *Ledger* office more than 30 years ago.

Twain, then 19 years old, briefly worked for the *Ledger* in 1854 as he visited the cities of the East Coast; during that year he also worked in Washington D.C. and New York City before returning to St. Louis to work for the *Evening News* (*MT: Bachelor Years* 82-93).

18 May (Monday)

"Women of the World"; p. 4

Mark Twain told the Vassar College students that his usual price for a reading was $500, but that there he was quite satisfied to take 50 cents and get the other $499.50 in looking at the girls.

18 May (Monday)

"Men of Mark"; p. 4

Mark Twain and George W. Cable are said to have quarreled over a division of the spoils from their lecturing tour and dissolved partnership.

Although the two may have quarreled over the profits from their tour since Twain made so much more money from it than did Cable, their falling out was primarily due to Cable's unrelenting piety. By this time in his life, Twain was a confirmed agnostic and had little use for people who ostentatiously displayed their faith, something Cable never failed to do (*Mr. Clemens & MT* 265-67).

8 June (Monday)
"Men of Mark"; p. 4

Mark Twain's brother, Orion Clemens, is an Iowa farmer, happier, healthier and more contented than Mark.

Orion Clemens (1825-97) possessed the same desire for fame and riches that his younger brother did, but he lacked any discernible talent or luck. Consequently, after he achieved a high point in 1861 when he was named secretary to the Nevada Territory (and frequently served as its acting governor), his life was a series of disappointments. He tried his hand at being a lawyer, an inventor, a writer, an orator, a politician, and a businessman. He failed at each of these professions and had to rely upon the charity of Twain to support him and his wife from the 1870s until his death. One of his more spectacular failures was as a chicken farmer. After he moved to Keokuk, Iowa, Orion persuaded Twain to loan him $3,000 to buy a chicken farm. Although he was able to sell his chickens for $1.25 a pair, it cost him $1.60 to raise them for market. Within a year or two, Orion was bankrupt again and decided to return to his law practice, where "he was a lawyer in name only and had no clients" (*Autobiography* 218-24). A few years later, Twain told Orion that he should write the story of his life and title it *Autobiography of a Damn Fool.*

8 June (Monday)
"Men of Mark"; p. 4

Mark Twain's wealth is stated thus: From the publication of his books, $200,000, the amount of the sum being due to the fact that he has always been practically his own publisher, and thereby made all the profit for himself; lecturing, $100,000; scrapbook $50,000; wife's fortune $75,000; total, $475,000. That is about the sum he now possesses.

In 1872, Twain invented "Mark Twain's Self-Pasting Scrap-Book," which was a book with pregummed pages that could be moistened to allow clippings or photographs to be displayed (*Mr. Clemens & MT* 150). Unlike most of his other business ventures, this invention was successfully marketed and did make money.

15 July (Wednesday)
"Men of Mark"; p. 4

The statement that Mark Twain has made $200,000 out of his books staggers a Boston critic who avers that he tried to read Mark's latest volume and could make nothing of it.

Twain's "latest" volume was *Huckleberry Finn.*

17 July (Friday)
"Mark Twain as a Pensioner"; p. 4

Mark Twain has turned up in the Pension Office as an applicant for a pension, and quite naturally his application is so worded as to seriously interrupt the business of the bureau. It seems that Mr. Samuel Clements of Elma, N.Y., was an applicant for a pension on account of rheumatism, sore eyes, and some other troubles. On June 29 Commissioner Black wrote Mr. Clements that the application was rejected because it did not state a pensionable disability. It seems Senator Hawley of Connecticut had something to do with the application, and the day before Gen. Black's letter was written he wrote to Mr. Clements at Elma, N.Y., congratulating him on the allowance of his pension, thinking it had been favorably considered. Now it happens that Mark Twain, otherwise Samuel L. Clemens, is at present at Elmira, N.Y., and Hawley's postal card, as well as Black's letter, went to Samuel Clemens at Elmira, instead of Samuel Clements at Elma. The result was the following letter:

"Elmira, N. Y., July 8, 1885—

"John C. Black, esq., Commissioner:

"Dear Sir—I have not applied for a pension. I have often wanted a pension—often, ever so often I may say; but inasmuch as the only military service I performed during the war was in the Confederate army, I have always felt a delicacy about asking you for it. However, since you have suggested the thing yourself, I feel strengthened. I haven't any very pensionable diseases myself, but I can furnish a substitute, a man who is just simply a chaos, a museum of all the different kinds of aches and pains, fractures, dislocations, distempers, distortions, contusions, and malformations there are, a man who would regard 'rheumatism and sore eyes' as mere recreation and refreshment after the serious occupations of his day.

"If you grant me the pension, dear sir, please hand it to Gen. Hawley, United States Senator—I mean hand him the certificate, not the money—and he will forward it to me. You will observe by his postal card herewith enclosed that he takes a friendly interest in the matter. He thinks I've already got a pension, whereas I've only got the rheumatism, but I didn't want that; I had that before. I wish it were catching. I know a man that I would load up with it pretty early. Lord!

We all feel that way sometimes. I've seen the day when—but never mind that; you may be busy. Just hand it to Hawley—the certificate, you understand, if not transferable. Very truly yours,

"S. L. Clemens,

"Known to the police as 'Mark Twain.'"

4 August (Tuesday)
"Men of Mark"; p. 4

Mark Twain says, not altogether without truth, that "wherever Grant's body lies that is national ground."

Following Gen. Grant's death on 23 July 1885, a debate ensued about where the national hero should be buried. It was resolved finally in favor of New York City.

13 August (Thursday)
"Men of Mark"; p. 4

Mark Twain is the richest author in America.

14 August (Friday)
"Men of Mark"; p. 4

It is a notable fact that the inventor of the Gatling gun peacefully resides in the same city with Mark Twain.

Richard Jordan Gatling (1818-1903), inventor of a rudimentary machine gun in 1862, built a gun factory in Hartford.

24 August (Monday)
"Men of Mark"; p. 4

The Albany *Times* says that Mark Twain pays taxes on less than $50,000 worth of property. If he is worth a quarter of a million, as reported, how does he manage to beat the assessors?

26 August (Wednesday)
"Men of Mark"; p. 4

Mark Twain and John T. Raymond are said to be out. The actor says that he never read any of the humorist's humor, not even the book out of which the play of *Colonel Sellers* was made, and Twain retorts that he can't endure the actor's acting of that or any other character. The ill feeling arises from a question of royalties on the drama out of which both have made fortunes.

Late in his life, Twain attacked Raymond as an inept actor who stumbled upon one role that fit him. He adds in *Autobiography*, "But Raymond was great in humorous portrayal only. In that he was superb, he was wonderful . . . in all things else he was a pygmy of pygmies" (19).

26 September (Saturday)
"Women of the World"; p. 4

It is Gen. Custer's widow's written opinion that the wife of Mark Twain is young and pretty, with lustrous black eyes, and a pervading air of delicate refinement.

21 November (Saturday)
"Book Notes"; p. 9

Mark Twain has written "The Private History of a Campaign that Failed" for the December *Century*. It contains an account of his own personal experiences as a youthful "rebel" in the early days of the war. This article is said to contain nearly as much tragedy as comedy, and will be illustrated by maps drawn by the author, and some striking pictures by Kemble.

After a decade of questions about his war record, Twain wrote a long essay to explain his two-week service in the Confederate Army. At this time, the country was swept by a wave of nostalgia about the Civil War. Every month, for example, the *Century* printed a first-person account of a battle; most of these essays stressed heroism and glory, but Twain's suggests that war is brutal, confusing, and frightening. E. W. Kemble (1861-1933), one of Twain's favorite illustrators, also created the engravings for *Huckleberry Finn*.

5 December (Saturday)
"Mark Twain's Troubles"; p. 5

Samuel L. Clemens, writing in the December *Century*, says: "Out West there was a good deal of confusion in men's minds during the first months of the great trouble—a good deal of unsettledness, of leaning first this way, then that, then the other way. It was hard for us to get our bearings. I call to mind an instance of this. I was piloting on the Mississippi when the news came that South Carolina had gone out of the Union on the 20th of December 1860. My pilot-mate was a New Yorker. He was strong for the Union; so was I. But he would not listen to me with any patience; my loyalty was smirched to his eye, because my father had owned slaves. I said, in palliation of this dark fact, that I had heard my father say, some years before he died, that slavery was a great wrong, and that he would free the solitary negro he then owned if he could think it right to give away the property of the family when he was so straitened in means. My mate retorted that a mere impulse was nothing—anybody could pretend to a good impulse; and went on decrying my unionism and libeling my ancestry. A month later the secession atmosphere had considerably thickened on the Lower Mississippi, and I became a rebel; so did he. We were together in New Orleans, the 26th of January, when Louisiana went out of the union. He did his full share of the rebel shouting, but was bitterly opposed to letting me do mine. He said that I came of a bad stock—of a father who had been willing to set slaves free. In the following summer he was piloting a Federal gunboat and shouting for the Union again, and I was in the Confederate Army. I held his note for some borrowed money. He was one of the most upright men I ever knew; but he repudiated that note without hesitation, because I was a rebel, and the son of a man who owned slaves."

This article excerpts the second paragraph from "The Private History of a Campaign that Failed."

8 December (Tuesday)
"Mark Twain's Birthday: He Was 50 Years Old Last Monday"; p. 2

Mark Twain, the genial humorist, passed his semi-centennial guidepost Monday and received the congratulations of his friends. Dr. Holmes clothed his in verse as follows:

To Mark Twain on His Fiftieth Birthday
Ah, Clemens, when I saw thee last—
    We both of us were younger—
How fondly mumbling o'er the past
    Is memory's toothless hunger:
So 50 years have fled, they say,
    Since first you took to drinking—
I mean in nature's milky way—
    Of course no ill I'm thinking.
But while of life's uneven road
    Your track you've been pursuing,
What fountains from your wit have flowed—
    What drinks you have been brewing!

I know whence all your magic came—
   Your secret I've discovered—
The source that fed your inward flame—
   The dreams that round you hovered:
Before you learned to bite or munch,
   Still rocking in your cradle,
The muses mixed a bowl of punch
   And Hebe seized the ladle.
Dear, babe, whose 50th year today,
   Your ripe half-century rounded.
Your books the precious draught betray
   The laughing nine compounded.
So mixed the sweet, the sharp, the strong,
   Each finds its faults amended,
The virtues that to each belong
   In happier union blended.
And what the flavor can surpass
   Of sugar, spirit, lemons?
So while one health fills every glass
   Mark Twain for Baby Clemens!
Boston, November 23.

   Frank R. Stockton, the storyteller wrote:

   My dear Mr. Clemens: In your first half-century you have made the world laugh more than any other man. May you repeat the whole performance and "mark twain."

   Charles Dudley Warner said:

   My dear Neighbor: You may think it an easy thing to be 50 years old, but will not find it so easy to stay there, and your next 50 years will slip away much faster than those just accomplished. After all, half a century is not much, and I wouldn't throw it up to you now only for the chance of saying that few living men have crowded so much into that space as you, and few have done so much for the entertainment and good fellowship of the world. And I am glad to see that you wear your years as lightly as your more abundant honors. Having successfully turned this corner I hope that we shall continue to be near neighbors and grow young together. Ever your friend,

   Charles Dudley Warner,
Hartford, November 22.

11 December (Friday)
"Gen. Grant and Mark Twain: Two Accounts of the Same Campaign From Opposite Points of View"; p. 3

Grant: "I took my regiment to Palmyra and remained there a few days, until relieved by the 19th Illinois Infantry. From Palmyra I proceeded to Salt River, the railroad bridge over which had been destroyed by the enemy. Col. John M. Palmer at that time commanded the 13th Illinois, which was acting as a guard to workmen who were engaged in rebuilding the bridge. Palmer was my senior and commanded the two regiments as long as we remained together. The bridge was finished in about two weeks, and I received orders to move against Col. Thomas Harris, who was said to be encamped at the little town of Florida, some 25 miles south of where we then were.

"As we approached the brow of the hill from which it was expected we could see Harris's camp, and possibly find his men ready formed to meet us, my heart kept getting higher and higher until it felt to me as though it was in my throat. I would have given anything then to have been back in Illinois, but I had not the usual courage to halt and consider what to do; I kept right on. When we reached a point from which the valley below was in full view, I halted. The place where Harris had been encamped a few days before was still there, and the marks of a recent engagement were plainly visible, but the troops were gone. My heart resumed its place. It occurred to me at once that Harris had been as much afraid of me as I had been of him. This was a view of the question I had never taken before; but it was one I never forgot afterward. From that event to the close of the war I never experienced trepidation upon confronting an enemy, though I felt more or less anxiety.

Inquiries at the village of Florida divulged the fact that Col. Harris, learning of my intended movement, while my transportation was being collected, took time by the forelock and left Florida before I had started from Salt River. He had increased the distance between us by 40 miles. The next day I started back to my old camp at Salt River.

* * *

Twain: "The rest of my war experiences was of a piece with which I have already told of it. We kept monotonously falling back upon one camp or another, and eating up the country. . . . The last camp we fell back upon was in a hollow near the village of Florida, where I was born—in Monroe County. Here we were warned one day that a Union colonel was sweeping down on us with a whole regiment at his heels. This looked decidedly serious. Our boys went apart and consulted; then we went back and told the other companies present that the war was a disappointment to us and we were going to disband. They were getting ready themselves to fall back on some place or other and were only waiting for Gen. Tom Harris, who was expected to arrive at any moment; so they tried to persuade us to wait a little while, but the majority of us said no, we were accustomed to falling back, and didn't need any of Tom Harris's help; we could get along perfectly well without him, and save time, too. So about half of our 15, including myself, mounted and left on the instant. An hour later we met Gen. Harris on the road. . . . Harris ordered us back, but we told him there was a Union colonel coming with a whole regiment in his wake, and it looked as if there was going to be a disturbance, so we had concluded to go home. . . . In time I came to know that Union colonel whose coming frightened us out of the war and crippled the Southern cause to that extent—General Grant. I came within a few hours of seeing him when he was as unknown as myself.

The paragraphs from Gen. Grant are excerpted from his memoirs, published by Twain's company in December 1885; the memoirs were an immense success and made a great deal of money for Twain and Grant's family (Grant died shortly before the book was published). The paragraph from Twain is an excerpt from "The Private History of a Campaign that Failed."

19 January (Tuesday)
"Tales of Type: Mark Twain's Speech at the Dinner of the Typothetic Society"; p. 1

New York, Jan. 19—

At the dinner of the Typothetic Society at Delmonico's last night a large number of old printers and publishers attended. Mark Twain, after a complimentary speech of J. H. Bailey, said: "I am staggered by the compliments so lavishly poured out upon me, and I am proud, as well as staggered. It is the first time that anyone has stood up in the presence of a large and respectable audience, such as this is, and confessed that I have told the truth once. If I could return the compliments, I'd do it. The historical reminiscences of the president have cast me into a reminiscent mood, for I also, in my small way, am an antiquity. It may be that I am among strangers, and that the printer of today is not the printer of 35 years ago. I knew him. I lit his fires. I dusted his office and drew his water from the village pump. I picked the type from under his stand in the mornings, and if he was there to see, I put the good type back in the case and the bad ones in the hellbox; and if he was not there, I dumped the lot with the 'pi.' I used to carry around the papers, and was the enduring target of all the dogs in the village. I wish I had a nickel for every dog bite I have got on me. I could keep M. Pasteur in business for a year. The subscribers for our paper paid in groceries, and the country ones paid in cabbages or cordwood. That was, when they did. When they did, we always mentioned it in the paper and gave them a puff. If we failed to do this, they stopped their paper. They all directed the policy of the paper. One man paid in cash, and he owned us body and soul. He changed our politics every which way, and changed our religion four times. If we attempted to reason, he threatened to stop his paper and that closed the discussion. We used to take out the telegraphic items and lay them on a galley. Then we'd change the dates and shove them in the paper day after day, until public interest in them was worn to the bone. I have seen a t.d. advertisement of a sheriff's sale booming along serenely two years after the sale had taken place. Our early ads were patent medicine electrotype and we used to fence with them when the column rules were worn out. When we pied a form we suspended until next week. We always suspended when fishing was good. The editor was a poet. When his intellects suppurated and discharged a poem, he would read it to the printers and ask them what they thought of it. They always scraped their rulers on their boxes while he was reading and when he was done they always said it was hogwash. They were a very frank and candid people. I can look back now and see that old office with its candle in the 'k' box. But perhaps I sing the glories of a forgotten age to unfamiliar ears and I will stop."

Twain delivered this speech about his experiences as a printer's devil at the Typothetae Dinner in New York City on 18 January. Early in 1850, three years after his father's death, the 14-year-old Twain was apprenticed to Joseph Ament, owner of the Hannibal *Courier* (*MT: Bachelor* 67). By his own account, Twain and the other apprentices made up for their lack of wages and poor clothing by doing as little work as possible, while still having fun (*Autobiography* 87-91). Of the jargon in the speech, the "hellbox" was where broken type was placed to be melted and recast, while "pi" refers to a box of random or mixed type; a "t.d." advertisement was an ad intended to run only for a short, specified time, such as for one week or during the Christmas season. Four years before this speech, Louis Pasteur (1822-95) had begun his well-publicized search for a vaccination to cure rabies. It was rare, indeed, for the *Post-Dispatch* to go a week without reporting an outbreak of hydrophobia somewhere in the United States. About this time in his life, Twain became more involved with a new invention that could set type by machine, thus saving a newspaper a great deal of labor and money. He began his investment into the Paige Typesetter with a modest $5,000 in 1880, but within six years he had sunk between $20,000 and $30,000 a year into the company. The machine's 18,000 parts, however, rarely moved in unison and the company's failure, along with some other bad investments, led to Twain's bankruptcy in 1894 (*Mr. Clemens & MT* 282-88).

28 January (Thursday)
"The Copyright Discussion"; p. 7
    Washington, D. C., Jan. 28—
       The Senate Patent Committee this morning listened to argument on the subject of international copyright. The committee-room was quite full, a number of ladies being present. Senator Pratt sat at the head of a long table, while at the other end sat Samuel Clemens (Mark Twain). The humorist was dressed in a rough suit of gray-mixed goods, the vest cut low and the ends of a stiff black tie hanging down the white shirt front. As the hearing proceeded he rested his elbows on the table, his head and whole upper half of his body moving uneasily. Occasionally he ventured into the discussion, but his delivery in speaking is slow and at times almost painful, and he made only one attempt to redeem his reputation as a humorist. Henry Holt of New York, on behalf of the book publishers; Rev. Howard Crosby and George W. Curtis, on behalf of the authors, and Horace E. Scudder of Cambridge, as representing in part both interests, made long arguments. Mr. Holt said that the standard of American literature had been greatly lower by the publication of 10- and 20-cent books. In order to keep up the periodical publication of these works, skin publishers found it necessary to print all kinds of trash, while reputable publishers could not afford to put out works really worthy of publication. Senator Hawley appeared before the committee to urge the introduction in the bill of a clause "For the protection of American printers." Mr. Clemens favored Mr. Hawley's idea, while Mr. Sedgwick opposed it. The Connecticut Senator resented rather sharply the use of Mr. Sedgwick of the term "pirates" applied to cheap book publishers. In the absence of Hon. James Russell Lowell, the hearing was adjourned to tomorrow. Among those present today were A. G. Sedgwick; Howard Crosby; E. C. Stedman; J. B. Gelder; Geo. Walton; Green; the executive committee of the American copyright league; S. L. Clemens; Richard Watson; Geider, editor of the *Century*; and other well-known writers.

6 February (Saturday)
"Men of Mark"; p. 5
       Mark Twain says he has received $52,000 as his profits on his latest book, *Huckleberry Finn*.

10 February (Wednesday)
"A Remarkable Case: Mr. Brewer's Suit Against a Bark for Being Bitten by a Hog"; p. 7

New Orleans, Feb. 10—

A most remarkable suit for damages has been instituted in the United States district court in this city. David G. Brewer of this city libels the bark *Mark Twain*, now lying at this port, alleging that on February 2 he went aboard said bark to visit the second mate. He stepped on board in company with the first mate and proceeded to the carpenter shop, where they remained in conversation for some time. The libelant, on returning ashore, was thrown down by a large and powerful hog, which tore his clothing and terribly lacerated him, the hog belonging to said bark. He claims to be irretrievably injured and demands such damages as the court may award. Admiralty process was ordered to issue.

If he knew of this lawsuit, Twain surely found it hilarious.

11 February (Thursday)
"Men of Mark"; p. 4

Mark Twain in Washington and in his favorite pepper and salt gray suit, with the gray streaking his long and bushy hair, is described as looking like "an unkept miller with a sprinkling of flour on his head."

13 February (Saturday)
no headline; p. 4

Mark Twain wears "a suit of pepper and salt." It might be prudent to perspire freely in such a suit.

23 February (Tuesday)
"Mark Twain's Queer War Record"; p. 4

Some of the Eastern literary papers seem to have just discovered that Mark Twain (Samuel L. Clemens) was a rebel bushwacker in the early part of the late war. The fact was published in Virginia, Nev., in 1864, during the hottest period of the war. And worse—the rival journal that published the fact went further and intimated in language not be to mistaken that Mark had violated his parole and was then a fit subject for a target for a detail of Union soldiers.

Lieut. Clemens, having been a pilot on the Mississippi

River, and therefore knowing the channel and being familiar with the points where steamboats would have to hug the shore, was detailed for the special duty of firing into the Federal transports plying that stream, and he performed that duty effectively. He was captured and paroled. While under parole, the account stated, he went ahead firing into Union boats. He was captured a second time, but by a different command, none of whom knew he was under parole, or he would have been shot on the spot. He was sent to St. Louis and imprisoned in a tobacco warehouse on Wash Street. He got to thinking the matter over—the probability of being sent to Grant's army, by which he was first captured, to be exchanged, and by which, if recognized, he would certainly be shot for a violation of his parole—and he skipped across the plains to the Territory of Nevada, of which his brother, Orion Clemens, was then secretary by appointment from President Lincoln. Fearing the influence of his brother would not be sufficient to save him if he should be recognized by passing officers or soldiers of the Union Army, he did not remain long in Carson City, but pushed on to the out-of-the-way mining camp of Aurora, where he remained until he fancied the storm had blown over.

When in Aurora he wrote a series of letters to the Virginia *Enterprise*, and subsequently accepted a place on the editorial staff of that journal. His sharp pen put a man named Willis, city editor of the Virginia *Union*, to hunting up his record, and the publication of the foregoing facts was the result. For this, Mark Twain sent Willis a challenge to mortal combat. The challenge was sent by Mark's "game" little friend, Steve Gillis. Willis would not accept—he would not meet anyone on the field of honor except a man of honor. This offended Gillis highly, and he challenged Willis. Willis would not accept, because he had no cause of quarrel with Gillis, but his "best man" then came in and challenged Mark Twain, who declined on the same ground given by Willis for not meeting Gillis. The three challenges all passed the same day—within a few hours, in fact—and as dueling had just been made popular by the Dog Valley meeting of Tom Fitch, "the silver-tongued" orator, and Joseph T. Goodman, the poetical editor-in-chief of the *Enterprise*, it looked as though Six-Mile Canyon was to be deluged with blood. But the matter was dropped, and Mark Twain was never called upon by drumhead court-martial to stand up and take the regulation dose of leaden pills.

This article by an anonymous writer was originally printed in the Nogales (Calif.) *Frontier*. The paragraphs about Twain being a bushwacker are certainly a libel as there is no evidence to support such a claim; the incidents related in the third paragraph are certainly just as false as those in the first two. While he was in Nevada, Twain's sharp pen offended quite a few people, including many journalists on competing newspapers. The Virginia City *Daily Union*, edited by Tom Fitch, became a particular target for Twain, who wrote for the *Territorial Enterprise*. (Fitch and Goodman had indeed fought a duel in 1863, with the result of Fitch being shot in the leg.) It is likely that the above account of Twain's service record was invented by a reporter on the *Union* who had wanted to insult Twain.

13 March (Saturday)
"The 10 Greatest Books"; p. 11

In early March the *Post-Dispatch* asked its readers to select the 10 greatest books of the 19th century, with a cash prize to be awarded to the "best" list. Over the next two weeks, the newspaper received nearly 2,000 entries. Of the first 237 lists, Mark Twain's *The Innocents Abroad* was picked four times by readers; none of his other works were selected. Various novels by Charles Dickens, George Eliot, and Victor Hugo were much more popular than Twain's.

29 April (Thursday)
"Mark Twain's Business Joke"; p. 4

> I learn from Mr. Clemens—Mark Twain—that he can manufacture each single volume of Gen. Grant's memoirs for about 45 cents. As the book is sold at $3.50, you can estimate the great profit derived from it. The profit is divided between Mrs. Grant, the agents, and the firm of Webster & Co. Mr. Clemens has, by long odds, the largest interest in that firm.

Twain had originally intended to publish his own works only, but because he believed the ex-president was being swindled by unscrupulous publishing houses, he offered early in 1885 to publish Grant's memoirs to ensure that his family would never lack money (*Autobiography* 236-41). Grant signed the contract with C. L. Webster & Co. on 28 February 1885 and, with Twain's help in editing and proofreading, was able to complete his memoirs by mid-July. He died of throat cancer on 23 July, but his memoirs—published in two volumes on 1 December 1885 and 10 May 1886—were immediate best-sellers. His family made approximately $450,000 from their sale, while Twain's profits amounted to $100,000.

29 May (Saturday)
"Men of Mark"; p. 4

Mark Twain professes to be better satisfied with his success as a publisher than with his reputation as a writer.

19 June (Saturday)
"Sharp Mark Twain"; p. 9

Mark Twain is a humorist, as everybody knows. But everybody does not know what a clever, sagacious, hard-headed man of business he is. He will soon be one of the richest publishers in America, and he seldom makes a blunder in trade. It may be taken for granted, therefore, that when he gave Mr. Daniel Frohman $1,000 not to produce his new play, *The American Claimant* (written in collaboration with Mr. Howells), he displayed extraordinary forethought. He came to the conclusion that, since he could not stand the play, the public would not be likely to stand it.

The play, originally entitled *Colonel Sellers as a Scientist*, was actually withdrawn in 1884 at the request of W. D. Howells. Twain subsequently rewrote the play and produced it himself in 1887. It failed, as the *Post-Dispatch* noted on 24 September 1887. Daniel Frohman (1851-1940) managed the Lyceum Theatre, one of the most prominent houses in New York City.

5 July (Monday)
"Men of Mark"; p. 4

Mark Twain is visiting his mother at Keokuk, Iowa.

Jane Clemens lived with Twain's older brother and his wife in that city. On 7 April 1885 the *Post-Dispatch* reprinted an interview with her.

8 July (Thursday)
"Men of Mark"; p. 4

Mr. Clemens reached Minneapolis just in time to escape a collusion with that other great humorist, Sam Jones.

Like many other newspapers, the *Post-Dispatch* regarded the Rev. Sam Jones (1849-1906), a prominant revivalist in the Midwest, as a charlatan because of his bombastic sermons.

24 July (Saturday)
"Mark Twain and His Roommate's Boots"; p. 11

Mark Twain and Dan De Quille roomed together in early Comstock days. One morning Dan missed his boots, and after a vain search he suspiciously inquired of Mark, who was lying in bed lazily smoking a clay pipe: "Mark, I can't find my boots; do you know anything about 'em?"

"Your boots?" complacently replied Mark. "Well, yes; I threw them at that blasted cat that was yowling around the house last night!"

"Threw my boots at the cat?" howled Dan, in a rage. "Why in h--- didn't you throw your own boots?"

"Dan," said Mark, after a reflective puff or two, "Dan, if there is anything I hate it is a selfish man. I have observed of late that you are getting selfish. What difference does it make whose boots were thrown at the cat?"

Attributed to the San Francisco *Post*, this anecdote might very well be true.

7 August (Saturday)
"Men of Mark"; p. 4

Mark Twain is a baseball enthusiast and contributes liberally to the support of the local nine in Hartford, Conn.

14 August (Saturday)
"Doctor, Plumber, Twain"; p. 3

By the way, I must tell you a story of a contretemps which proved a rather serious joke to that arch jester, Mark Twain. It has never been put into print I think, but comes from the best authority to me. Everyone has heard of that house on Farmington Avenue in Hartford, which is so peculiar and picturesque that tourists go to see it aside from the interest attaching to the home of an American author. It is called a combination of Mark Twain and Queen Anne architecture, and is a most attractive and comfortable domicile. Some years ago, when Mr. Clemens was absent for several months from home, Mrs. Clemens, who is a lady of quiet tastes and a devoted mother, thought that she perceived that her little girls were ailing. Filled with quick alarm she sent for the family physician, who, a prominent practitioner, had a large-sized bee in his bonnet which was named "sewer gas." He told the lady that her darlings were doubtless suffering from malarial troubles induced by imperfect drainage, and that the plumbing of the house was probably defective or out of repair. She was much alarmed and in a sad quandary in her husband's absence, the more so as she knew he had taken great pains to secure perfect sanitation in the household arrangements. Sending for a plumber, of course the rival of the man who had put in the pipes, she asked him to make an examination. The good man was horror-stricken at the condition in which he found things. He condemned the whole system and was given the contract to tear out and replace the plumbing and make secure the safety of the inmates of the house. Of course the expense was enormous, but the doctor said it was justifiable, and the plumber was righteously indignant at the man who originally did the job. About the time the change was completed Clemens arrived home and the wife flew to his arms with an account of their narrow escape from illness, and perhaps death. It was then that the funny man arose in his wrath, and the manner in which he cursed sewer gas, doctor, and plumber was said to have been an education in the comprehensive possibilities of the English language. The fact was that in order to avoid possible danger he had made his house drain into the river that passes below his grounds. The pipes were not connected with any sewer, and the really fine work of the best plumber in town had been torn out and far poorer work put in to ease the fond fears of a loving mother, carry out the whims of a too scientific physician, and add some $1,500 to the pile of a rapacious plumber.

Attributed to the Hartford correspondent of the Boston *Saturday Globe*, the details of this anecdote were probably supplied by Twain himself, who certainly would have been the "best authority" in the matter.

18 August (Wednesday)
no headline; p. 4

Mark Twain was defeated in his legal attempt to restrain John Wanamaker from selling Grant's memoirs at a reduced price. It is thought that this will cast a gloom over Mark's next joke.

John Wanamaker (1838-1922), a prominent Philadelphia merchant who Twain describes as an "unco-pious butter-mouthed Sunday school-slobbering thief," aroused the humorist's ire by discounting

Grant's memoirs in his store, thus allegedly cutting into its royalty payments (qtd. in *Mr. Clemens & MT* 273). Judge Butler of the U. S. Circuit Court decided that Wanamaker had legally purchased the books from agents hired by Twain's company and, consequently, could sell them as he chose.

28 August (Saturday)
"Literary Aliases"; p. 11

In this long article, a reporter gives the pseudonyms of various authors and tries to explain why they felt the need to disguise their true identities. He has one sentence about Twain, but does not explain the significance of his nom de plume:

> Apropos few people who know of "Mark Twain" are not aware that his name is Samuel L. Clemens; but few know that the L. stands for Langhorne.

31 August (Tuesday)
no headline; p. 4

The Grant memoirs continue to have a phenomenal sale despite the fact that they are published by an ex-Confederate soldier.

See 29 April for details about Twain's publishing of Grant's memoirs.

7 October (Thursday)
"Women of the World"; p. 4

Mark Twain's mother says of him: "He was always a good boy, Samuel was, though prone to be mischievous. He's always been the same to me—the best son a mother ever had."

27 October (Wednesday)
"Men of Mark"; p. 4

Mark Twain and Bret Harte began their literary careers as book canvassers.

Actually, both men got their starts as newspaper reporters—Twain in Nevada and Harte in California.

12 November (Friday)
"Mark Twain's Latest: The Autobiography of Sir Robert Smith of Camelot"; p. 5

New York, Nov. 12—

Last night's monthly meeting of the Military Service Institution on Governor's Island was made entertaining by Mark

Twain who read a paper, the announcement of which caused
the thronging of the old Museum Hall. Gen. W. T. Sherman
and Gen. Schofield were present. Gen. James B. Fry presided.
Mr. Clemens said that what he was about to read was part of a
still uncompleted book, of which he would give the first
chapter by way of explanation and follow it with selected
fragments, "or outline the rest of it in bulk, so to speak; do as
the dying cowboy admonished his spiritual adviser to do:
'Just leave out the details and heave in the bottom facts.'"
Mr. Clemens's story is the autobiography of Sir Robert Smith
of Camelot, one of King Arthur's knights, formerly a manufacturer of Hartford, Conn. Robert Smith says of himself: "I
am a Yankee of the Yankees, a practical man, nearly barren of
sentiment or poetry; in other words my father was a blacksmith, my uncle was a horse-doctor, and I was both. Then I
went over to the Great Arms factory and learned my real
trade—learned to make everything, guns, revolvers, can-
nons, boilers, engines, electric machines, anything in short
that anybody wanted anywhere in this world. * * * I became
head boss and had a thousand men under me. Well, a man
like that is full of fight, that goes without saying. With a
thousand rough men under one, one has plenty of that sort
of amusement. Well, at last I met my match; I got my dose.
It was during a misunderstanding conducted with iron crow-
bars with a fellow we used to call Hercules. He laid me out
with a crusher alongside the head that made everything crack
and seemed to make every joint of my skull lap over on its
neighbor and then the world went out in darkness and I felt
nothing more for a while, and when I came to again I was
standing under a naked tree on the grass with a beautiful
country, a landscape spread out before me—all to myself. No,
not quite, not entirely to myself. There was a fellow on a
horse looking down at me—a fellow fresh out of picture
book. He was in old-time armor from his head to his heel.
He had a helmet on like a cheese box, with slits in it and he
carried a shield and a sword. And his horse had armor on,
too, and gorgeous silken trapping that hung around him like
a bed-gown to the ground. And this apparition said to me:
'Fair sir, will you joust?' Said I: 'Will I which?' 'Will you
joust? Will you break a lance for land or lady?'

    "Said I: 'What are you giving me? You go along back to
your circus or I'll report you.' Now what does that fellow do

but fall back a couple of hundred yards and then came tilting at me as hard as he could drive, his long spear pointed straight at me. I saw he meant business, so I was up the tree when he arrived. Well, he allowed I was his property; the captive of his spear. Well, there was argument on his side, and the bulk of the advantage, so I judged it best to humor him and we fixed up an agreement. I was to go along with him and he was not to hurt me. So I came down and we started away, I walking by the side of his horse. It puzzled me ever so much that we did not come to any circus or any sign of one, so I gave up the idea of a circus and concluded that he was from an asylum, so I was up a stump as you may say."

And so the two wandered on together, and amid signs of human life that afford the author many opportunities for quaint philosophic contrasts and dry humor until they came to Camelot, to the court of King Arthur. Fanciful and curious are the reflections of the transposed Yankee about that place—which he at first thinks must be an asylum. In its country of soft, reposeful summer landscape as lovely as a dream and as lonesome as Sunday; where the air was full of the smell of flowers and the twittering of birds, and there were no people, or wagons, or life, or anything going on. Very vividly he portrays the scene at Camelot where King Arthur with his knights sit at a round table as big as a circus ring, and 300 dogs howling for bones around them, while the musicians are in one gallery high aloft and the ladies in another. But before he gets in there he seeks information from a plain-looking man in the outer court, saying to him:

"'Now, my friend, do me a kindness. Tell me, do you belong to the asylum, or are you just here on a visit or something like that?' And he looked me over and said:

"'Marry, fair sir.'

"'Oh,' I said, 'that will do. I guess you are a patient.'

"To another he said: 'Now, my friend, if I could see the head keeper just a minute, only a minute.'

"He said: 'Prithee do not let me.'

"'Let you what?'

"'Do not hinder me, if the word please thee better,' and he was an undercock and had no time to talk, though he would like to any time for it would just comfort his very liver to know where I got my clothes.

"Then another, a lad, came along to him saying that he

was a page. 'Oh, go 'long,' I said, 'you ain't more than a paragraph.' The page happened to mention that he was born in
the beginning of the year 513. It made the cold chills creep
over me. I stopped and said a little faintly, 'Now, maybe I did
not hear you just right. Would you say that again, and say it
slow. What year did you say it is?'

"'513.'

"'And according to your notions, according to your lights
and superstitions, what year is it now?'

"'Why,' he said, 'the year 528, the 19th of June.' Well, I
felt a mournful sinking of the heart and muttered: 'I shall
never see my friends again; never see my friends any more;
they won't be born for as much as a thousand years.

The speaker had often been interrupted by laughter, but at
the originality and fun of that conceit his auditors laughed
until they cried.

How the cute Yankee determined to get at the bottom facts
about the year, by watching for a total eclipse of the sun that
he remembered the almanac of 1884 had spoken of as having
occurred in 528, will have to be learned from the book when
it appears.

"Well, I made up my mind to two things. If it was still in
the 19th century and I was among lunatics I would boss that
asylum or know the reason, and if on the other hand it was
really the sixth century all right, I did not want any better
thing. I would boss the whole country inside of three
months for I judged I'd have a start on the best educated man
by 1,300 years. * * *

"But I'm not a man to waste time, so I said to the boy:
'Clarence, if your name should happen to be Clarence, what's
the name of this duck, that galoot who brought me here?'"
The galoot turned out to be Sir Kay, the Senescal. In the natural course of the story came the charming descriptions of the
king's castle leading up to a royally funny account of the
competitive lying of the gallant knights about their feats at
arms. The transposed Smith looked upon the knights as a
sort of white Indians, admired their bigness and simplicity
and eventually concluded: There did not seem to be brains
enough in the entire nursery to bait a fishhook. But you did-
n't mind that after a little while, for you saw that brains were
not needed in a society like that and would have marred its
symmetry and spoiled it. Everybody goes to sleep when Mer-

lin reels off that same old story about Excalibur. Guinevere makes eyes at Launcelot in a way that would have got him shot in Arkansas. King Arthur orders the Yankee to go to some unknown place not down on any map, capture a castle, kill the colossal saucer-eyed ogre who owned it, and release 60 royal princesses. Of course he went, but reflected: "Well, of all the d--d contracts, this is the boss. I offered to sublet it to Sir Lancelot, to let him have it at 90 days, with no margin but 'No' he had got a better thing. He was going to a menagerie of one-eyed giants and a cottage of princesses." It occurs to him finally, after wondering if a compromise with the ogre would not work, simply to go back and tell the King that he had killed the ogre. He does so, and, of course, the King and his knights, who are used to swallowing each other's huge lies, readily take in his, and a brilliant career opens before him as the boss liar of the Court.

He took a contract from the King to kill off at one of the great tournaments 15 kings and many acres of hostile armoured knights. When, lance in rest, they charged by squadrons upon him, he, behind the protection of a barbed wire fence charged with electricity, mowed them down with Gatling guns that he had made for the occasion. He found that the "education of the 19th century is plenty enough capital to go into business in the sixth century with." And the next year he was running the kingdom all by himself on a moderate royalty of 40 percent. He spoiled the ogre business, cleared out the fuss and flummery of romance, and put King Arthur's kingdom on a strictly business basis. Inside of three years the improvement was complete. Cast iron clothes had gone out of fashion, Sir Launcelot was running a kind of Louisiana lottery. The search for the Holy Grail had been given up for the Northwest passage. King Arthur's 140 illustrious knights had turned themselves into a stock board, and a seat at the round table was worth $30,000.

This account of Twain's reading was relayed to the *Post-Dispatch* by its New York correspondent. Twain's new novel, which he had been working on for only a month or so when he delivered this reading of an early draft, would eventually become *A Connecticut Yankee in King Arthur's Court*. He made many revisions in his drafts, however, including changing his hero's name to "Hank Morgan." The finished novel was published 10 December 1889.

15 November (Monday)
"Men of Mark"; p. 4

Mark Twain is getting old very fast, but he does not like to be told of it. His hair is nearly white, but Mark persists that this was caused by sitting in damp churches out in California.

16 November (Tuesday)
"Men of Mark"; p. 4

Mark Twain is said to be worth $1,200,000.

This estimate of Twain's worth is exaggerated. Although he lived like a millionaire, in actuality he had little money saved. Reports like this one, however, help to explain why his financial troubles in the next decade so shocked the public.

7 December (Tuesday)
"Men of Mark"; p. 4

Mark Twain is now said to be worth something like a million and a half.

23 December (Thursday)
"Men of Mark"; p. 4

Mark Twain has recently been elected reader to a Browning Club at Hartford, and he says he is practicing on some of the easy pieces of the obscure poem.

The club began with just a few female members in the mid-1880s, but Twain's readings of Robert Browning—especially of *The Ring and the Book*—proved to be so popular that it grew until it regularly filled a room in the Twain mansion (*Nook Farm* 104-05).

24 December (Friday)
"Women of the World"; p. 4

Mark Twain said to a friend the other day that he did not like to come to New York with his wife. "She is very anxious to have everyone think she dresses like a New Yorker," he said, "and yet whenever she buys anything in a store in this city the clerk is sure to ask, 'What hotel shall I send this to, ma'am?'"

24 December (Friday)
"Men of Mark"; p. 4

Mark Twain is considering a proposition from one of the magazines to conduct a humorous department.

5 January (Wednesday)
"People of Note"; p. 4

The widely circulated item to the effect that Mark Twain is worth $1,500,000 is not true. Mr. Clemens is a wealthy man, but his fortune does not nearly reach that figure.

6 January (Thursday)
"Mark Twain's Lost Idea"; p. 2

Mark Twain says that the funniest thing he ever wrote came to an untimely end and was lost entirely to the world. It was in his early Western days when he was reporter on the *Chronicle* of Virginia City, Nev. In those days, when the saloon was the social center of the town, and the opening of each new one a matter of general interest, it was the custom of the proprietor of a new venture in liquid refreshments to send a basket of his choicest wares to the newspaper office, and for the editor to return the compliment by giving a glowing account of the opening. One day a basket of unusually choice wines from a saloon that was to be of an unusually aristocratic order inspired Mark with a brilliant idea. He wrote a few lines in straight good English, but the next began to be pretty badly mixed, and as he represented one bottle after another as having been sampled, approved and emptied, he drifted on into worse and worse confusion, until he finally brought up in such an inextricable tangle of incoherency, such as might be supposed to possess the brain of a man who had drank a basket of mixed wine. But when the paper came out he searched it over and over in vain for his cherished article. It was not there. But he did find a brief paragraph setting forth in the most commonplace, conventional way imaginable the fact that a basket of wines had been received from Mr. ---, that they were very fine, and that "we bespeak for him the liberal patronage that he deserves." With fire in his eye and profanity on his lips Mark started on an investigation, and soon settled the blame on the head of one of the printers.

"Why," said the fellow, "I couldn't make head nor tail out of the copy, and I concluded Mr. Clemens must have been pretty full when he wrote it. I heard the editor say last week that if he got drunk again he'd discharge him, and I thought if that stuff got into the paper he'd have to go sure. So I tore it up and wrote this myself. Just thought I'd save his place for him if I could."

Before this honest friend, whose zeal for his welfare had not left a piece of his prized article as big as a nickle, Mark could say no more. But he could not reproduce it. It had been the swift and brilliant inspiration of the moment, and was completely gone. But he mourned long over the fate of what he always believed his most brilliant production.

Originally printed in the Pittsburgh *Dispatch*, this anecdote is probably true since Twain's drinking while in Nevada was prodigious. During one binge, for example, Twain, Artemus Ward, and Dan De Quille— hopping from one frost-covered roof to another—went for a moonlit stroll across the top of Virginia City (*MT: Bachelor* 218-19).

20 January (Thursday)
"Men of Mark"; p. 4

Mark Twain said recently, when asked whether it was true that he proposed to start a newspaper in Hartford: "Heavens, no! I shall never start a newspaper so long as I can buy three for less than it costs to have my boots blackened."

11 February (Friday)
"Twain Tickled 'Em: The Humorist Entertains the New York Stationers' Board of Trade"; p. 8

The 12th annual dinner of the Stationers' Board of Trade was given last evening at the Hotel Brunswick. There were about 150 persons present. The feature of the entertainment which followed the dinner was the speech of Mark Twain. Mark Twain said:

"Gents—I find this an evening of surprises. I came here through an understanding with the chairman that I was not to break over pledges made and drift into an after-dinner speech, unless I saw immoralities or crimes being committed, and lo, I have waited in constant expectation that something would be said or done that would compel me to speak. But concerning what has been said and done here, I am bound to say that thus far there have been mere misdemeanors. I have been introduced to you as an example of the author and publisher. I am one of the latest publishers, and I am one of the oldest authors and certainly one of the best. (Laughter.) When I came here I expected to remain in some humble capacity outside of the door and never dreamt of being made conspicuous by taking a high seat among the distinguished guests. But then I am used to being made conspicuous. (More laughter.) As I say, I have found really nothing to attack. I expected Mr. Breman to commit himself—lawyers are always committing themselves—But Mr. Breman was—the fact is that his speech can actually be complimented. (Laughter.) As to his attacking Ben, that is to say Ben Franklin, an old, dead man, that can be explained. Franklin was sober because he lived in Philadelphia. Why, Philadelphia is a sober city today. What must it have been in Franklin's time? (Great laughter.) Why, it is as good as Sunday to be in Philadelphia now. (More laughter.) Franklin was frugal, and he says himself he had no vices, because, though he little suspected it, he made a vice of frugality. You saw this. Mr. Breman told you how he did, but when he mentions why he did it he gives himself away, and finally he wishes that at the last he may be shoved into a barrel of Madeira, but if he had lived here instead of in Philadelphia, he would have wanted to get the barrel of Madeira into him. (Roars of laughter.) I am here in the character of author and publisher, but I think I will let that rest." (Renewed laughter.)

Referring to a previous remark of the chairman of the board who was about to establish a legal department, Mr. Twain said: "You want a chaplain more than you want a lawyer." As to his capacity as a publisher, he said: "Oh, I can tell you a great deal about publishing, but I don't think I will. I am rather too fresh yet. I am at the honest stage now, but after a while, when I graduate and grow rich, I will tell you about it." (Continued laughter.)

Turning his attention to education, he said: "It is so common that an education is within the grasp of everyone, and if he does not want to pay for it, why here is the state ready to pay for it for him. But sometimes I want to inquire what an education is. I remember myself that when I went to school I was told than an adjective is an adverb and it must be governed by the third person singular, and all that sort of thing. (Laughter). And when I got out of school I straightaway forgot all about it. (More laughter.) In my combined character of publisher and author, I receive a great many manuscripts from people who say they want a candid opinion whether that is good literature or not. That is all a lie. What they want is a compliment. But as to this matter of education, the first that strikes you is how much teaching has really been done and how much is worthless cramming. You have all seen a little book called *English as She is Spoke*. Now, in my capacity as publisher, I recently received a manuscript from a teacher which embodied a number of answers given by her pupils to questions propounded. These answers show that the children had nothing but the sound to go by; the sense was perfectly empty. Here are some of their answers to words they were asked to define:

"'Auriferous—Pertaining to an orifice.' (Laughter.)

"'Ammonia—A food of the gods.' (Renewed laughter.)

"'Equestrian—One who asked questions.'

"'Parasite—A kind of umbrella.' (Roars of laughter.)

"'Ipecac—A man who likes a good dinner.' (Shouts of laughter.)

"'And here is the definition of an ancient word honored by a great party: 'Republican—A sinner mentioned in the Bible.' (Shouts of laughter.)

"And here is an innocent deliverance of a zoological kind: 'There are a good many donkeys in the theological gardens.'

"Here also is a definition which really is not very bad in its way: 'Demagogue—a vessel containing beer and other liquids.' (Prolonged laughter.)

"Here, too, is a sample of a boy's composition on girls, which I must say I rather like:

"'Girls are very stuck-up and dignified in their maner and behavyour. They think more of dress than anything and like to play with dowls and rags. They cry if they see a cow in the far distance and are afraid of guns. They stay at home all the time and go to church every sunday. They are al-ways sick. They are al-ways funy and making fun of boys hands and they say how dirty. They cant play marbles. I pity them poor things. They make fun of boys and then turn round and love them. I don't belave they ever killed a cat or anything. They look out every nite and say, 'Oh, ant the moon lovely.' Thir is one ting I have not told and that is they al-ways now their lessons bettern boys.'"

"Mr. Breman" is a misprint for Charles Cotesworth Beaman (1840-1900), a prominent New York City lawyer. Twain accepted for publication the book of cute juvenile expressions, which he later published as *English as She is Taught*. Parts of it were incorporated into an essay under the same title; it is reprinted in *Complete Essays* (36-47).

16 February (Wednesday)
"Men of Mark"; p. 4
Mark Twain is said to have a $1,000,000 safely invested in such a way that he can't be taxed a red cent on it, and his wife can't marry again if he dies and enjoy a dollar of it.

17 March (Thursday)
"Men of Mark"; p. 4
Mark Twain is, it is said, in Germany the most popular of all American writers.

21 March (Monday)
"Men of Mark"; p. 4
Mark Twain talks of endowing a home for pumped-out humorists.

22 March (Tuesday)
"Men of Mark"; p. 4
Mark Twain is said to be thoroughly agnostic in his religious views. He, however, attends church regularly, being fond of the eloquent sermons of his friend, Dr. Twichell.

Twain enjoyed Twichell's services at the Asylum Hill Congregational Church even though he had indeed become agnostic in his beliefs.

29 March (Tuesday)
"As to the Innocents at Home"; p. 4
Mark Twain talks of endowing a home for pumped-out humorists, and there are those who believe that Twain ought to be given a front room in it.

1 April (Friday)
"Telegraphic Brevities"; p. 8

There were readings at Boston yesterday by prominent authors for the benefit of the Longfellow memorial. Those who participated were Mark Twain, Oliver Wendell Holmes, Julia Ward Howe, Edward Everett Hale, George William Curtis, T. B. Aldrich, W. D. Howells, Cal Higginson, and James Russell Lowell. About $10,000 was realized by the entertainment.

28 April (Thursday)
"Men of Mark"; p. 4

At the Trinity College athletic meeting recently Mark Twain made a witty speech in the course of which he remarked that he had had a clerk who went into athletics and afterwards stole $30,000.

30 April (Saturday)
"Mark Twain's Record: The Humorist Gives a Complete Account of His Service in the War"; p. 11

When your secretary invited me to this reunion of the Union veterans of Maryland, he requested me to come prepared to clear up a matter which he said had long been a subject of dispute and bad blood in war circles in this country—to wit: the true dimensions of my military services in the Civil War, and the effect which they had upon the general result. I recognize the importance of this thing to history, and I have come prepared. Here are the details: I was in the Civil War two weeks. In that brief time I rose from private to second lieutenant. The monumental feature of my campaign was the one battle in which was my command—it was in the summer of '61. If I do say it, it was the bloodiest battle ever fought in human history; there is nothing approaching it for destruction of human life in the field, if you take in consideration the forces engaged, and the proportion of death to survival. And yet you do not even know the name of that battle. Neither do I. It had a name, but I have forgotten it. It is no use to keep private information which you can't show off. Now look at the way history does. It takes the Battle of Boonville, fought nearby about the date of our slaughter, and shouts its teeth loose over it, and yet never even mentions ours; doesn't even call it an "affair," doesn't call it anything at all; never even heard of it. Whereas, what are the facts?

Why, these: In the Battle of Boonville there were 2,000 men engaged on the Union side and about as many on the other—supposed to be. The casualties, all told, were two men; and not all of them were killed outright, but only half of them for the other man died in the hospital next day. I know that because his great-uncle was second cousin to my grandfather, who spoke three languages and was perfectly honorable and upright, though he had warts all over him and used to—but never mind about that, the facts are just as I say and I can prove it. Two men killed in that Battle of Boonville, that's the whole result. All the others got away—on both sides. Now then, in our battle there were just 15 men engaged on our side—all brigadier generals but me, and I was a second lieutenant. On the other side there was but one man. He was a stranger. We killed him. It was night, and we thought he was an army of observation; he looked like an army of observation—in fact, he looked bigger than any army of observation would in the daytime; and some of us believed he was trying to surround us, and some thought he was going to try to turn our position, and so we shot him. Poor fellow, he probably wasn't an army of observation, after all, but that wasn't our fault; as I say, he had all the look of it in that dim light. It was a sorrowful circumstance, but he took the chances of war, and he drew the wrong card; so we buried him with the honors of war, and took his things. So began and ended the only battle in the history of the world where the opposing force was utterly exterminated. And yet you don't know the name of that battle; you don't even know the name of that man.

Now, then, for the argument. Suppose I had continued in the war and gone on as I had began and exterminated the opposing force every time—every two weeks—where would your war have been? Why, you see yourself the conflict would have been too one-sided. There was but one honorable course for me to pursue, and I pursued it. I withdrew to private life and gave the Union cause a chance. There, now, you have the whole thing in a nutshell; it was not my presence in the Civil War that determined that tremendous contest—it was my retirement. It left the Confederate side too weak. And yet, when I stop and think, I cannot regret my course. No, when I look abroad over this happy land, with its wounds healed and its enmities forgotten, this reunited sisterhood of majestic states; this freest of free commonwealths the sun in his course shines upon; this one sole country nameable in history or tradition where a man is a man and manhood the only royalty; this people ruled by the justest and wholesomest laws and government yet devised by the wisdom of men; this mightiest of the civilized empires of the earth in numbers, in prosperity, in progress and in promise, and reflect that there is no North, no South any more, but that as in the old time, it is now and remains forever in the hearts and speech of Americans our land, our country, our giant empire, and the flag floating in the firmament our flag, I would not wish it otherwise. No, when I look about me and contemplate these sublime results, I feel deep down in my heart that I acted for the best when I took my shoulder out from under the Confederacy and let it come down.

Twain's speech, reprinted from the Baltimore *American*, burlesques the account of shooting a civilian which was narrated without humor in "The Private History of a Campaign That Failed." Perhaps Twain tells a funny version of the story to a group of honored Civil War veterans to deemphasize that after the killing he deserted. The notion of utterly destroying an enemy probably comes from the fact that Twain, at the time of his speech, was immersed in the writing of *A Connecticut Yankee*, which concludes with a complete slaughter: Hank Morgan and his handful of boys with Gatling guns and dynamite kill 25,000 armored knights and stand as masters of England. While one may laugh at the destruction in *A Connecticut Yankee*, or chuckle at Twain's speech, both show clearly Twain's sense of horror about war, as well as his growing pessimism.

23 May (Monday)
"Mark Twain's Scholarly Attainments"; p. 3

People who know Samuel L. Clemens only as Mark Twain, the humorist, have no idea about the scholarly attainments of the man. Reading his books of travel, one gets only the impression of a newspaperman. A brilliant and witty one, it is true, but with the shallow flippancy, the careless irreverence that is the characteristic of many journalists who hold few things sacred and would sacrifice most things to point a funny paragraph. Dora Wheeler, who has painted the portraits of most of the literary men and women of today, painted Twain's not long ago, and said of him that she had never had among all of her literary sitters one more thoughtful, learned, and scholarly. He would pass like a flash from the maddest and most irreverent waggery to a grave discussion of abstruse thought, and his favorite poet was—mirabile dictu—Robert Browning. If one can picture anything apparently more at the antipodes of thought than Twain's trenchant, obvious, aggressive humor and the subtle, introspective, involved processes of Browning's mind, they may be able to comprehend how far one is from knowing a man solely by his published work.

Attributed to the Brooklyn *Eagle*, this anecdote shows how difficult it was for Twain to be accepted by his readers as anything but a "funny man." Dora Wheeler, an American painter, was noted for her portraits of authors; in addition to Twain, she painted Thomas Hardy, Frank Stockton, and Charles Dudley Warner.

18 July (Monday)
"Men of Mark"; p. 4

Mark Twain is spending the summer at his country home near Elmira, N. Y., and is busily engaged on a new book. He is rich, but he wants more money. He does not work for fun.

20 July (Wednesday)
"Men of Mark"; p. 4

It is said that Mark Twain tries a new hotel whenever he comes to New York. This gives greater freshness to the jokes that he sprinkles along the corridors.

8 August (Monday)
"Telegraphic Brevities"; p. 8

A tremendous meeting of anarchists, presided over by a Mr. Clemens, cousin to Samuel L. Clemens (Mark Twain), was held at Topeka, Kan., yesterday, at which a newspaperman came near to being mobbed.

There is no evidence that any of Twain's relatives were political extremists.

19 August (Friday)
"Men of Mark"; p. 4

Mark Twain takes his summer dress question by the horns. He is, according to one who has seen him lately, not only robed in white "like the angels," but his suits are made of fine linen such as one sees constantly on the men in the streets of Havana, and his hats are of the lightest straw.

22 August (Monday)
"Mark Twain as a Cub: Captain Horace Bixby Tells How the Humorist Learned the Mississippi River"; p. 6

Capt. Horace Bixby of the magnificent steamer *City of Baton Rouge* is the most popular man on Southern waters. Capt. Bixby is a well-preserved relic of the golden age of the river, and has been a constant student of currents and chutes for 40 years. Horace Bixby is the man who taught Mark Twain how to steer a steamboat, and the success of his whilom cub has reflected considerable glory on the tutor. That was away back in the '50s when Bixby was a pilot, and after all these years he is now of the opinion that a pilot is a bigger man than a captain any day, and especially on a dark night in a tight place. Capt. Bixby is now 61 years of age, and he says, "I am just nine and a half years older than Sam Clemens." When in a reminiscent mood the other day he said:

"It was quite remarkable how Sam Clemens happened to become a pilot. He has written a great deal about it himself, but I don't believe he ever told it all. It was in the spring of 1857. I was then running regularly between St. Louis and New Orleans, and occasionally doing an outside job on the Ohio River from Cincinnati to New Orleans. It was on one of these outside trips that I first met Clemens. I was taking the *Paul Jones* down from Cincinnati and he was a passenger on board. In those days the pilothouse was a great loafing place for passengers and pilots out of work. They came in, spit all over the wheel, swapped lies, and then left the pilot on duty to slosh around in the debris. I didn't like it a bit, and I was mighty short with all passengers who attempted to talk with me. One morning, when the boat reached Island No. 35 in the Mississippi River, and we were booming along at a good rate, a young man walked into the pilothouse and, after watching me for a few minutes, said: 'G-o-o-d m-o-r-n-i-n-g,' in a drawling voice.

"I said 'Good morning' mighty sharp, thinking it would freeze him out. But it didn't. He said:

"'D-o-n-'t y-o-u w-a-n-t a b-o-y t-o l-e-a-r-n t-h-e r-i-v-e-r?'

"'No; don't want any boy to learn the river. What are you pulling your words that way for?'

"'I d-o-n-'t k-n-o-w. Y-o-u w-i-l-l h-a-v-e t-o a-s-k m-y m-o-t-h-e-r. S-h-e d-o-e-s t-h-e s-a-m-e t-h-i-n-g.'

"I thought he was chaffing me when he said that, and I looked up, but his face was just as sober as a preacher's. He then asked me if I knew the Bowens who were on the river. I told him that I did and worked with one of them in 1853. He told me that the Bowens lived next door to his father, Judge Clemens of Hannibal, Mo. In his drawling way he told me of his plans. He had learned printing at Hannibal on his brother's paper, but it did not agree with him, and he was going to South America for his health. He liked the river, however, and would abandon his projected invasion of South America for an opportunity to become a pilot.

"'There is only one thing that would induce me to teach you the river,' said I.

"'W-h-a-t's t-h-a-t?' he asked.

"'Money,' said I.

"'Mone-y?' he echoed.

"'That's just it,' I answered.

"'H-o-w m-u-c-h?' he gasped.

"'Five hundred dollars,' I said.

"'We-ll, I ai-n't go-t that mu-ch,' said he.

"'Then you better get it if you want to learn the river,' I replied.

"'I've go-t ei-g-h-t l-o-t-s up in K-e-o-k-u-k, I-owa, but I don't know w-hat they wo-uld bring, an' I've go-t 2,000 acres of l-and in Tenness-ee that I can get 25 cents an acre for,' said he, summing up his assets. We talked for some time, and he impressed me very favorably. It was finally agreed that he was to pay me $100 down and $75 every six months until the debt was paid. I told him that he would have to provide his own clothes and board while in port. On the river he would receive his board and lodging free. He started in as a cub on the *Aleck Scott*, and he learned rapidly. He was then just past 21, and rather eccentric. He always had writing paper and pencil around the pilothouse, and was eternally scribbling away at something. I seldom ever tried to investigate the mysteries of the manuscript, but I soon turned his talent to good account. In those days pilots made out reports of the condition of the channel, and Clemens at once developed into a brillant and picturesque river reporter. His reports were humorous and contained all the information, and were frequently copied into the papers just as he wrote them. This, I think, was the first public writing that he did, except, perhaps, some squibs for the Hannibal paper. He was a good boy, not addicted to dissipation, and obeyed orders. He hated suspenders and used to enjoy himself in very loose clothes, with his hair roached back. We steered together on many trips, and then he changed around and in two years received a license that made him a full-fledged pilot. His first boat was the *Alonzo Child*, under Capt. De Haven, and he kept turning the wheel until the war broke out. His boat was then in the South, and he piloted three months for the Confederacy. Then he got through the lines and went home, but after a short stay at Hannibal he went as a volunteer for three months in the army of Gen. Sterling Price, the Missouri Confederate. He fought for the Confederacy three more months on land, and then retreated in good order, with his right resting on St. Louis. His brother, Orion Clemens, was at that time nominated secretary of the Territory of Nevada, and Sam accompanied him West. Everybody knows the rest."

Originally printed in the Chicago *Tribune*, this interview is virtually identical to an interview with Bixby printed 9 May 1882. The Bowen brothers—Sam, Will, and Hart—that Twain uses as references were buddies from his schooldays in Hannibal; all three brothers grew up to be pilots on the Mississippi (*Sam Clemens* 140-41). Will Bowen, in particular, remained a good friend throughout Twain's life; they corresponded regularly and Twain often used Will to jog his memory about their boyhood adventures, many of which were later worked into fiction (*Mr. Clemens & MT* 114-15).

3 September (Saturday)
"Men of Mark"; p. 4

Mark Twain is said to be engaged in the most gigantic financial enterprise of his life. There is never anything funny in Mark Twain's money ventures—that is, for other people.

This piece of gossip probably refers to Twain's heavy investment in the Paige Typesetter, a burden that was to bankrupt him in 1894. See 19 January 1886.

15 September (Thursday)
"Men of Mark"; p. 4

Mark Twain will be 52 years of age in November.

24 September (Saturday)
"Mark Twain's New Play: Nym Crinkle Scores the Three-Act
Farcical Monologue";' p. 8
New York, Sept. 24—

It is rather late in the day to point out that Mark Twain is
as destitute of the dramatic instinct as a parish clerk. Mr.
Howells himself is not as unspotted in this respect as Mark
Twain, and there would be no earthly sense in referring to
the well-known fact again if Mark Twain had not again challenged the reference. His *Colonel Sellers*, one of the funniest
hodgepodges ever put upon the stage, and I believe one of the
most successful, was as far from being a drama as is a comic
counting-house almanac. It would be futile to wade through
all that Mark Twain has written with the purpose of finding
therein one remote excuse for his talent taking to the theater;
that he is droll no one ever disputed; that he can make a
dramatic story, no one in the possession of his senses ever
dreamed. But, as if this fact had not been sufficiently
pounded into us by Mark Twain's voluminous work, he
again takes the boards and yesterday there was presented at
the Lyceum Theatre, through the medium of a special mati-
nee, a so-called farcical comedy in three acts by this innocent,
who never before in all his comical wanderings got so far
abroad. *The American Claimant*, as it is called, is not even a
farcical comedy. It is a three-act farcical monologue, in which
Mr. A. P. Burbank, with commendable modesty, undertook
to do the annex business to Col. Sellers. The fate of this new
Col. Sellers is not unlike that which usually befalls a funny
joke when it is revived and amplified. You can beat a gold
dollar out to cover a backyard, but the currency is destroyed.
Col. Mulberry Sellers, originally made famous all over this
continent by John T. Raymond, in whom nature had written
the character before Mark Twain had met him, is now shown
settled down in Washington, surrounded by innumerable
patents of his own invention, most of which are as far beyond the realm of sober reason as anything Rider Haggard
has invented. The three acts of the monologue take place
without the change of a chair in the same room, and Col.
Sellers has the floor all the time. He is "accompanied,"
thanks to Mrs. Langtry for the word, by four persons. He has
a daughter, Mary Sellers; a wife, Mrs. Sellers; a friend from
Missouri, Lafayette Hawkins; and a "nigger" servant, Aunt

Sally. There is also a lover of Mary who stands around. The plot of the piece is this:

The family is miserably poor, owing to Col. Sellers's monomania. The mother and daughter have to make shift with the same dress to receive company by turns. Col. Sellers has invented a method of materializing all the dead of the past and letting them out as policemen. His first attempt brings Mary's lover to the house. Col. Sellers thinks that the lover was dead and his process has materialized him. On the contrary, the lover has called in the most natural manner, and when the family is at the lowest point of destitution buys one of the Colonel's patents as an excuse for obtaining the daughter. This is told without situation, without action, without crisis, without suspense, without surprise, without emotion, and without other human interest than attends the hilarious insanity of the Colonel himself. And here I might as well say at once that Col. Sellers, as now presented, is hopelessly insane, and it is quite in keeping with much of Mark Twain's humor to be utterly indifferent to the fact that insanity, like all other misfortunes, ceases to be funny under deliberate exhibition. The only feeling that can supervene if the part is well acted is pity for the subject. Every madhouse is full of such characters, and while it is possible to smile at the wretch who sits in the sun and believes the world is reverencing him as the Deity, any attempt to make a public exhibition of his hallucination will excite only commiseration. But, this consideration aside, the construction of *The American Claimant* is so utterly defiant of all laws of dramatic representation that nothing but the desire of a rather clever "monologist" to get before the public with something more solid than a lecture-room platform to stand on could have paved the way to its presentment in the theater. The Mark Twain humor which abounds in it consists of the vagaries of Col. Sellers and his descriptions of his inventions. An example of the latter is his machine called the marine phonograph, which stored up blasphemy for use at sea. With four or five of these machines in action on board a vessel, he claims there will be swearing enough to take her through any storm. The absurdity of this is distinctly American, but it is in no sense dramatic and belongs to the department of comic journalism with cuts.

Mr. Burbank played the part of Col. Sellers with sufficient

skill of portrayal to make everyone wish it had been worthier of his care and ambition, but he was not well "accompanied," save in the person of the traditional Negro wench, admirably done by W. H. Lytell. The young lady who played the part of Mary Sellers, Miss Alice King Hamilton, and who is apparently pretty and intelligent enough, so overacted the part and rolled her eyes and gesticulated without cause that she ruined the only single need of sentiment in the piece with an emphasis as irrational as was the life and character of her stage father. It was a rare case in which a bright and charming girl insisted on not being bright and charming at all, and succeeded in distorting nature with a wholly uncalled for display of elocution.

Nym Crinkle.

Nym Crinkle, the *Post-Dispatch's* New York City theater critic, was not the only person to dislike the play; other reviewers unanimously considered it a disaster, too, although Alfred P. Burbank (1846-94) in the lead received occasional good notices. Comparing the play to the works of H. Rider Haggard (1856-1925), however, may have attracted some people to the performances as Haggard's sensationalistic novels enjoyed a brief vogue at this time.

4 October (Tuesday)
"Defeated but Hopeful"; p. 4

In a long column of miscellaneous news, headed by a report of a yacht race in England, there is a short item about Twain:

Mark Twain is now residing at Buckenham Hall near Norwich, which he has taken for a year and is equally enjoying himself yachting on the Norfolk broads, entertaining a party of Dutch friends and editing his *Library of Wit and Humor*, upon which he has been engaged for some time.

Twain desultorily worked on *Mark Twain's Library of Humor*—which he, W. D. Howells, and Charles H. Clark coedited—for about six years, from 1881 when he initially conceived the idea of an anthology of American humorists until December 1887 when it was finally published by Twain's own publishing house. A lack of publicity, however, kept the book from being a success (*Autobiography* 255-56).

17 November (Thursday)
"Men of Mark"; p. 4

Charles Dickens and his wife were the guests of Mark

Twain in Hartford, Conn.

Charles Dickens Jr. (1837-96) toured the country in 1887 to read from his father's works. He stopped in St. Louis later that year.

24 November (Thursday)
"International Copyright: Bill Nye's Effort to Give the Cause a New and Attractive Name"; p. 2

In an article announcing that authors would read from their works on 28 and 29 November in New York City to publicize the copyright problems they faced, popular humorist Bill Nye devotes one paragraph to Twain:

> Mr. Samuel L. Clemens will give voice to a few passionate utterances, which will offset the flippant, yet droll remarks of Mr. Curtis and Dr. Edward Eggleston. Samuel L. Twain is well worth a journey from the interior of the state to witness. He will make use of some remarks which he has thought of especially for this occasion.

In addition to George William Curtis and Edward Eggleston (both of whom were noted for their sobriety), James Russell Lowell, Charles Dudley Warner, W. D. Howells, Frank Stockton, George W. Cable, and James Whitcomb Riley were slated to be on the program. On 11 December, the *Post-Dispatch* carried a lengthy report about the event. Throughout his professional career Twain fought for the rights of authors by appearing at such benefits and by testifying before the U.S. Congress and Britain's House of Lords. He believed that a man should own his words just as surely as a man could legally own an invention; he wanted copyright laws to be similiar to patent laws to ensure a book could not be copied and sold without royalties paid to its author (*Autobiography* 279-83). As one of the most popular authors of his day, Twain did in fact lose a fortune to literary pirates.

27 November (Sunday)
"Literary Notes"; p. 15

> Mark Twain has written something in the form of a play entitled *Meisterschaft*, which will appear in an early number of the *Century*. The play, as may be supposed, is in two languages.

Twain originally wrote the comic play as a translation exercise for a German-language study group which met regularly at his home in Hartford; *Meisterschaft* subsequently appeared in the January 1888 issue of the *Century* (*MT & the Theatre* 86). Although he often struggled with the language—and even poked fun at it in such essays as

"The Awful German Language" (1880)—Twain enjoyed studying German and then attempting to speak it on his frequent trips to Europe.

11 December (Sunday)
"Our Popular Authors: The Men Who Write Songs and Weave Stories that Delight Us"; p. 20

In a long story about a benefit for the International Copyright League, two paragraphs are devoted to Twain's performance:

> Samuel L. Clemens, "Mark Twain," when exhibited in an authors' show, presents the spectacle of a man who seems to be constantly saying to himself: "Why don't they label us?" Mark Twain does not grow older in looks as rapidly as most men. He advanced to the desk with that peculiar shambling step of his, ran one hand down into his trousers pocket, and stuck the thumb of the other hand into the armhole of his waistcoat. He always does this before he speaks a word. Sometimes he does it more. The last time the writer heard him lecture, after having thus got rid of his hands, he stood before the house as still and silent as an unopened oyster. The audience was as still as he. After a long pause, during which everyone was painfully wondering what ailed him, he said, "H'm!" and immediately relapsed into silence. A full minute went by during which he remained perfectly quiet with his eyes staring straight before him. Then he said "H'm!" again. At last, someone started a little ripple of applause. Mark looked up, radiant with smiles. "Thank you," he said, "I was waiting for you to begin!"
>
> Mr. Clemens tells his intimate friends that this assumption of supreme impudence comes hard with him, that he has to brace himself up for each encounter. His success under these circumstances is quite remarkable, for a more fascinating picture of cheerful "cheek," so to speak, than he presents cannot be conceived. An American audience likes this when it is well done and detests it when poorly done. He told the story of Horace Greeley's ride with "Hank" Monk and told it admirably. The professional reader seldom ventures to essay this story. It is one of the most difficult of recitations. The least timidity or nervousness ruins it. Mr. Clemens went right on with it until everyone was convulsed with laughter and when he had done, his hearers were holding their sides.

The *Post Dispatch* printed a caricature of Twain to illustrate his stance as described in the first paragraph. The story of Horace Greeley (1811-72), a popular newspaper editor and politician, and the wild stagecoach ride Hank Monk allegedly gave him, is one of Twain's most famous lectures. He first delivered it in San Francisco on 16 November 1866 and it stayed in his repertoire throughout his professional career; he tells the Greeley-Monk story in chapter 20 of *Roughing It*.

1888

3 March (Saturday)
no headline; p. 4

A number of authors have already been invited to take part in another authors' reading in New York City to be given for the benefit of the international copyright movement. Among those invited are Mr. Howells and Mr. Frank Stockton. Both these gentlemen took part in the last reading, and, while they were as distinguished as any present, it was shown clearly that they cannot read for public. It would appear, therefore, that the management is not acting fairly with the public in inviting authors who, however widely known through their books, can really contribute nothing towards such entertainments as these readings. However, Mark Twain, J. W. Riley, and G. W. Cable, who are professional readers as well as writers, will be among the readers and will be sure to please.

18 March (Sunday)
"Authors in Public: A. M. Palmer's Literary Combination in the National Capital"; p. 10

Washington, D. C., Mar. 17—

"Palmers' Barnstormers" is what Mark Twain calls the group of distinguished authors who come here to give readings from their works in two entertainments for the benefit of the American Copyright League. A. M. Palmer, the sympathetic friend of the authors in their struggle for international copyright, is the business manager of the combination, and he is to be congratulated, not only upon the personnel of the company, but upon the acceptability of the entertainment which they present.

The first of the readings took place today in the Congregational Church before an audience not only large but most distinguished in character. The President had another engagement, but Mrs. Cleveland was there, coming unostentatiously and gleefully, enjoying every feature of the entertainment. Congress did not attend in a body, but many members did, and so did representatives of all the best elements of society of the national capital.

The authors were a show in their very appearance as they filed upon the platform with all the dignity of justices of the Supreme Court, the venerable George Bancroft at the head and the youthful editor of the *Century* bringing up the rear. A good-looking set of men they were and their kinds of good looks were as varied as the character of their works. The group consisted of George Bancroft, Samuel L. Clemens (Mark Twain), William D. Howells, H. H. Boysen, Edward Eggleston, James Whitcomb Riley, E. C. Stedman, Frank R. Stockton, R. W. Gilder, Richard M. Johnston, and Col. Thomas W. Knox.

Mr. Stedman, in fashionable morning dress and with his grizzled whiskers neatly parted in the middle and pointed at the ends, made a capital introductory address equally logical and witty. Referring to the combination of authors whom he was to introduce, he said that while only one of them was like Mark Twain, his own "Harper & Bros. and Edwin Booth combined," they might be collectively described as the Howells and Bishop Realistic Combination, or the Gilder and Warner Minstrels, or the Johnston and Page Old Dominion Varieties, or the Eggleston and Whitcomb Riley dialect Comedians, etc., as each auditor might choose.

There were eight numbers on the programme. Mr. Eggleston read "A Bold Stroke for a Horse," an unpublished chapter from his serial *The Graysons*, and Mr. Howells the chapter from *The Minister's Charge* giving the interviews between the minister and Lemuel. Mr. Gilder read most effectively his poem on "The Life Work of Lincoln" and "The Burial of Grant."

Then there was a break in the programme owing to Charles Dudley Warner's absence. His place was taken by Mark Twain, who explained that Warner and the railroad that he lived on, together with the state of Connecticut, were buried under many feet of snow, but that 8,000 men were at work digging them all out. He said, however, that he was a neighbor of Warner, and in many respects a better man. After much more impromptu fun he told in his drawling way the story of how he became an anti-duelist.

"Now," said he in closing an appeal to every young man and young woman in the audience to beware of duelling, "if a man should challenge me I would go to him like a brother and take him by the hand, lead him to a secluded spot and kill him."

Col. Knox read "An Adventure with a Grizzly," appearing as a substitute for H. C. Bunner, and J. Whitcomb Riley concluded the entertainment with a rendition of two of his dialect poems in a way that showed him to be an actor as well as poet and humorist. Twain and Riley, in fact, made the great successes of the day.

The entertainment realized a good sum for the Copyright League. On Monday, Stedman, Richard Malcolm, Johnston, Clemens, Boysen, Stockton and Page will read. Receptions in honor of the visiting authors will be given by Mrs. Cleveland, Mrs. John Hay, Mrs. Senator Hawley and Mrs. Senator Hearst.

This account of the performance was relayed to St. Louis via telegraph by a *Post-Dispatch* reporter. The piece that Twain read—"How I Escaped Being Killed in a Duel"—was printed in the *Post-Dispatch* on 10 April 1876.

25 March (Sunday)

"People Who Write: Washington Invaded by American Novelists and Humorists"; p. 11

This long report about a reception for the authors who read for the International Copyright League contains a paragraph about Twain and his wife:

Mr. and Mrs. Clemens held a reception of their own in the bow-window. Mark Twain was surrounded with interested faces listening to his droll conversation, "long drawn out." He has a fund of ready wit which he introduces very pleasantly. We always think of him as the author of *Tom Sawyer*, but never as that of *Huckleberry Finn*. In alluding to *Tom Sawyer*, he admitted the absence of a moral in it, but said he wrote it for the sole purpose of enjoyment. One of the very noticeable features about him was the slight clipping of that bushy appendage to his head which he is pleased to call hair. He has agreeable manners and is easily approached. Mrs.

Clemens is a slight, little woman, bright and entertaining in conversation. Her features are delicately cut, and her bright, blue eyes gleam through glasses. She was with her husband in the reserved gallery of the Senate the early part of the week and watched with much interest the rather unentertaining proceeding of the introduction of bills.

25 March (Sunday)
"The Favorite Novel"; p. 11
   About the close of the last year the assistant librarians at the Public Library put their heads together and decided it would prove an interesting experiment, not only for themselves but also for the reading public, to determine popular sentiment on the question of the favorite works of fiction. To this end the assistants agreed to note down and make a list of the books drawn most often from the library desk, and the results given below are somewhat surprising. When the 1st of February had arrived the assistants compared notes, and this is what they found: During the month of January the biggest demand by any one work was for *Ben-Hur* by Wallace. Of this work, 46 different copies had been drawn. Next to *Ben-Hur* came Dickens's *David Copperfield*, which found 34 admirers, and the third place on the list was captured by two books, each with a record of 28 entries, namely *The Last Days of Pompeii* by Lord Lytton and Victor Hugo's *Les Miserables*. Hawthorne's *Scarlet Letter* came next with 27 entries, and close on the heels of this work came the *Count of Monte Cristo* with 26 votes for popular favor. The standard of excellence observed throughout the above books drops a trifle in the seventh with Mark Twain's *Huckleberry Finn*, which had 24 readers during the month.

Following *Huckleberry Finn* in popularity, the *Post-Dispatch* notes further, were *Ramona, Vanity Fair,* and *Ivanhoe,* among others.

30 September (Sunday)
"Longfellow: Ceremonies Attending the Unveiling of the Statue"; p. 9

In a story relayed by telegraph to the *Post-Dispatch*, a reporter notes that Twain, along with such other luminaries as George W. Cable, E. C. Stedman, and Thomas B. Aldrich, sent a letter of condolences to the ceremony which took place on 29 September.

5 November (Monday)
"Men of Mark"; p. 4

Samuel L. Clemens ("Mark Twain") is an enthusiastic tariff reformer and will vote for Cleveland and Thurman. As an offset to his vote Robert J. Burdette will cast a ballot for Harrison and Morton.

17 November (Saturday)
"Men of Mark"; p. 4

Samuel L. Clemens ("Mark Twain") claims that his speech on tariff reform in Hartford carried Connecticut for the Democracy.

1 December (Saturday)
"Mark Twain's Clever Daughter: She Kept a Diary Until She Suspected Her Father of a Mean Trick"; p. 6

Mark Twain, if he is in the mood, will tell the story of his own courtship in the manner worthy of the greatest of living humorists. When he first met the lady who afterward became his wife he was not so distinguished as now; his origin was humble, and for some years of his life he had been a pilot on the Mississippi River. The future Mrs. Clemens was a woman of position and fortune; her father was a judge, and doubtless, expected "family" and social importance in his son-in-law. Clemens, however, became interested in his daughter, and after a while proposed, but was rejected.

"Well," he said to the lady, "I didn't much believe you'd have me, but I thought I'd try."

After a while he "tried" again with the same result and then remarked with his celebrated drawl, "I think a great deal more of you than if you said 'Yes,' but it's hard to bear." A third time he met with better fortune and then came to the most difficult part of his task, to address the old gentleman.

"Judge," he said to the dignified millionaire, "have you seen anything going on between Miss Lizzy and myself?"

"What? What?" exclaimed the judge rather sharply, apparently not understanding the situation, yet doubtless getting a glimpse of it.

"Have you seen anything going on between Miss Lizzy and myself?"

"No, no, indeed!" replied the magnate, sternly. "No, sir, I have not."

"Well! Look sharp and you will," said the author of *Innocents Abroad*; and that's the way he asked the judicial luminary for his daughter's hand.

Mark has a child who inherits some of her father's brightness. She kept a diary at one time in which she noted the occurrences in the family, and among other things, the sayings of her parents. On one page she wrote that father sometimes used stronger words when mother wasn't by and he thought "we" didn't hear. Mrs. Clemens found the diary and showed it to her husband, probably thinking the particular page worth his notice. After this Clemens did and said several things that were intended to attract the child's attention, and found them duly noted afterward. But one day the following entry occurred:

"I don't think I'll put down anything more about father, for I think he does things to have me notice him, and I believe he reads this dairy." She was Mark's own child.

Originally printed in the New York *Mail and Express*, the anonymous author of this piece perhaps misheard the anecdote about Twain's courtship and thus mistakes "Livy," Twain's pet name for his wife Olivia, for "Lizzy." The best source for information about Twain's long courtship of Livy is *MT: Bachelor* (398-423). The final two paragraphs of this newspaper report refers to the diary kept by Twain's eldest daughter—Susy was sixteen in 1888—about her famous father. He quotes from it at length in *Autobiography* (201-14); it was published by Doubleday as *Papa: An Intimate Biography of Mark Twain* (1985). The best source for additional information about Susy and her relationship with Twain is *Susy & MT*.

1889

26 January (Saturday)
"Men of Mark"; p. 4

Mark Twain is said by one who knows him well to be the most miserable of men. He is possessed by a wild, mad fear that ill-luck is bound to overtake him and deprive him of his fortune. It is said that he shed tears of despair when an old $14 cow died a short time ago.

While the bit of gossip about a cow is not true, certainly Twain had overinvested his money into various schemes; he may indeed have worried about his finances in January of 1889.

4 February (Monday)
"Men of Mark"; p. 4

Mark Twain denies the story that "he cried like a child when his old cow recently died." He says he never owned an old cow, but buys directly from a milk can at 6 cents a quart.

27 April (Saturday)
"Authors who Live in Hartford: The Literary Lights of the Monday Evening Club and *Backlog Studies*"; p. 3

Some years ago, says the March *Book Buyer*, Mr. Charles Dudley Warner bought in Hartford a newer and larger house, which he has practically rebuilt. It stands next door on one side to Mrs. Stowe and on the other side to Mark Twain's, and between Mr. Clemens's and Mr. Warner's houses the path shows signs of constant use. The Warner home, which is marked as much by Mrs. Warner's tastes as by her husband's, is distinctively theirs. No other house is like it. The very porch and doorway are an invitation to enter, which all are only too eager to accept; and within, it is full of light and comfort and an easy informality both in its appearance and its atmosphere. On the walls hang relics of the journeys about the world, gathered in Nubia, Egypt, Northern Africa, Spain and all over the continent of Europe; the portieres and rugs are of interesting Oriental workmanship; and whether it is a picture, a bit of china or porcelain—whatever object takes the eye—the inquirers find it has a history and associations of its own. Open fireplaces are there, of course, for it was the writer of the *Backlog Studies* who offered the ridiculous picture of an artist putting on canvas "a happy family gathered round a hole in the floor called a register." In the *Backlog Studies* Mr. Warner introduces, under thin veils that do not disguise them, Mark Twain, their pastor, Rev. J. H. Twichell, and the common friend of all of them, Rev. Dr. E. P. Parker. These four and Gen. Hawley, Gen. Franklin, Judge Shipman of the United States District Court, Hon. H. C. Robinson, President Smith of Trinity College and others, 20 in all, form the Monday Evening Club of Hartford, which meets alternate Mondays, between October and May. Rev. Dr. Bushnell, Dr. J. Trumbull and others founded the club 25 years ago, and it has been an important literary force in the city ever since.

The Monday Evening Club, founded in the 1860s to foster intellectual discussion and debate among the leading male citizens of Hartford, met every other Monday during the winter and spring months. Soon after he moved to Hartford in 1871, Twain was invited to join, which he did without hesitation. The club proved to be an excellent place for him to work out his more controversial ideas about the nature of man, politics, and religion. However heterodoxical he was, and he certainly expressed some radical ideas at times, Twain could be assured of an audience that considered his points carefully rather than rejecting them out of hand (*Nook Farm* 102-04). Twain and Warner—whose *Backlog Studies* was published in 1873—enlisted linguist Dr. J. Hammond Trumbull (1821-97), to write the chapter epigraphs in different languages for *The Gilded Age*. In November 1897, Twain told the *Century* that he believed Trumbull was "the richest man in America in the matter of knowledge—knowledge of all values, from copper up to government bonds."

13 May (Monday)

"Tattoo Marks: Mark Twain Tells How They May be Removed by Fire"; p. 7

A tattoo mark is easily removed, writes Mark Twain. When I was a small boy I had my share of warts. I tried in turn the 368 ways of removing them, but without results; indeed, I seemed to get wartier and wartier right along. But at last somebody revealed to me the 369th way, and I tried it. Thus: I drove a needle down to the basement of the wart, then held the other end of the needle in the flame of a candle some little time: The needle became red hot throughout its length and proceeded to cook the wart. Presently I drew the needle out; if it had white atoms like nits sticking about its point, that wart was done; if the point was clear, I drove it in again and cooked till I got those white things. They were the roots of the wart. Twenty-four hours later the wart would become soft and flabby, and I removed it with a single wipe of my hand. Where it had been was a clear surface now, which quickly healed and left no scar. Within two days I was wartless, and have so remained until this day.

Well, a long time afterward, when I was 16 years old, a sailor tattooed an anchor and rope on the back of my left hand with India ink. The color was a deep, dark blue, and extravagantly conspicuous. I was proud of it for awhile, but by the time I had worn it nine years I was tired of it and ashamed of it. I could find nobody who could tell me how to get rid of it, but at last my wart experience of near half a generation before occurred to me, and I got me several needles and a candle straightaway. I drove the needles along just under the surface of the skin and tolerable close together, and made them include the whole tattoo mark; then I fired up on them and cooked that device thoroughly. Next day I wiped the device off with my hand. The place quickly healed and left no scar. A faint bluish tint remained, and I was reminded to begin again and cook that out; but as it was hardly detectable and not noticeable, it did not seem worth the fuel, and so I left it there, and there it is yet though I suppose I am the only member of my tribe that knows it.

This piece is reprinted from the Boston *Herald*.

19 May (Sunday)
"Mark Twain Chatty: He Tells of His Former Life as a Reporter"; p. 20

Washington, D. C., May 17—

Met Mark Twain the other day wandering around the Capitol and looking at pictures 50 years old as if they were new, and inspecting with the interest of a rustic stranger the vivid bronze doors whose Columbian glories had bleared his eyeballs more than two decades ago. He strayed into the press gallery, threw back his gray overcoat, adjusted his gold spectacles on his nose, and looked around.

"A good deal changed," he said, glancing at the life-size photographs of Whitelaw Reid and younger editors which now decorate the walls, "and it seems a hundred years ago."

I asked when he was here.

"I had a seat in the press gallery," he meditated, "let's see—in 1867—and now I suppose all the veterans are gone—all the newspaper fellows who were here when I was, Reid and Horace White and Ramsdell and Adams and Townsend."

"The ones you name happen to all to be gone," I admitted, "some to the control of newspapers and some to where Dr. Potter says there are no newspapers, but some of the real veterans are still here. On those pegs in the corner some of the ancients still hang up their coats—Gen. Boynton and Byington and Uriah Painter and Judge Noah, the king of the Jews and dean of the corps. Most of the old fellows are dead—Whitely of the *Herald*, Crouse of the *Times*, Adams of the *World*, Henry of the *Tribune*, Gobright of the Associated Press. Jim Young is executive clerk of the Senate, John Russell Young is a journalist at large, Ed Stedman has grown to be a banker poet, and Henry Villard—well, you know all about him and his fortunes."

"Yes; some of these men I never knew in Washington; a few of them were here before my time. In fact, I was rather new and shy, and I did not mingle in the festivities of Newspaper Row. Probably most of the men you mention were perfectly unconscious to my existence. The *Morning Call* and the *Enterprise* did not make much of a commotion in the United States.

"I roomed in a house which also sheltered George Alfred Townsend, Ramsdell, George Adams and Riley of the San Francisco *Alta*. I represented the Virginia (Nev.) *Enterprise*. Also, I was private secretary to Senator Stewart, but a capabler man did the work. A little later that winter William Swinton and I housed together. Swinton invented the idea—at least it was new to me—of manifolding correspondence. I mean of sending duplicates of a letter to various widely separated newspapers. We projected an extensive business, but for some reason or other we took it out in dreaming—never really tried it." Here Mark walked into the gallery and looked down at the vacant senatorial seats.

"I was here last," he went on, "in 1868. I had been on that lark to the Mediterranean and had written a few letters to the San Francisco *Alta* that had been copied past all calculation and to my utter astonishment, a publisher wanted a book. I came back here to write it.

"Why, I was offered an office in that ancient time by the California senators—minister to China. Think of that! It wasn't a time when they hunted around for competent people. No, only one qualification was required: You must please Andy Johnson and the Senate. Nearly anybody could please one of them, but to please both—well, it took an angel to do that. However, I declined to try for the prize. I hadn't anything against the Chinese, and besides, we couldn't spare any angels then."

"A pretty good place to write," I remarked as we took seats.

"Some things," he said, "but an awfully bad place for a newspaper man to write a book as the publisher demanded. I tried it hard, but my chum was a storyteller, and both he and the stove smoked incessantly. And as we were located handy for the boys to run in, the room was always full of the boys who leaned back in my chairs, put their feet complacent on my manuscript, and smoked till I could not breath."

"Is that the way you wrote *Innocents Abroad*?" I asked.

"No; that is the way I didn't write it. My publisher prodded me for copy which I couldn't produce till at last I arose and kicked Washington behind me and ran off to San Francisco. There I got elbow room and quiet."

"It was apparently a wise move," I concurred, "but you could write here now, and this is exactly the place for a man like you. More intellectual society is attainable here than in any other city in the world. The only big mistake of your successful life, Clemens"—for only his intimate friends address him as "Mark"—"is not coming to Washington to live. Why, all over the United States people of leisure and culture are"—

"Yes, I know, I know," broke in Clemens, "but don't tantalize me. Do you take a fiendish enjoyment in making me suffer? I know perfectly well what I am about, and I appreciate what I am losing. Washington is no doubt the boss town in the country for a man to live in who wants to get all the pleasure he can in a given number of months. But I wasn't built that way. I don't want the earth at one gulp. All of us are always losing some pleasure that we might have if we could be everywhere at once.

"I lose Washington, for instance, for the privilege of saving my life. My doctor told me that if I wanted my three score and 10, I must go to bed early, keep out of social excitements, and behave myself. You can't do that in Washington. Nobody does. Look at John Hay. Just fading away, I have no doubt, amid these scenes of mad revelry. My wife, you know, is practically an invalid, too, so that neither of us could keep up with the procession. No, the best place for us is quiet and beautiful Hartford, though there is a good deal of the society of Washington that I should delight in."

"I suppose you have been pirated a good deal," I said to Mr. Clemens. "I do not mean by illegal publication of your works, but by private individuals claiming to write your writings?"

"Oh, yes," he said, "considerably—some scores of cases, I suppose. One ambitious individual in the West still claims to have written the 'Jumping Frog of Calaveras County,' and another is sure that he produced that classic work known as 'Jim Wolfe and the Cats.' I suppose either would face me down with it; and their conduct has led me to conjecture that a man may possibly claim a piece of property so long and persistently that he at last comes honestly to believe it is his own. You know that poor fellow in New Jersey, so weakminded as to declare that he wrote 'Beautiful Snow,' and going to his coffin with tearful protests? And you know about Col. Joyce and Ella Wheeler, and 'laugh and the world laughs with you'?

"But I haven't been bothered that way so much as I have been by personators. In a good many places men have appeared, represented that they were Mark Twain and have corroborated the claim by borrowing money and immediately disappearing. Such personators do not always borrow money. Sometimes they seem to be actuated by a sort of idiotic vanity.

"Why, a fellow stopped at a hotel in an English city, registered as Mark Twain, struck up an acquaintance with the landlord and guests, recited for them and was about to accept a public dinner of welcome to the city when some mere acci-

dent exposed him. Yet I myself had stopped for weeks at that
same inn and was well known to the landlord and citizens.
His effrontery was amazing."

"Did he resemble you?"

"I do not know. I hope and believe that he did not. Parties whom I have since been inclined to regard as my enemies had the indecency to say that he did.

"The same thing happened in Boston and several other
cities. It was not pleasant to have bills coming in for money
lent me in Albany, Charleston, Mexico, Honolulu and other
places, and my calm explanation that I was not there bringing
sarcastic letters in reply with 'Oh, of course not! I didn't see
you with my own eyes, did I?', etc., and I resolved that I
would follow up the next swindle I heard of. I had not long
to wait. A dispatch came from Des Moines, Iowa:

"'Is Mark Twain at home?'

"'Yes, I am here and have not been away,' I answered.

"'Man personated you—got $250 from audience—shall I
catch him'" came back, bearing the signature of a lawyer.

"'Yes,' I telegraphed in reply, 'have sent you check for expenses.'

"He was a good while catching him—some weeks—perhaps months, and then he made me an elaborate report, giving the route of his labyrinthine and serpentine chase of the
swindler, the money he had expended, and the information
that he did not entirely and completely catch him, though he
'got near him several times.' I was out some hundreds of
dollars.

"I was disgusted; and when I got another dispatch—from
New Orleans, I think it was—

"'Man swindled audience with pretended lecture here last
night, claiming to be you. What shall I do?' I telegraphed
back unanimously, 'Let him go! Let him go !'

"I'd give $100, though, to see one of these dopplegängers
who personate me before an audience, just to see what they
look like."

Mark Twain comes down every winter to work for the
passage of an international copyright law in conjunction with
Edward Eggleston, Gilder, and other authors. Senator Reagan
of Texas, a friend of Mark's, but an opponent of his pet measure, greeted him cordially last winter with, "How are you,
Mark? How are you? Right glad to see you. Glad to see you.

Hope to see you here every session as long as you live!"

One of Mark Twain's' favorite amusements here, they say, is turning himself into an amateur guide and explaining to his friends the various objects of interest in the Capitol. He is particularly facetious over the pictures in the rotunda and the stone people in "Statuary Hall." Arriving opposite the marble statue of Fulton, seated and intently examining the model of a steamboat in his hands, he indulges in a wide-sweeping gesture and exclaims: "This, ladies and gentlemen, is Pennsylvania's favorite son, Robert Fulton. Observe his easy and unconventional attitude. Notice his serene and contented expression, caught by the artist at the moment when he made up his mind to steal John Fitch's steamboat."

The humorist dresses a great deal more carefully than formerly; this is made necessary by his increasing amplitude, by his vast shock of gray hair, by his boisterous and ungovernable moustache, and by his turbulent eyebrows that cover his gray eyes like a dissolute thatch. And when he talks he talks slowly and extracts each of his vowels with a corkscrew twist that would make even the announcement of a funeral sound like a joke.

This interview by W. A. Croffut was telegraphed to the *Post-Dispatch*. Included with the interview are two caricatures of Twain.

26 May (Sunday)
"These are Their Favorite Authors"; p. 26

In late May the *Post-Dispatch* surveyed 1,500 of its readers to discover who were their favorite writers. Not surprisingly, Twain was mentioned quite often. One reader, R. M. Johnson, said, "Mark Twain by all means. I have read *Huckleberry Finn* five times and can read it again and enjoy it." Another person, P. H. Montgomery, said, "Mark Twain is my favorite by long odds. When reading his books I become so interested that I forget where I am."

30 May (Thursday)
"Men of Mark"; p. 4

Mark Twain, the humorist, is reported to have an income of $80,000 a year from his books and his business investments.

16 June (Sunday)
"Bill Nye on Writers"; p. 21

Edgar Wilson Nye (1856-1896), a popular humorist of the late 1880s, wrote a column for the Sunday *Post-Dispatch*. The topics for his columns varied widely, but they usually turned on his subtle observations of human nature. For one such column, Nye discusses authors—including Twain—that he had met. After a few paragraphs about authors who compose on a typewriter, which was a novelty at the time, he devotes one paragraph to Twain.

Mark Twain is not above using the pen. He smokes a pipe while working. It is not a strong pipe, but yet there is something about it which encourages people to let him alone when he is smoking, doing what little business they have on hand by means of the telephone. When he does not feel well he fasts. Many other authors do that way also, but they go without generally, in order that their publishers may have pie six times a day and sweetcakes for breakfast. Mr. Clemens, being himself a publisher, is enabled to eat oftener than an author who is dependent. Another advantage to this system is that it enables Mr. Clemens, the publisher, to reject the manuscript of Mark Twain, if he thinks best, without hurting the author's feelings. Mr. Clemens is the Vanderbilt of literature and does much good by means of his wealth. He looks cross, but behind a frowning countenance he hides a smiling face. Possibly I am a little mixed in the above quotation, as I am writing this on board the train and some overzealous passenger has taken away the "Read and Return" copy of the Bible, forgetting to bring it back. This leaves me practically helpless when I desire to quote from the Scriptures.

The *Post-Dispatch* prints a caricature of Twain—puffing a huge pipe and hunched over a desk—with the column. Cornelius Vanderbilt (1794-1877), one of the richest men in America, had gained fame for his philanthropy.

18 September (Wednesday)
"The Fame of Mark Twain"; p. 3

The only American you are sure of meeting in every town of Europe is Mark Twain. On board our Danish ship the captain and first mate used to spend hours exchanging stories from *Innocents Abroad*, *Roughing It*, *A Tramp Abroad*, and so on. That was not a point to be wondered at, for they touched New York once a month. But after we had heard the name of Mark Twain in small country villages of Norway and Sweden, in Denmark, all the way through Germany, and at every little way station in Switzerland, we realized that neither Hartford, nor Connecticut, nor the United States owned Mr. Clemens. At Geneva yesterday we met a German professor who had been staying a while in Argentiere, a bit of the village near Chamounix. On our inquiring if he knew the English lady there who ascended Mont Blanc in January and afterward married her guide, he said that he had just come from her home. He added that an American, "Mr. Twain," had written up the history of the ascent and marriage and there were some slight inaccuracies in the details. The account had been sent on from Germany and a sort of family council had been held, to which the guests of the houses had been admitted, Mr. Jansen, the famous Parisian scientist, and our professor, among others. Mme. Charlet insisted that she did not freeze three of her fingers, as is stated by Mr. Twain, and the professor trusts that a correction will be made in the next edition of the work.

This article, by an anonymous author, was originally printed in the Hartford *Courant*. Twain discusses the "English lady"—a Miss Stratton—who scaled Mont Blanc in chapter 16 of the second volume of *A Tramp Abroad*. Upon his visit to the famous mountain in 1878, however, Twain was more cautious than Miss Stratton: He "scaled" it by telescope only.

3 November (Sunday)
"Accused of Plagiarism: Critics say Mark Twain Has Stolen His Last Story"; p. 8
Philadelphia, Pa., Nov. 2—
Literary people in Philadelphia are charging Mark Twain with plagiarism. He is said to have appropriated the entire plot and most of the incidents of his latest story, *A Connecticut Yankee in King Arthur's Court*, from the charming short story *The Fortunate Island*, written in 1882 by "Max Adeler" (Charles Heber Clarke), now editor of the *Textile Record* and *Manufacturer's Record* of Philadelphia. In a morning paper today over two columns were devoted to excerpts from the advance sheets of Twain's story, which will appear in the forthcoming number of the *Century*. The plot and many of the incidents coincide with those of *The Fortunate Island*, which was published by Lee & Shepperd of Boston in 1882,

and in this country had a phenomenally small sale. The proceeds to Mr. Clarke were actually not more than $57. Mr. Clarke when interviewed said that no one could help noticing the coincidence, but said that he did not care to enter into a controversy, as he had given up humorous writing.

This story was telegraphed to the *Post-Dispatch*. Twain's novel, published 10 December 1889, enjoyed moderate sales; nothing came from this charge of plagiarism.

14 November (Thursday)
"Men of Mark"; p. 4

Mark Twain, who has never been accused of excessive modesty, will be tempted to indulge in "the big head." He has been charged with plagiarism.

22 November (Friday)
"Mark Twain and His Wife"; p. 2

Mark Twain lives an idle, easygoing sort of existence during nine months of the year. Unlike most authors, he works in summer and rests all the remainder of the year. His home at Hartford, Conn., is a handsome red-brick Queen Anne villa, the principal attraction of which is a large library on the first floor. Here Mark Twain may be found any day during his loafing season, sitting in a comfortable armchair, with his feet on the windowsill, partly hid by a cloud of tobacco smoke. Mrs. Clemens is a sweet, lovely, refined woman, but a serious drawback to her husband's happiness is the fact that she cannot appreciate his jokes.

This report was reprinted from the Rochester *Democrat*.

14 December (Saturday)
"Women of the World"; p. 4

Mark Twain's wife has written a book under a fictitious name.

This report is not true.

28 December (Saturday)
"Men of Mark"; p. 4

Mark Twain is reputed to be growing indolent with his advancing years. He retires early to bed and never breakfasts before 10 o' clock.

1 January (Wednesday)
"Men of Mark"; p. 4
　　Mark Twain's income is $80,000 a year.

Although his income may have been this high, Twain's expenditures more than equalled it.

24 January (Friday)
"That's Mark Twain: An Amusing Incident of the Famous Beecher Trial"; p. 8
　　New York, Jan. 24—
　　The current issue of the *Shoe and Leather Reporter* has this:
　　"A New York banker was relating the other day an incident of the Beecher trial. He was a warm friend of the great preacher, but he was also acquainted with Mr. Fullerton, one of the counsel for the other side. Mr. Fullerton made an appointment with him to take him over to Brooklyn during the time Mr. Beecher was a witness. After he filed into court with the anti-Beecher procession—Fullerton, Beach, Tilton, and others—he had the uncomfortable feeling that he was in a false position, and he imagined there was reproach in Mr. Beecher's eye as he observed him. Near the prosecuting group sat the man whom the gentlemen were talking of, and whom he took for granted to be the 'mutual friend,' Moulton. The fellow's face had a strange fascination for him. He could not keep his eyes off of him, and the more he looked the more he wondered how a man so near Beecher's caliber could have trusted a person with a countenance as that. This distrust and dislike of his grew as long as he sat where he could get a view of him. After a while, he said to someone near him, 'That's Moulton, of course,' pointing in the direc-

tion whither his eyes had been so long bent. 'I should not think a jury would put much confidence in anything he testified to.'

"'Why, that is not Moulton, ' replied the party he had spoken to, 'that's Mark Twain.'"

Henry Ward Beecher (1813-87), the most prominent minister of his day, was sued by Theodore Tilton in January 1875 for having an adulterous relationship with his wife. Twain did in fact attend some sessions of the trial, which eventually ended in a hung jury in June 1875 although Beecher's reputation had already been destroyed. The trial itself, and how the press reveled in it, disgusted Twain (*Mr. Clemens & MT* 157-58). There is no evidence to suggest that Twain actually resembled Frank Moulton, a friend of Tilton's who had succeeded in tricking Beecher into confessing his sins.

26 January (Sunday)
no headline; p. 4

The *Saturday Review* says that Mark Twain's latest book is a triumph of dullness, vulgarity, and ignorance. Twain can make use of this effectively as an advertisement because it is proof that his humor is entirely different from what is called humor in England.

The book that so offended the *Saturday Review* was *A Connecticut Yankee*, published in December of 1889. Twain had refused to delete any of its sarcasms about English history or tradition for its British publication.

4 February (Tuesday)
"Harriet Beecher Stowe"; p. 4

This profile of Stowe (1811-96) mentions that she often enjoyed visiting her Hartford neighbors, including Mark Twain. By 1890, however, she was extremely senile and had an annoying habit of entering a house, sneaking up on a person and, as Twain later remembered, "fetch[ing] a war whoop that would jump that person out of his clothes" (qtd. in *Nook Farm* 88).

9 March (Sunday)
"Mark Twain Enjoined"; p. 3

New York, March 8—

Author and playwright Edward H. House has been successful in his suit to enjoin Samuel S. [sic] Clemens (Mark Twain), Mrs. Abby Sage Richardson, and Daniel Frohman from producing *The Prince and the Pauper*. An injunction against the defendants was granted today by Judge Daly.

After he was unable to write a stageable version of *The Prince and the Pauper* for professional actors, in late 1886 Twain urged his friend E. W. House (1836-1901) to dramatize the novel if he could (*MT & the Theatre* 84). House later claimed that he had immediately begun work on the project, but on 13 May 1889 Twain signed a contract giving dramatization rights to Abby Sage Richardson (1837-1900) for a production to be staged at the Lyceum Theatre, which was owned by Daniel Frohman (1851-1904). As soon as he learned of the production, House copyrighted his version and threatened suit. Twain and his lawyers attempted to compromise with House (pointing out that no written contract existed), but he rejected all settlements. Meanwhile, Richardson's *The Prince and the Pauper* premiered 24 December 1889 in Philadelphia to a large audience; it seemed as if the play would be a huge success. House then filed suit to stop the production. Eventually, a compromise was reached by which House would receive a percentage of the profits (*MT & the Theatre* 87-89). The play subsequently went on to become a modest success, although it never achieved the acclaim that *Colonel Sellers* had attained.

23 March (Sunday)
no headline; p. 4

A relationship has been discovered between that great German of "Blood and Iron" and the distinguished American of "Nerve and Brass" by translating Bismarck Schoenhausen into Mark Twain Prettyhouse.

27 April (Sunday)
no headline; p. 20

For the humor page, a *Post-Dispatch* artist drew two caricatures of Twain, one with his trademark bushy moustache and one without. Under the picture of a clean-shaven humorist, a verse is printed:
Shorn or unshorn, the fact remains
That they're identically the same,
And that they're one, although they're Twain.

29 April (Tuesday)
"Men of Mark"; p. 4

Mark Twain says he once quit smoking. It was when he began to write *Roughing It* and it took him three weeks to write three chapters. He resumed smoking and finished the book in three months.

Twain's reputation for smoking cigars and pipes became legendary, and he was never slow to exploit his habit. In a speech at a banquet to honor his 70th birthday, for example, Twain remarked that he had made a point "never to smoke when asleep, and never to refrain when awake."

24 May (Saturday)
"Men of Mark"; p. 4

Mark Twain's success in life, says a correspondent of the Chicago *Times*, seems to have made him crusty and sour. He is worth considerably over $2,000,000.

This statement vastly overestimates Twain's fortune, which in fact was nearly depleted due to his investment in the Paige Typesetter.

24 September (Wednesday)
"Men of Mark"; p. 4

Mark Twain received $60,000 in royalties from the play in which the famous Mulberry Sellers appeared.

This statement of Twain's wealth, unlike that of 24 May, is probably true.

29 October (Wednesday)
"Killed by a Train—A Doctor's Advertisement—Mark Twain's Mother"; p. 8

In a paragraph of miscellaneous news, a brief obituary of Jane Clemens appears:

Hannibal, Oct. 29—

The remains of Mrs. Jane Clemens, mother of Mark Twain, will arrive here tomorrow morning from Keokuk. The funeral service will be held in the First Presbyterian Church, and the interment will be in Mount Olivet Cemetery. Hannibal was the home of Mrs. Clemens years ago, and the scene of Mark Twain's boyhood days.

25 December (Thursday)
"Authors' Christmas Greetings: Sentiments of a Number of Well-Known Writers"; p. 8

Along with greetings from Oliver Wendell Holmes, James Whitcomb Riley, and Frank Stockton, there is one from Twain:

It is my heartwarm and world-embracing Christmas hope

and aspiration that all of us—the high, the low, the rich, the poor, the admired, the despised, the loved, the hated, the civilized, the savage—may eventually be gathered together in a heaven of loving feast and peace and bliss—except the inventor of the telephone.

Hartford, Dec. 23,

Mark Twain.

In the spring of 1877, Twain, who had $23,000 to invest, rejected overtures from an agent of Alexander Graham Bell who wanted him to buy stock in the telephone. Twain, convinced it was only a "wildcat speculation," declined and later sank a good deal of his money into the Paige Typesetter. Ironically, he realized the value of the telephone too late. As he remembers in *Autobiography*, "About the end of the year (or possibly in the beginning of 1878) I put up a telephone wire from my house down to the *Courant* office, the only telephone wire in town, and the *first* one that was ever used in a private house in the world" (232-33).

1891

23 February (Monday)
"Men of Mark"; p. 4

Mark Twain, among other equally big investments, has $170,000 sunk in a typesetting machine.

See 19 January 1886 and 3 September 1887 for other reports of the Paige Typesetter.

20 May (Wednesday)
"Men of Mark"; p. 4

Mark Twain is going abroad and will take his family along with him. He proposes to remain away for some years.

Twain closed his house in Hartford because of the enormous expenses of running it. Although he intended to return after his financial situation improved, he never lived in it again. On 6 June, the family sailed to Europe.

21 June (Sunday)
"The Book Table"; p. 13

Mark Twain has gone to Europe with his family. He expects to remain abroad several years.

13 July (Monday)
"Men of Mark"; p. 4

Mark Twain is in Paris. As he cannot write French, the gay city is open to congratulations.

8 August (Saturday)
"Men of Mark"; p. 4

Mark Twain is at Aix nursing a cramped wrist, bathing to recover his health, and generally finding life around the rouge et noir tables as dull as criticism upon his own works.

Although Twain himself suffered from rheumatism in his arm, the baths at Aix-les-Baines—and later at Marienbad—were primarily intended for his wife, who had developed heart trouble. Twain wrote an essay about his visit to Aix which was printed in the *Post-Dispatch* on 8 November.

22 October (Thursday)
"Made Mark Twain Laugh"; p. 12

Mark Twain says the following is the best boy's composition he ever read:

"On Girls

"Girls are very stuck-up and dignefied in their maner and behaveyour.

"They think more of dress than anything, and like to play with dowls and rags. They cry if they see a cow in afar distance and are afraid of guns. They stay at home all the time and go to church every Sunday. They are al-ways sick. They are al-ways funny and making fun of boy's hands and they say how dirty. They can't play marbles. I pity them poor things. They make fun of boys and then turn around and love them.

"I don't beleave they ever kiled a cat or anything. They look out every night and say oh ant the moon lovely. There is one thing I have not told and that is they al-ways now their lessons bettern boys."

This anecdote is excerpted from one of Twain's essays entitled "English as She is Taught"; see 10 February 1887 for further excerpts from his essay.

8 November (Sunday)
"Paradise of the Rheumatics: Mark Twain's Observations on the Baths and the Use of Kings for Advertising Purposes"; p. 12

Aix-les-Bains, Oct. 26—

Certainly Aix-les-Bains is an enchanting place. It is a strong word, but I think the facts justify it. True, there is a rabble of nobilities, big and little, here all the time, and often a king or two, but as these behave quite nicely and also keep mainly to themselves, they are little or no annoyance. And then a king makes the best advertisement there is, and the cheapest. All he costs is a reception at the station by the mayor and the police in their Sunday uniforms, shop-front decorations along the route from station to hotel, brass band at the hotel, fireworks in the evening, free bath in the morning. This is the whole expense; and in return for it he goes away from here with the broad of his back metaphorically stenciled over with display ads, which shout to all nations of the earth, assisted by the telegraph:

Rheumatism routed at Aix-les-Bains!

Gout admonished. Nerves braced up!

All Diseases welcomed, and satisfaction given

or the money returned at the door!

We leave nature's noble cliffs and crags undefiled and uninsulted by the advertiser's paintbrush. We use the back of a king, which is better and properer, and more effective, too, for the cliff stands still and few see it, but the king moves across the fields of the world and is visible from all points like a constellation. We are out of kings this week, but one will be along soon—possibly his Satanic Majesty of Russia. There's a colossus for you! A mysterious and terrible form that towers up into unsearchable space and cast a shadow across the universe like a planet in eclipse. There will be one absorbing spectacle in this world when we stencil him and start him out.

This is an old valley, this of Aix, both in the history of man and in the geologic records of the rocks. Its little lake of Bourget carries the human history back to the lake dwellers, furnishing seven groups of their habitations, and Dr. Graveyard says in his interesting local guidebook that the mountains round about furnish "geologically, a veritable epitome of the globe." The stratified chapters of the earth's history are clearly and permanently written on the sides of the roaring bulk of the Dent du Chat, but many of the layers of race, religion, and government, which in turn have flourished and perished here between the lake dweller of several thousand years ago and the French republican government of today, are ill-defined and uninforming by comparison. There were several varieties of pagans. They went their way, one after the other, down into night and oblivion, leaving no account of themselves, no memorials. The Romans arrived 2,300 years ago; other parts of France are rich with remembrances of their eight centuries of occupation, but not many are here. Other pagans followed the Romans. By and by, Christianity arrived, some 400 years after the time of Christ. The long procession of races, languages and religions, and dynasties demolished each other's monuments and obliterated each other's records—it is man's way, always.

As a result, nothing is left of the handiwork of the remoter inhabitants of the region except the constructions of the lake dwellers and some Roman odds and ends. There is part of a small Roman temple, there is part of a Roman bath, there is a graceful and battered Roman arch. It stands on a turfy level over the way from the present great bath house, is surrounded by magnolia trees, and is both a picturesque and suggestive object. It has stood there some 1,000 years. Its nearest neighbor, not 20 steps away, is a Catholic church. They are symbols of the two chief eras in the history of Aix. Yes, and of the European world. I judge that the venerable arch is held in reverent esteem by everybody, and that this esteem is sufficient protection from insult, for it is the only public structure I have yet seen in France which lacks the sign, "It is forbidden to post bills here." Its neighbor, the church, has that sign on more than one of its sides, and the other signs, too, forbidding certain other sorts of desecration.

The arch's next nearest neighbor—just at its elbow, like the church—is the telegraph office. So there you have the three great eras bunched together—the era of war, the era of theology, the era of business. You pass under the arch, and the buried Caesars seems to rise from the dust of the centuries and flit before you; you pass by that old battered church, and are in touch with the middle ages, and with another step you can put down 10 francs and shake hands with Oshkosh under the Atlantic.

It is curious to think what changes the last of the three symbols stands for; changes in men's ways and thoughts, changes in material civilization, changes in the Deity—or in men's conception of the Deity, if that is an exacter way of putting it. The second of the symbols arrived in the earth at a time when the Deity's possessions consisted of a small sky freckled with mustard seed stars, and under it a patch of landed estate not so big as the holdings of the Czar today, and all his time was taken up in trying to keep a handful of Jews in some sort of order—exactly the same number of them that the Czar has lately been dealing with in a more abrupt and far less loving and long-suffering way. At a later time—a time within all old men's memories—the Deity was otherwise engaged. He was dreaming his eternities away on his great white throne, steeped in the soft bliss of hymns of praise wafted aloft without ceasing from choirs of ransomed souls, Presbyterians and the rest. This was a Deity proper enough to the size and condition of things, no doubt a provincial Deity with provincial tastes. The change since has been inconceivably vast. His empire has been unimaginably enlarged. Today he is master of a universe made up of myriads upon myriads of gigantic suns, and among them, lost in that limitless sea of light, floats that atom, his earth, which once seemed so good and satisfactory and cost so many days of patient labor to build, a mere cork adrift in the waters of a shoreless Atlantic. This is the business era, and no doubt he is governing his huge empire now, not by dreaming the time away in the buzz of hymning choirs, with occasional explosions of arbitrary power disproportioned to the size of the annoyance, but, by applying laws of a sort proper and necessary to the sane and successful management of a complex and prodigious establishment, and by seeing to it that the exact and constant operation of these laws is not interfered with for the accommodation of any individual or political or religious faction or nation.

Mighty has been the advance of the nations and the liberalization of thought. A result of it is a changed Deity, a Deity of a dignity and sublimity proportioned to the majesty of his office and the magnitude of his empire, a Deity who has been freed from a hundred fretting chains and will in time be freed from the rest by several ecclesiastical bodies who have these matters in charge. It was, without a doubt, a mistake and a step backward when the Presbyterian Synods of America recently decided by vote to leave him still embarrassed with the dogma of infant damnation. Situated as we are, we cannot at present know with how much of anxiety he watched the balloting, nor with how much of grieved disappointment he observed the result.

Well, all these eras above spoken of are modern, they are of last week, they are of yesterday, they are of this morning, so to speak. The springs, the healing waters that gush up from under this hillside village, indeed, are ancient; they, indeed, are a genuine antiquity; they antedate all these fresh human matters by processions of centuries; they were born with the fossils of the Dent du Chat, and they have always been limpid and always abundant. They furnished a million gallons a day to wash the lake dwellers with, the same to wash the Caesars with, no less to wash Balzac with, and have not diminished on my account. A million gallons a day—for how many days? Figures cannot set forth the number. The delivery in the aggregate has amounted to an Atlantic. And there is still an Atlantic down in there. By Dr. Graveyard's calculation, that Atlantic is three quarters of a mile down in the earth. The calculation is based upon the temperature of the water, which is 114 deg. to 117 deg. Fahrenheit, the natural law being that below a certain depth heat augments at the rate of one degree for every 60 feet of descent.

Aix is handsome and is handsomely situated, too, on its hill slope with its stately prospect of mountain range and plain spread out before it and about it. The streets are mainly narrow and steep and crooked and interesting and offer considerable variety in the way of names. On the corner of one of them you read this: "Rue du Puits d'Enfer—Pit of Hell Street. Some of the sidewalks are only 18 inches wide; they are for the cats, probably. There is a pleasant park, and there are spacious and beautiful grounds connected with the two great pleasure resorts, the Cercle and the Villa des Fleurs. The town consists of big hotels, little hotels, and pensions. The season lasts about six months, beginning with May. When it is at its height, there are thousands of visitors here, and in the course of the season as many as 20,000 in the aggregate come and go.

These are not all here for the baths; some come for the gambling facilities and some for the climate. It is a climate where the field strawberry flourishes through the spring, summer, and fall. It is hot in the summer, and hot in earnest; but this is only in the daytime; it is not hot at night. The English season is May and June; they get a good deal of rain then, and they like that. The Americans take July, and the French take August. By the 1st of July the open air music and the evening concerts and operas and plays are fairly under way, and from that time onward the rush of pleasure has a steadily increasing boom. It is said that in August the great grounds and the gambling rooms are crowded all the time and no end of ostensible fun is going on.

It is a good place for rest and sleep and general recuperation of forces. The book of Dr. Graveyard says there is something about this atmosphere which is the deadly enemy of insomnia, and I think this must be true, for if I am any judge this town is at times the noisiest in Europe, and yet a body gets more sleep here than he could at home. I don't care where his home is. Now, we are living at a most comfortable and satisfactory pension, with a garden of shade trees and flowers and shrubs, and a convincing air of quiet and repose. But just across the narrow street is the little market square, and at a corner of that is the church that is neighbor to the Roman arch, and that narrow street and that billiard table of a marketplace and that church are able, on a bet, to turn out more noise to the cubic yard at the wrong time than any other similar combination in the earth or out of it. In the street you have the skull-bursting thunder of the passing hack, a volume of sound not producible by six hacks anywhere else; on the hack is a lunatic with a whip, which he cracks to notify the public to get out of his way. This crack is as keen and sharp and penetrating and ear-splitting as a pistol shot at close range, and the lunatic delivers it in volleys, not single shots. You think you will not be able to live till he gets by, and when he does get by he only leaves a vacancy for the bandit who sells *Le Petit Journal* to fill with his strange and awful yell. He arrives with the early morning and the market people, and there is a dog who arrives at about the same time and barks steadily at nothing till he dies, and they fetch another dog just like him. The bark of this breed is the twin of the whip volley, and stabs like a knife. By and by, what is left of you the church bell gets. There are many bells, and apparently 6,000 or 7,000 town clocks, and as they are all five minutes apart—probably by law—there are no intervals. Some of them are striking all the time—at least, after you go to bed they are. There is one clock that strikes the hour, and then strikes it over again to see if it was right. Then for evenings and Sundays there is a chime—a chime that starts in pleasantly and musically, then suddenly breaks into a frantic roar and boom, and the crash of warring sounds makes you think Paris is up and the revolution come again. And yet, as I have said, one sleeps here—sleeps like the dead. Once he gets his grip on his sleep, neither hack, nor whip, nor news fiend, nor dog, nor bell cyclone, nor all of them together can wrench it loose or mar its deep and tranquil continuity. Yes, there is indeed something in this air that is death to insomnia.

The buildings of the Cercle and the Villa des Fleurs are huge in size and each has a theater in it and a great restaurant, also conveniences for gambling and general and variegated entertainment. They stand in ornamental grounds of great extent and beauty. The multitudes of fashionable folk sit at refreshment tables in the open air afternoons and listen to the music, and it is there that they mainly go to break the Sabbath.

To get the privilege of entering these grounds and buildings you buy a ticket for a few francs which is good for the whole season. You are then free to go and come at all hours, attend the plays and concerts free, except on special occasions, gamble, buy refreshments, and make yourself symmetrically comfortable.

Nothing could be handier than those two little theaters. The curtain doesn't rise until 8:30. Then between the acts one can idle for half an hour in the other departments of the building, damaging his appetite in the restaurants or his pocket in the baccarat room. The singers and actors are from Paris and their performance is beyond praise.

I was never in a fashionable gambling hall until I came here. I had read several millions of descriptions of such places, but the reality was new to me. I very much wanted to see this animal, especially the now historic game of baccarat, and this was a good place for Aix ranks next to Monte Carlo for high play and plenty of it. But the result was what I might have expected—the interest of the looker-on perishes with the novelty of the spectacle—that is to say, in a few minutes. A permanent and intense interest is acquirable in baccarat or in any other game, but you have to buy it. You don't get it by standing around looking on.

The baccarat table is covered with green cloth and is marked off in divisions with chalk or something. The banker sits in the middle, the croupier opposite. The customers fill all the chairs at the table, and the rest of the crowd are massed at their backs and leaning over them to deposit chips or gold coins. Constantly, money and chips are flung upon the table, and the game seems to consist in the croupier's reaching for those things with a flexible sculling oar and raking them home. It appeared to be a rational enough game for him, and if I could have borrowed his oar I would have staid, but I didn't see where the entertainment of the others came in. This is because I saw without perceiving and observed without understanding. For the widow and the orphan and the others do win money there. Once, an old gray mother in Israel or elsewhere pulled out, and I heard her say to her daughter or her granddaughter as they passed me: "There, now I've won six louis, and I'm going to quit while I'm ahead." Also, there was this statistic. A friend pointed to young man with the dead stub of a cigar in his mouth, which he kept munching nervously all the time and pitching $100 chips on the board while two sweet young girls reached down over his shoulder to deposit modest little gold pieces, and said: "He's only funning now; wasting a few hundred to pass the time—waiting for the 'gold room' to open, you know, which won't be until well after midnight—then you'll see him bet! He won £14,000 there last night. They don't bet anything there but big money."

The thing I chiefly missed was the haggard people with the intense eye, the hunted look, the desperate mien, candidates for suicide and the pauper's grave. They are in the descriptions, as a rule, but they were off-duty that night. All the gamblers, male and female, old and young, looked abnormally cheerful and prosperous.

However, all the nations were there, clothed richly, and speaking all the languages. Some of the women were painted and were evidently shaky as to character. These items tallied with the descriptions well enough.

The etiquette of the place was difficult to master. In the brilliant and populous halls and corridors you don't smoke, and you wear your hat, no matter how many ladies are in the thick throng of drifting humanity; but the moment you cross the sacred threshold and enter the gambling hall, off the hat must come, and everybody lights his cigar and goes to suffocating the ladies.

But what I came here for five weeks ago was the baths. My right arm was disabled with rheumatisim. To sit at home in America and guess out the European bath best fitted for a particular ailment or combination of ailments, it is not possible, and it would not be a good idea to experiment in that way, anyhow. There are a great many curative baths on the continent, and some are good for one disease but bad for another. So it is necessary to let a physician name your bath for you. As a rule, Americans go to London to get this advice, and South Americans go to Paris for it. Now and then an economist chooses his bath himself and does a thousand miles of railroading to get to it, and then the local physicians tell him he has come to the wrong place. He sees that he has lost time and money and strength, and almost the minute he realizes this he loses his temper. I had the rheumatism and was advised to go to Aix, not so much because I had that disease as because I had the promise of certain others. What they were was not explained to me, but they are either in the following menu, or I have been sent to the wrong place. Dr. Graveyard's book says:

"We know the class of maladies benefited by the water and baths at Aix are those due to defect of nutrition, debility of the nervous system, or to a gouty, rheumatic, herpetic, or scrofulous diathesis—all diseases extremely debilitating and requiring a tonic, and not a depressing action of the remedy. This it seems to find here, as recorded experience and daily action can testify. . . . According to the line of treatment, followed particularly with due regard to the temperature, the action of Aix waters can be made sedative, exciting, derivative, or alternative and tonic."

The "Establishment" is the property of France, and all the officers and servants are employees of the French government. The bath house is a huge and massive pile of white marble masonry, and looks more like a temple than anything else. It has several floors and each is full of bath cabinets. There is every kind of bath—for the nose, the ears, the throat, vapor baths, tube baths, swimming baths, and all people's favorite, the douche. It is a good building to get lost in when you are not familiar with it. From early morning until nearly noon people are streaming in and streaming out without halt. The majority come afoot, but great numbers are brought in sedan chairs, a sufficiently ugly contrivance whose cover is a steep little tent made of striped canvas. You see nothing of the patient in this diving-bell as the bearers tramp along, except a glimpse of his ankles bound together and swathed around with blankets or towels to that generous degree that the result suggests a sore piano leg. By attention and practice the pall-bearers have got so that they can keep out of step the whole time—and they do it. As a consequence their veiled churn goes rocking, tilting, swaying along like a bell-buoy in a ground swell. It makes the oldest sailor seasick to look at that spectacle.

The "course" is usually 15 douche baths and five tub baths. You take the douche three days in a succession, then knock off and take a tub. You keep up this distribution through the course. If one course does not cure you, you take another one after an interval. You seek a local physician and he examines your case and prescribes the kind of bath required for it, with various other particulars; then you buy your course tickets and pay for them in advance—$9. With the tickets you get a memorandum book with your dates and the hours all set down in it. The doctor takes you into the bath the first morning and gives some instructions to the two doucheurs who are to handle you through the course. The pour boires are about 10 cents to each of the men for each of the baths, payable at the end of the course. Also, at the end of the course, you pay three or four francs to the superintendent of your department of the bath house. These are useful particulars to know and are not to be found in the books. A servant of your hotel carries your towels and sheet to the bath daily and brings them away again. They are the property of the hotel; the French government doesn't furnish these things.

You meet all sorts of people at a place like this, and if you give them a chance they will submerge you under their experiences, for they are either glad or sorry they came and they want to spread their feelings out and enjoy them. One of these said to me:

"It's great, these baths. I didn't come here for my health—I only came to find out if there was anything the matter with me. The doctor told me if there was, the symptoms would soon appear. After the first douche I had sharp pains in all my muscles. The doctor said it was different varieties of rheumatism, and the best varieties there were, too. After my second bath I had aches in my bones and skull and around. The doctor said it was different varieties of neuralgia, and the best in the market—anybody could tell me so. I got many new kinds of pain out of my third douche. These were in my joints. The doctor said it was gout, complicated with heart disease, and encouraged me to go on. Then we had the fourth douche, and I came out on a stretcher that time and fetched with me one vast, diversified, undulating, continental kind of pain, with horizons to it and zones and parallels of latitude and meridians of longitude and isothermal belts and variations on the compass—O, everything tidy and right up to the latest developments, you know. The doctor said it was inflammation of the soul, and just the very thing. Well, I went right on gathering them in—toothache, liver complaint, softening of the brain, nostalgia, bronchitis, osteology, fits, coleoptera, hydrangea, cyclopedia britannica, delirium tremens, and a lot of other things that I've got down in my list that I'll show you, and you can keep it if you like and tally off the bric-a-brac as you lay in.

"The doctor said I was grand proof of what these baths could do; said I had come here as innocent of disease as a grindstone, and inside of three weeks these baths had sluiced out of me every important ailment known to medical science, along with considerable more that were entirely new and patentable. Why, he wanted to exhibit me in his bay window."

There seems to be a good many liars this year. I began to take the baths and found them most enjoyable; so enjoyable that if I hadn't a disease I would have borrowed one just to have a pretext for going on. They took me to a stone-floored basin about 14 feet square, which had enough strange-looking pipes and things in it to make it look like a torture chamber. The two half-naked men seated me on a pine stool and kept a couple of warm-water jets as thick as one's wrist playing upon me while they kneaded me, stroked me, twisted me, and applied all the other details of the scientific massage to me for seven or eight minutes. Then they stood me up and played a powerful jet upon me all around for another minute. The cool shower bath came next, and the thing was over. I came out of the bath house a few minutes later feeling younger and fresher and finer than I have felt since I was a boy. The spring and cheer and delight of this exaltation lasted three hours, and the same uplifting effect followed the other 20 douches which I have taken since.

After my first douche I went to the chemist's on the corner, as per instructions, and asked for half a glass of Challe water. It comes from a spring 16 miles from here. It was furnished to me, but, perceiving that there was something the matter with it, I offered to wait till they could get some that was fresh, but they said it always smelt that way. They said that the reason that this was so much more rank than the sulphur water of the bath was that it contained 32 times as much sulphur as that. It may be true, but in my opinion that water comes from a cemetery, and not a fresh cemetery either. History says that one of the early Roman generals lost an army down there, somewhere. If he could come back now I think this water would help him find it again. However, I drank the Challe, and have drunk it once or twice every day since. I suppose that it is all right, but I wish I knew what was the matter with those Romans.

My first baths developed plenty of pain, but the subsequent ones removed almost all of it. I have got back the use of my arm these last few days, and I am going away now.

There are many beautiful drives around Aix, many interesting places to visit, and much pleasure to be found in paddling about the little Lake Bourget on the small steamers, but the excursion which satisfied me best was a trip to Annecy and its neighborhood. You go to Annecy in an hour by rail, through a garden land that has not had its equal for beauty, perhaps, since Eden; and certainly Eden was not as cultivated as this garden is. The charm and loveliness of the whole region are bewildering. Picturesque rocks, forest-clothed hills, slopes richly bright in the cleanest and greenest grass, fields of grain without fleck or flaw, dainty of color, and as shiny and shimmery as silk, old gray mansions and towers half-buried in foliage and sunny eminences, deep chasms with precipitous walls, and a swift stream of pale blue water between, with now and then a tumbling cascade, and always noble mountains in view, with vagrant white clouds curling about their summits.

Then at the end of an hour you come to Annecy and rattle through its old crooked lanes, built solidly up with curious old houses that are a dream of the middle ages, and presently you come to the main object of your trip, Lake Annecy. It is a revelation, it is a miracle. It brings the tears to a body's eyes it is so enchanting. That is to say, it affects you just as all things that you instantly recognize as perfect affect you—perfect music, perfect eloquence, perfect art, perfect joy, perfect grief. It stretches itself out there in the caressing sunlight, and away toward its border of majestic mountains, a crisped and radiant plain of water of the divinest blue that can be imagined. All the blues are there, from the faintest shoal water suggestion of the color, detectable only in the shadow of some

overhanging object, all the way through a little blue and a little bluer still, and again a shade bluer till you strike the deep,
rich Mediterranean splendor which breaks the heart in your
bosom it is so beautiful.

And the mountains, as you skim along on the steamboat,
how stately their forms, how noble their proportions, how
green their velvet slopes, how soft the mottlings of sun and
shadow that play about the rocky ramparts that crown them,
how opaline the vast upheavals of snow banked against the
sky in the remotenesses beyond—Mont Blanc and the others—how shall anybody describe? Why, not even the painter
can quite do it, and the most the pen can do is to suggest.

Up the lake there is an old abbey—Talloires—relic of the
middle ages. We stopped there; stepped from the sparkling
water and the rush and boom and fret and fever of the 19th
century into the solemnity and the silence and the soft gloom
and the brooding mystery of a remote antiquity. The stone
step at the water's edge had the traces of a well-worn inscription on it; the wide flight of stone steps that led up to the
front door was polished smooth by the passing feet of forgotten centuries, and there was not an unbroken stone among
them all. Within the pile was the old square cloister with
covered arcade all around it where the monks of ancient
times used to sit and meditate, and now and then welcome to
their hospitalities the wandering knight with his tin breeches
on, and on the middle of the square court (open to the sky)
was a stone well curb, cracked and slick with age and use, and
all about were weeds, and among the weeds moldy brickbats
that the Crusaders used to throw at each other. A passage at
the further side of the cloister led to another weedy and roof-
less little enclosure beyond, where there was a ruined wall
clothed to the top with masses of ivy, and flanking it was a
battered and picturesque arch. All over the building there
were comfortable rooms and comfortable beds, and clean
plank floors with no carpets on them. In one bedroom up-
stairs were a half a dozen portraits, dimming relics of the
vanished centuries—portraits of abbots who used to be as
grand as princes in their old day and very rich and much
worshipped and very holy; and in the next room there was a
howling chromo and an electric bell. Downstairs there was
an ancient wood carving with a Latin word commanding silence, and there was a new piano close by. Two elderly

French women, with the kindest and honestest and sincerest faces have the abbey now and they board and lodge people who are tired of the roar of cities and want to be where the dead silence and serenity and peace of this old nest will heal their blistered spirits and patch up their ragged minds. They fed us well, they slept us well, and I wish I could have staid there a few years and got a solid rest.

This essay is the first in a series of six letters Twain wrote to the *Post-Dispatch* and other newspapers about his European travels in 1891-92; included with this essay is a drawing of Twain. Aix-les-Baines, still popular as a resort today, is in the south of France approximately 50 miles west of Lyon.

17 November (Tuesday)
"Handwriting Talks"; p. 12

In a long article, an anonymous graphologist analyzes the signatures of famous American men; among those he considers are Horace Greeley, Presidents Grant and Garfield, and Mark Twain. A paragraph is devoted to Twain:

> A love of jocosity is strongly marked in the handwriting of Mark Twain. It is deduced from the turned-up finals, which indicate wit. As in the majority of instances of handwriting of this kind, there is a marked eccentricity in the forms of the letters, filled with considerable will and obstinacy. The long bar to the "t" indicates energy, its height above the letter vivacity, while the hook at the end is an indication of quick temper.

An illustration of Twain's signature is printed with this piece. Although this paragraph is a perceptive analysis of his character, if Twain knew of graphology he surely discounted it as a measure of a man—just as he ridiculed phrenology and palm reading (*Autobiography* 63-67).

3 December (Thursday)
"Men of Mark"; p. 4

> Mark Twain, who went to Berlin recently, has been the object of great interest to the people of Germany's capital.

Although he was immensely popular throughout Europe, Germany had an especial love for Twain's writings.

6 December (Sunday)
"Mark Twain Criticises *Parsifal*: The American Humorist Wants
to See a Wagner Opera in Pantomime"; p. 12
Bayreuth, Aug. 2—

It was at Nuremberg that we struck the inundation of mu-
sic-mad strangers that was rolling down upon Bayreuth. It
had been long since we had seen such multitudes of excited
and struggling people. It took a good half hour to pack them
and pair them into the train—and it was the longest train we
have yet seen in Europe. Nuremberg had been witnessing
this sort of experience a couple of times a day for about two
weeks. It gives one an impressive sense of the magnitude of
the biennial pilgrimage. For a pilgrimage is what it is. The
devotees come from the very ends of the earth to worship
their prophet in his own Kaaba in his own Mecca.

If you are living in New York or San Francisco or Chicago
or anywhere else in America, and you conclude by the middle of May that you would like to attend the Bayreuth opera
two months and half later, you must use the cable and get
about it immediately, or you will get no seats, and you must
cable for lodgings, too. Then if you are lucky, you will get
seats in the last row and lodgings on the fringe of the town. If
you stop to write, you will get nothing. There were plenty of
people in Nuremberg when we passed through who had
come on pilgrimage without first securing seats and lodgings.
They had found neither in Bayreuth; they had walked
Bayreuth streets a while in sorrow, then gone to Nuremberg
and found neither beds, nor standing room and had walked
those quaint streets all night waiting for the hotels to open
and empty their guests into the trains and so make room for
these, their defeated brethren and sisters in the faith. They
had endured from 30 to 40 hours railroading on the Continent of Europe—with all that implies of worry, fatigue, and
financial impoverishment—and all they had got, and all they
were to get for it, was handiness and accuracy in kicking
themselves, acquired by practice in the back streets of the two
towns when other people were in bed, for back they must go
over that unspeakable journey with their pious mission un-
fulfilled. These humilated outcasts had the frowsy and un-
brushed and apologetic look of wet cats, and their eyes were
glazed with drowsiness, their bodies were adroop from crown
to sole, and all kindhearted people refrained from asking

them if they had been to Bayreuth and failed to connect, as knowing they would lie.

We reached here (Bayreuth) about mid-afternoon on a rainy Saturday. We were of the wise, and had secured lodgings and opera seats months in advance.

I am not a musical critic and did not come here to write essays about the operas and deliver judgments upon their merits. The little children of Bayreuth could do that with a finer sympathy and a broader intelligence than I. I only care to bring four or five pilgrims to the operas, pilgrims able to appreciate them and enjoy them. What I might write about the performances to put in my odd time would be offered to the public as merely a cat's eye view of a king and not of didactic value.

Next day, which was Sunday, we left for the operahouse— that is to say, the Wagner temple—a little after the middle of the afternoon. The great building stands all by itself, grand and lovely, on high ground outside the town. We were warned that if we arrived after 4 o'clock we should be obliged to pay $2.50 apiece extra by way of fine. We saved that; and it may be remarked here that this is the only opportunity Europe offers of saving money. There was a big crowd in the grounds about the buildings, and the ladies' dresses took the sun with fine effect. I do not mean to intimate that the ladies were in full dress, for that was not so. The dresses were pretty, but neither sex was in evening dress.

The interior of the building is simple—severely so; but there is no occasion for color or decoration since the people sit in the dark. The auditorium has the shape of a keystone, with the stage at the narrow end. There is an aisle on each side, but no aisle in the body of the house. Each row of seats extends in an unbroken curve from one side of the house to the other. There are seven entrance doors on each side of the theater and four at the butt end, 18 doors to admit and emit 1,650 persons. The number of the particular door by which you are to enter the house and leave it is printed on your ticket, and you can use no door but that one. Thus, crowding and confusion are impossible. Not so many as 100 people use any one door. This is better than the usual (and useless) elaborate fireproof arrangements. It is the model theater of the world. It can be emptied while the second hand of a watch makes its circuit. It would be entirely safe, even if it were built of lucifer matches.

If your seat is near the center of a row and you enter late, you must work your way along a rank of about 25 ladies and gentlemen to do it. Yet this causes no trouble, for everybody stands up until all the seats are full; the filling is accomplished in a very few minutes. Then all sit down, and you have a solid mass of 1,500 heads, making a steep cellar-door slant from the rear of the house down to the stage.

All the lights were turned low, so low that the congregation sat in deep and silent gloom. The funeral rustling of dresses and the low buzz of conversation begin to die swiftly down, and presently not the ghost of a sound was left. This profound and increasingly impressive stillness endured for some time—the best precaution for music, spectacle, or speech conceivable. I should think our show people would have invented or imported that simple and impressive device for securing and solidifying the attention of an audience long ago; instead of which they continue to this day to open a performance against a deadly competition in the form of noise, confusion, and a scattered interest.

Finally, out of darkness and distance and mystery soft rich notes rose upon the stillness, and from this grave the dead magician began to weave his spells about his disciples and steep their souls in his enchantments. There was something strangely impressive in the fancy which kept intruding itself that the composer was conscious in his grave of what was going on here, and that these divine sounds were the clothing of thoughts which were at this moment passing through his brain and not recognized and familiar ones which had issued from it at some former time.

The entire overture, long as it was, was played to a dark house with the curtain down. It was exquisite; it was delicious. But straightaway thereafter, of course, came the singing, and it does seem to me that nothing can make a Wagner opera absolutely perfect and satisfactory to the untutored but to leave out the vocal parts. I wish I could see a Wagner opera done in pantomime once. Then one would have the lovely orchestration unvexed to listen to and bathe his spirit in and the bewilderingly beautiful scenery to intoxicate his eyes with, and the dumb acting couldn't mar these pleasures, because there isn't often anything in the Wagner opera that one could call by such a violent name as acting; as a rule all you would see would be a couple of silent people, one of them standing still, the other catching flies. Of course, I do not really mean that he would be catching flies; I only mean that the usual operatic gestures which consist in reaching out first one hand out into the air and then the other might suggest the sport I speak of if the operator attended strictly to business and uttered no sound.

This present opera was *Parsifal*. Madam Wagner does not permit its representation anywhere but here in Bayreuth. The first act of the three occupied two hours, and I enjoyed that in spite of the singing.

I trust that I know as well as anybody that singing is one of the most entrancing and bewitching and moving and eloquent of all the vehicles invented by man for the conveying of feeling; but it seems to me that the chief virtue in song is melody, air, tune, rhythm, or what you please to call it, and that when this feature is absent what remains is a picture with the color left out. I was not able to detect in the vocal parts of *Parsifal* anything that might with confidence be called rhythm or tune or melody; one person performed at a time— and a long time, too—often in a noble, and always in a high-priced, voice; but he only pulled out long notes, then some short ones, then another long one, then a sharp, quick, peremptory bark or two—and so on and so on; and when he was done you saw the information he had conveyed had not compensated for the disturbance. Not always, but pretty often. If two of them would but put in a duet occasionally and blend their voices; but no, they don't do that. The great master, who knew so well how to make 100 instruments rejoice in unison and pour out their souls in mingled and melodious tides of delicious sounds, deals only in barren solos when he put in the vocal parts. It may be that he was deep and only added the singing to his operas for the sake of contrast it would make with the music. Singing! It does seem the wrong name to apply to it. Strictly described, it is a practicing of difficult and unpleasant intervals, mainly. An ignorant person gets tired of listening to gymnastic intervals in the long run, no matter how pleasant they may be. In *Parsifal*, there is a hermit named Gurnemanz who stands on the stage in one spot and practices by the hour, while first one and then another character of the cast endures what he can of it and then retires to die.

During the evening there was an intermission of three-quarters of an hour after the first act and one an hour long after the second. In both instances the theater was totally emptied. People who had previously engaged tables in the sole eating-house were able to put in their time very satisfactorily; the other 1,000 went hungry. The opera was concluded at 10 in the evening or a little later. When we reached home, we had been gone more than seven hours. Seven hours at $5 a ticket is almost too much for the money.

While browsing about the front yard among the crowd between the acts I encountered 12 or 15 friends from different parts of America, and those of them who were most familiar with Wagner said that *Parsifal* seldom pleased at first, but after one had heard it several times it was almost sure to become a favorite. It seemed impossible, but it was true for the statement came from people whose word was not to be doubted.

And I gathered some further information. On the ground I found part of a German musical magazine, and in it a letter written by Uhlic 33 years ago in which he defends the scorned and abused Wagner against people like me who found fault with the comprehensive absence of what our kind regard as singing. Uhlic says Wagner despised "*Jene plapperude musik*," and therefore "runs, trills, and *schnorkel* are disgarded by him." I don't know what a *schnorkel* is, but now that I know it has been left out of these operas I never have missed so much in my life. And Uhlic further says that Wagner's song is true song: that it is "simply emphasized intoned speech." That certainly describes it—in *Parsifal* and some of the other operas; and if I understand Uhlic's elaborate German he apologizes for the beautiful airs in *Tannhauser*. Very well; now that Wagner and I understand each other, perhaps we shall get along better, and I shall stop calling him Waggner, on the American plan, and therefore call him Voggner, as per German custom for I feel entirely friendly now. The minute we get reconciled to a person, how willing we are to throw aside little needless punctilios and pronounce his name right!

Of course, I came home wondering why people should come from all corners of America to hear these operas when we have lately had a season or two of them in New York with these same singers in the several parts and possibly the same orchestra. I resolved to think that out at all hazards.

Tuesday—Yesterday they played the only operatic favorite I have ever had—an opera which has always driven me mad with ignorant delight whenever I have heard it—*Tannhauser*. I heard it first when I was a youth; I heard it next in the last German season in New York. I was busy yesterday and I did not intend to go, knowing that I should have another *Tannhauser* opportunity in a few days; but after 5 o'clock I found myself free and walked out to the operahouse and arrived about the beginning of the second act. My opera ticket admitted me to the grounds in front, past the policeman and the chain, and I thought I would take a rest on a bench for an hour or two and wait for the third act.

In a moment or so the first bugles blew, and the multitude began to crumble apart and melt into the theater. I will explain that this bugle-call is one of the pretty features here. You see, the theater is empty and hundreds of the audience are a good way off in the feeding-house; the first bugle-call is blown about a quarter of an hour before time for the curtain to rise. This company of buglers in uniform march out with military step and send out over the landscape a few bars of the theme of the approaching act, piercing the distances with the gracious notes, then they march to the other entrance and repeat. Presently, they do this over again. Yesterday, only about 200 people were still left in front of the house when the second call was blown; in another half-minute they would have been in the house, but then a thing happened which delayed them—the one solitary thing in this world which could be relied on with certainty to accomplish it, I suppose—an imperial princess appeared in the balcony above them. They stopped dead in their tracks and began to gaze in a stupor of gratitude and satisfaction. The lady presently saw that she must disappear or the doors would be closed upon these worshipers, so she returned to her box. This daughter-in-law of an emperor was pretty; she had a kind face; she was without airs; she is known to be full of common human sympathies. There are many kinds of princesses, but this kind is the most harmful of all, for wherever they go they reconcile people to monarchy and set back the clock of progress. The valuable princes, the desirable princes, are the czars and their sort. By their mere dumb presence in the world they cover with derision every argument that can be invented in favor of royalty by the most ingenious casuist. In his time the husband of this princess was valuable. He led a degraded life; he ended it with his own hand in circumstances and surroundings of a hideous sort, and was buried like a god.

In the operahouse there is a long loft back of the audience, a kind of open gallery in which princes are displayed. It is sacred to them; it is the holy of the holies. As soon as the filling of the house is about complete, the standing multitude turn and fix their eyes upon the princely layout and gaze mutely and longingly and adoringly and regretfully like sinners looking into heaven. They become rapt, unconscious, steeped in worship. There is no spectacle anywhere that is more pathetic than this. It is worth crossing many oceans to see. It is somehow not the same gaze that people rivet upon a Victor Hugo, or Niagara, or the bone of the mastodon, or the guillotine of the Revolution, or the Great Pyramid, or distant Vesuvius smoking in the sky, or any man long celebrated to you by his genius and achievements, or thing long celebrated to you by the praises of books and pictures, no, that gaze is only the gaze of intense curiosity, interest, wonder, engaged in drinking delicious deep draughts that taste good all the way down and appease and satisfy the thirst of a lifetime. Satisfy it—that is the word. Hugo and the mastodon still will have a degree of intense interest thereafter when encountered but never anything approaching the ecstacy of that first view. The interest of a prince is different. It may be envy, it may be worship, doubtless it is a mixture of both— and it does not satisfy its thirst with one view, or even noticeably diminish it. Perhaps the essence of the thing is the value which men attach to a valuable something which has come by luck and not been earned. A dollar picked up in the road is more satisfying to you than the 99 which you had to work for, and money won at faro or in stocks snuggles into your heart in the same way. A prince picks up grandeur, power and a permanent holiday and gratis support by pure accident, the accident of birth, and he stand always before the grieved eye of poverty and obscurity a monumental representative of luck. And then—supremest value of all—his is the only high fortune on the earth which is secure. The commercial millionaire may become a beggar; the illustrious statesman can make a vital mistake and be dropped and forgotten; the illustrious general can lose a decisive battle and with it the consideration of men; but once a prince always a prince—that is to say, an imitation god, and neither hard fortune nor an infamous character nor an addled brain nor the speech of an ass can undeify him. By common consent of all the nations and all the ages the most valuable thing in this world is the homage of men, whether deserved or undeserved. It follows without doubt or question, then, that the most desirable position possible is that of a prince. And I think it also follows that the so-called usurpations with which history is littered are the most excusable misdemeanors which men have committed. To usurp a usurpation—that is all it amounts to, isn't it?

A prince is not to us what he is to a European, of course. We have not been taught to regard him as a god, and so one good look at him is likely to so nearly appease our curiosity as to make him an object of no greater interest the next time. We want a fresh one. But it is not so with the European. I am quite sure of it. The same old one will answer; he never stales. Eighteen years ago I was in London, and I called at an Englishman's house on a bleak and foggy and dismal December afternoon to visit his wife and married daughter by appointment. I waited half an hour and then they arrived, frozen. They explained that they had been delayed by an unlooked-for circumstance: while passing in the neighborhood of Marlborough House they saw a crowd gathering and were told that the Prince of Wales was about to drive out, so they stopped to get a sight of him. They had waited half an hour on the sidewalk, freezing with the crowd, but were disappointed at last—the prince had changed his mind. I said, with a good deal of surprise, "Is it possible that you two have lived in London all your lives and have never seen the Prince of Wales?"

Apparently, it was their turn to be surprised, for they exclaimed: "What an idea! Why, we have seen him hundreds of times."

They had seen him hundreds of time, yet they had waited half an hour in the gloom and the bitter cold, in the midst of a jam of patients from the same asylum, on the chance of seeing him again. It was a stupefying statement, but one is obliged to believe the English, even when they say a thing like that. I fumbled around for a remark, and got out this one:

"I can't understand it at all. If I had never seen Gen. Grant I doubt if I would do that even to get a sight of him." With a slight emphasis on the last word.

Their blank faces showed that they wondered where the parallel came in. Then they said blankly: "Of course not. He is only a president."

It is doubtless a fact that a prince is a permanent interest, an interest not subject to deterioration. The general who was never defeated, the general who never held a council of war, the only general who had ever commanded a connected battlefront 1,200 miles long, the smith who had welded together the broken parts of a great republic and reestablished it where it is quite likely to outlast all the monarchies present and to come, was really a person of no serious consequence to these people. To them, with their training, my general was only a man after all, while their prince was clearly much more than that—a being of wholly unsimiliar construction and constitution, and being no more blood and kinship with men than are the serene eternal lights of the firmament with the poor dull tallow candles of commerce that sputter and die and leave nothing behind but a pinch of ashes and a stink.

I saw the last act of *Tannhauser*. I sat in the gloom and the deep stillness, waiting—one minute, two minutes I do not know exactly how long—then the soft music of the hidden orchestra began to breath its rich, long sighs out from under the distant stage, and by and by the drop-curtain parted in the middle and was drawn softly aside, disclosing the twilighted wood and a wayside shrine with a white-robed girl praying and a man standing near. Presently, that noble chorus of men's voices was heard approaching, and from that moment until the closing of the curtain it was music, just music—music to make one drunk with pleasure, music to make one take scrip and staff and beg his way round the globe to hear it.

To such as are intending to come here in the Wagner season next year I wish to say, bring your dinnerpail with you. If you do, you will never cease to be thankful. If you do not, you will find it a hard fight to save yourself from famishing in Bayreuth. Bayreuth is merely a large village and has no very large hotels or eating-houses. The principle inns are the Golden Anchor and the Sun. At either of these places you can get an excellent meal—no, I mean you can go there and see other people get it. There is no charge for this. The town is littered with restaurants, but they are small and bad and they are overdriven with custom. You must secure a table hours beforehand, and often when you arrive you will find somebody occupying it. We have had this experience. We have had a daily scramble for life; and when I say we, I include shoals of people. I have the impression that the only people who do not have to scramble are the veterans—the disciples who have been here before and know the ropes. I think they arrive about a week before the first opera and engage all the tables for the season. My tribe have tried all kinds of places—some outside of the town, a mile or two— and have captured only nibblings and odds and ends, never in any instance a complete and satisfying meal. Digestible? No, the reverse. These odds and ends are going to serve as souvenirs of Bayreuth, and in that regard their value is not to be overestimated. Photographs fade, bric-a-brac gets lost, busts of Wagner get broken, but once you absorb a Bayreuth-restaurant meal it is your possession and your property until the time comes to embalm the rest of you. Some of these pilgrims have become, in effect, cabinets; cabinets of souvenirs of Bayreuth. It is believed among scientists that you could examine the crop of a dead Bayreuth pilgrim anywhere in the earth and tell where he came from. But I like this ballast. I think a "hermitage" scrape-up at eight in the evening, when all the famine-breeders have been there and laid in their mementoes and gone, it is the quietest thing you can lay on your keelson except gravel.

Thursday—They keep two teams of singers in stock for the chief roles, and of these is composed of the most renowned artists in the world with Materna and Alvary in the lead. I suppose a double team is necessary; doubtless a single team would die of exhaustion in a week, for all the plays last from four in the afternoon till 10 at night. Nearly all the labor falls upon the half-dozen head singers, and apparently they are required to furnish all the noise they can for the money. If they feel a soft, whispery, mysterious feeling they are required to open out and let the public know it. Operas are given only on Sundays, Mondays, Wednesdays, and Thursdays, with three days of ostensible rest a week and two teams to do the four operas; but the ostensible rest is devoted largely to rehearsing. It is said that the off days are devoted to

rehearsing from some time in the morning till 10 at night.
Are there two orchestras, too? It is quite likely since there are
110 names in the orchestra list.

Yesterday, the opera was *Tristan and Isolde*. I have seen
all sorts of audiences—at theaters, operas, concerts, lectures,
sermons, funerals—but none which was twin to the Wagner
audience of Bayreuth for fixed and reverential attention. Absolute attention and petrified retention to the end of an act is
an attitude assumed at the beginning of it. You detect no
movement in the solid mass of heads and shoulders. You
seem to sit with the dead in the gloom of a tomb. You know
that they are being stirred to their profoundest depths; that
there are times when they want to rise and wave handkerchiefs and shout their approbation, and times when tears are
running down their face and it would be a relief to free their
pent emotions in sobs or screams; yet you hear not one utter-
ance till the curtain swings together and the closing strains
have slowly faded out and died; then the dead rise with one
impulse and shake the building with their applause. Every
seat is full in the first act; there is not a vacant one in the last.
If a man would be conspicuous, let him come here and retire
from the house in the midst of an act. It would make him
celebrated.

The audience reminds me of nothing I have ever seen
and of nothing I have read about except the city in the Ara-
bian tale where all the inhabitants have been turned to brass
and the traveler finds them after centuries mute, motionless,
and still retaining the attitudes which they last knew in life.
Here the Wagner audience dress as they please and sit in the
dark and worship in silence. At the Metropolitan in New
York they sit in a glare and wear their showiest harness; they
hum airs, they squeak fans, they titter, and they gabble all the
time. In some of the boxes the conversation and laughter are
so loud as to divide the attention of the house with the stage.
In large measure, the Metropolitan is a showcase for rich
fashionables who are not trained in Wagnerian music and
have no reverence for it, but who like to promote art and
show their clothes.

Can that be an agreeable atmosphere to persons in whom
this music produces a sort of divine ecstasy and to whom its
creator is a very deity, his stage a temple, the works of his
brain and hands consecrated things, and the partaking of

them with eye and ear a sacred solemnity? Manifestly, no.
Then, perhaps the temporary expatriation, the tedious
traversing of seas and continents, the pilgrimage to Bayreuth
stands explained. These devotees would worship in an atmosphere of devotion. It is only here that they can find it
without fleck or blemish or any worldly pollution. In this
remote village there are no sights to see, there is no newspaper to intrude the worries of the distant world, there is nothing going on, it is always Sunday. The pilgrim wends to his
temple out of town, sits out his moving service, returns to
his bed with his heart and soul and his body exhausted by
long hours of tremendous emotion, and he is in no fit condition to do anything but to lie torpid and slowly gather back
life and strength for the next service. This opera of *Tristan
and Isolde* last night broke the hearts of all witnesses who
were of the faith, and I know of some who have heard of
many who could not sleep after it but cried the night away. I
feel strongly out of place here. Sometimes, I feel like the sane
person in a community of the mad; sometimes I feel like the
one blind man where all the others see; the one groping
savage in the college of the learned, and always during
service, I feel like a heretic in heaven.

But by no means do I ever overlook or minify the facts
that this is one of the most extraordinary experiences of my
life. I have never seen anything like this before. I have
never seen anything so great and so fine and real as this
devotion.

Friday—Yesterday's opera was *Parsifal* again. The others
went and they show marked advance in appreciation; but I
went hunting for relics and reminders of the Margravine
Wilhelmina, she of the imperishable *Memoirs*. I am
properly grateful to her for her (unconscious) satire upon
monarchy and nobility, and therefore nothing which her
hand touched or her eye looked upon is indifferent to me. I
am her pilgrim; the rest of the multitude are Wagner's.

Tuesday—I have seen my last two operas; my season is
ended and we cross over to Bohemia this afternoon. I was
supposing that my musical regeneration was accomplished
and perfected because I enjoyed both of these operas, singing
and all, and, moreover, one of them was *Parsifal*, but the
experts have disenchanted me. They say:

"Singing! That wasn't singing; that was the wailing,

screeching of third-rate obscurities, palmed off in the interest of economy."

Well, I ought to have recognized the sign—the old, sure sign that has never failed me in matters of art. Whenever I enjoy anything in art it means that it is mighty poor. The private knowledge of this fact has saved me from going to pieces with enthusiasm in front of many and many a chromo. However, my base instinct does bring me profit sometimes; I was the only man out of 3,200 who got his money back on those two operas.

Richard Wagner (1813-83) selected Bayreuth, about 60 miles northeast of Nuremburg, to house a theater devoted to the performance of his works. Construction of the Festspielhaus began in 1872 and after many financial difficulties was completed four years later. Wagner himself directed many of the annual productions until his death in 1883. *Parsifal*, written between 1876 and 1882, was his last major work and only was performed at Bayreuth under the personal supervision of his widow. Twain, as this essay makes clear, felt disgust for the notion that one man could be considered superior to another man by virtue of their respective births. He especially despised Czar Alexander III (1845-94), who seemed intent to rule Russia by brutally repressing the Jews and other religious minorities in order to set up a state in which dissent or free speech was not allowed. In *Autobiography*, for example, Twain criticizes the czar by noting that as "[c]ruel and pitiful as was life throughout Christendom in the Middle Ages, it was not as cruel, nor as pitiful as is life in Russia today (271-72).

Appendix

This appendix, in chronological order, reprints three articles about Mark Twain from the St. Louis *Globe-Democrat*, the *Post-Dispatch's* primary competitor among the daily newspapers of St. Louis.

13 May 1882 (Saturday)
"Mark Twain's Travels"; p. 8

Samuel L. Clemens (Mark Twain), Hartford, Conn., accompanied by James R. Osgood, the Boston book publisher, and R. H. Phelps, of Hartford, the humorist's stenographer, are at the Southern, having arrived in the city yesterday morning from New Orleans on the Anchor Line boat *Baton Rouge*. It was the intention of the party to leave in the afternoon for Hannibal, Mo., on the steamer *Bald Eagle*, but not making the arrangements expected, they deferred their departure until this afternoon, when they will take the *Green City*. From Hannibal they will go to St. Paul, then to Chicago, and by way of the lakes make their way east.

"I go by water," said Mr. Clemens to a reporter last evening, "because I don't like the railroads. I wouldn't go to heaven by rail if the chance was offered me."

The reporter then reminded Mr. Clemens of a chance meeting two years ago, at the time of the reception in Chicago for Gen. Grant, when that distinguished personage was returning from his trip around the world. One of the special features of the elaborate programme prepared was a speech by "Mark Twain" at McVicker's Theatre, on the subject, announced beforehand, of "Babies." The humorist was stopping at the Palmer House, and, in the course of newspaper events, it became necessary to anticipate some portion of what he was to say. A call at the hotel found him still in bed,

although late in the morning, with the room properly littered with manuscript.

"I am preparing my address now," said Mark cheerily,
when the caller's errand was made known, "and if you'll
wait awhile you can take a copy. This is the way, you know,
we prepare impromptu speeches."

Mr. Clemens remembered it well, and expressed pleasure
at the judicious way in which the "applause" was worked in.
"I was here three weeks ago," he went on, and passed twenty-
four hours in the city without anyone knowing it outside of
one or two friends. Stopped a night right here at the Southern, registering as C. L. Samuels, New York. The three of us
were prowling under fictitious names, and we remained here
just as long as we dared. I am writing a new book, and a tour
of observation down the Mississippi River was necessary in
connection with it. To make such a tour incognito seemed
best, and so we have been dodging people, making our way by
stealth and keeping up a sort of swindle day by day."

"When will your new book be out?"

"Probably about New Year's. I have had a very pleasant
trip, and have been much interested in examining the spread
of the flood and hearing the stories told in connection with it.
I think it would be a capital thing to send a good man down
the river and pick up all the yarns told about it. It seemed to
me that every time they told some incident they added something to it. Then there are men with theories that we have
listened to for hours, and known less when we got through
than when we began."

"What do you think of calling your new book?"

"It hasn't been thought of yet. I was in hopes to get away
this afternoon, but cannot before tomorrow."

"I've a clean night-shirt at your disposal, if all your baggage is at the boat and you want it," broke in Clerk Keith, who
happened to approach.

"I shall want a night-shirt," replied Mr. Clemens, "and I'll
take it."

10 January 1885 (Saturday)
"Mark Twain and George W. Cable"; p. 10

Mark Twain and George W. Cable entertained about 700 of
their admirers in Mercantile Library Hall last night. They
gave recitals of selections from their respective work, Mark

Twain having four pieces on the programme and Mr. Cable the same number. Cable chose passages from his novel *Dr. Sevier*, in which he aimed to illustrate the characters of Narcisse, the Creole, Kate Riley and Mary Richley. All his recitals were successful in pleasing the audience, and before the evening was at an end the author of *Creole Days* was a strong favorite with all present. Mark Twain did not fail, however, to hold his own. He kept the assemblage in excellent humor with his literary surprises, and in the "King Sollemum" passage from *Huckleberry Finn*, the "Tragic Tale of a Fishwife," in which he illustrated the reckless distribution of genders among the nouns of the German language, and in the other selections he tickled the risibles of the audience to an extent that satisfactorily established the popular quality of his humor at least. Mr. Cable is quietly dramatic in his manner, and has a pleasant, pliable voice. His dialectic efforts, too, are very fair. Twain's voice has the resonance of a cracked steamboat whistle. He enunciates slowly, gesticulates with his head, and keeps either hand in a pants pocket during his stay on the stage. Last night's programme will be repeated this afternoon, and tonight new selections will be given.

11 January 1885 (Sunday)
"'Mark Twain'—Cable"; p. 12

"This literary conspiracy," as Mark Twain describes the entertainment given by Mr. George W. Cable and himself, is really a very novel and agreeable affair. The idea of an author reading selections from his own works is not a new one, to be sure; Dickens introduced it many years ago, with pronounced success, and others have since adopted it from time to time, with results of various kinds. But this is the first case, we believe, in which two authors have "joined teams" for reading purposes; and certainly no more two widely-read and popular current authors, and yet two writers more distinctly unlike in their literary methods and their personal characteristics, could easily be brought together as a platform attraction. One is blunt, audacious and strongly individualized; the other is delicate, decorous, and not at all self-assertive except in the sense of aiming to do well what is set before him. They appeal to an audience in ways entirely different, just as they are known to write from entirely different points of view; and not the least interesting feature of the entertainment is the chance it affords for noting the shifting and denoting manner in which their recitations—for they recite almost all of their "readings"—are received in turn by their hearers. One compels outright laughter, while the other seldom achieves more than smiles and a light murmur of gratification. Those who applaud the one do not always applaud the other; and yet it is hard to tell at the end which has seemed to make the surer impression, so much depends upon the fact that they must be judged together to be judged definitely.

The first thing, perhaps, which strikes the observer as to Mr. Cable is his small stature. There is an impression somehow that a man who writes big books should be physically commanding, though there is no logic in such a thought; and Mr. Cable is remarkable rather for being diminutive than surpassing in that respect. He does not come up the ordinary standard either in height or bulk, but is noticeably short, thin, and light in movement, and at first glance just a trifle disappointing. It does not appear quite reasonable that a man so daintily constructed can be the author of those vigorous and powerful stories of Creole life. His head is a good one, however, and his face radiant and reassuring. It is not what would be called a handsome face; it is too pallid, and it is whiskered out of proper proportion, and the long moustache has a tendency to twitch after a fashion that makes it too obviously superfluous. Mr. Cable is a Southern man, but he does not show it in any way. He looks more like a Jerseyman, and still more like an average New Yorker of sedentary employment and severe social tastes. Even his voice is not Southern; but it is very clear and pleasant; and his enunciation is more than usually distinct. He goes about his work with a relish that is infectious, as if he really believed in the characters and scenes which he portrays; and it is quite evident that he has carefully studied all the means by which character is to be specified and picturesque circumstances made vivid and impressive.

Mark Twain, on the other hand, very nearly realizes the idea one would form of him from reading his books. That is to say, he is robust, unconcerned, careless in gait and gesture, and ludicrously solemn of visage—a peculiarity which there is reason to believe he cultivates for business purposes. His voice is harsh, and his habit of nasal drawling is disagreeable, and there are moments when one wishes that he did not find it necessary to do so much hesitating between words and phrases. It is to be inferred, of course, that he thinks his stories good or he would not stand up and tell them night after night in preference to those of anybody else; but it is impossible to avoid wondering now and then if his disinterested and stolid manner is entirely assumed. When Cable is talking it is easy to see that he is not only anxious to be entertaining, but that it is an enjoyment to him at the same time; but nothing of that kind is perceptible in the great humorist's case. His general air is that of man who is fundamentally tired, and who would gladly skip the performance if he could. But it may be that in this very appearance of being bored with his own grotesque yarns lies the secret of persuading other people to laugh at them. We should not like to say that such a thing is out of the range of reasonable probability. And still we have a notion that some, at least, of the stories he tells would be more certain to hit the mark if the audience could be made to feel that he is himself convinced that they are actually and sufficiently funny.

It is to be regretted, we think, that Mr. Cable chooses to make most of his selections from *Dr. Sevier*. It is not generally regarded as his best work, whatever he may think of it, and his admirers would be more pleased, we must believe, if he would present scenes and characters from those of his stories that are both more familiar and more satisfactory. We venture to say, further, than even if he must make *Dr. Sevier* the basis of his readings, he should not give preference to the merely minor persons and incidents. The widow Riley is well enough in her way, and he mimicks her acceptably, but she is of little consequence at best. And so of the suave and deceptive Narcisse, for whom Mr. Cable seems to have a special partiality, but which is shared, we can warrant him, by very few of his readers. There is room to suspect that he has conceived the idea that it is amusement which the people mostly expect, and that it is therefore incumbent upon him to choose in the main such scenes and characters as can be turned to account in that one respect. If so, then he is mistaken, and the mistake is one that is calculated to disparage his standing as an author. He is not in an exact sense a humorist. His reputation has been won in a wholly different field, and through gifts of a wholly different nature. His strength is in the line of the dramatic, the picturesque, the pathetic; and these qualities, we cannot help thinking, should appear more conspicuously in his readings—for otherwise the value of his work is not properly shown, nor his books fitly recommended.

The order of Mark Twain's humor, unlike that of Mr. Cable's, is such that it can be readily adapted to platform uses. It is bold, distinct, imperative, and deals in quick and sharp surprises. Mr. Cable's method, on the contrary, is groping, artificial, and entirely lacking in the element of suddenness, so to speak. Humor of that sort serves an excellent purpose in lightening the pages of a work of serious fiction, and it is useful also in the respect of emphasizing certain forms of character, but when it is subjected to the test of public reading or recitation its want of inherent force and genuineness is at once manifest. Mark Twain's processes of thought lead inevitably to absurd conclusions; he could not avoid such results if he tried. This is not saying that everything he does is bound to be thoroughly laughable and deserving of high praise. He frequently writes trash, and it is necessary to discriminate in passing judgment upon his various contributions to the literature of the period. The fact remains, however, that he is essentially and at all times a humorist, and a very broad and aggressive one. He does not simply reproduce amusing things that he has seen, and report personal peculiarities with which he has come in contact; he originates and invents, and extracts drollery from things not in themselves of a humorous quality. Mr. Cable has no power of that kind; and therefore his humorous efforts suffer by comparison with those of his fellow-reader, and he is obliged to resort to expedients for making his points that are a confession of weakness.

Neither Mark Twain nor Mr. Cable could take a prize in an oratorical contest. The former is particularly not such an orator as Brutus was. He has defects that are natural and ineradicable, but also permits himself to indulge many faults that he might correct. It would hardly be possible for a man to handle himself more ungracefully than he does. His feet get in his way at every turn, and his hands are a continual burden and perplexity to him. Mr. Cable does some better in this regard, and seems to be properly aware that he should sacrifice something of daily habit and prejudices to the requirements of platform dignity and propriety; but he, too, has much difficulty with his hands, and some of his attitudes—as when he is portraying the courtship of Ristofalo and the widow Riley, for instance—are more graphic than exact and elegant. Both of them, singularly enough, speak in a halting manner; but Mr. Cable is nervous about it, as if he had suddenly forgotten his part, while with Mark Twain it seems to be quite the right thing, since he talks in such a slow and unwilling way that the listener easily believes the pauses necessary, like rests to a musician. And, speaking of music, we must not forget to say that Mr. Cable's Creole songs are very effective and very suggestive. He sings them with fine feeling and precision, in an admirable tenor voice; and we are not sure but he makes with them the most decided and lasting impression of the whole entertainment.

Two days before this article was printed, the *Globe-Democrat* carried a page-one advertisement for the reading. This advertisement, simply a large picture of the two men, is reprinted in *Mr. Clemens & MT* under the title of "Twins of Genius."

Index